Sweet and Sour

Life in Chinese Family Restaurants

Best wishes,
John Jung

John Jung

 Yin and Yang Press

ISBN   061534545X   978-0-615-34545-1
LCCN 2009940541

Printed in the United States of America.

Jung, John, 1937-
Sweet and Sour: Life in Chinese Family Restaurants
/ John Jung

p.   cm.

Second Printing

Credits: Front Cover Graphics, Courtesy of Karen Tam, MFA.
Top: *Shangri-la Café Installation, Toronto, 2006*
Bottom: *Gold Mountain Restaurant Montagne d'Or Installation, Montreal, 2004*

Back Cover Photographs, Courtesy of:
Top (l-r) Mike Krzeszak, Chris Jepson, Greg Schuler, Jim Belfield
Bottom (l-r) Michael Lehet, Jess Jackson, Joe Murayama, Katherine Moriarty

Online orders: http://tinyurl.com/johnjung

Praise for *Sweet and Sour: Life in Chinese Family Restaurants*

John Jung has taken us down another memory lane and this time we brought along our appetite. Sweet & Sour evoked hundreds of memories of China-towns, favorite soul food dishes, haunts of opulent and garish banquet halls and the more frequented and beloved hole-in-the walls. These are the collective memories shared by families and friends. Sweet & Sour is also an anthropo-logical study. Chinese cooks across these United States and Canada created an everlasting love for Chinese food enjoyed by all cultures. Find a "chop suey" house and generations upon generations will cite their favorites, be it chow mein, fried rice, beef brisket stew or even chicken feet. Without a doubt this is by far Jung's best work and with the greatest universal appeal.

Sylvia Sun Minnick, *Samfow: The San Joaquin Chinese Legacy*

John Jung again demonstrates a marvelous ability to blend archival data with fascinating first-person accounts to bring to life the family-operated Chinese eateries that are quickly disappearing from today's society. Following solid his-torical groundwork, Jung uses narratives of 10 individuals who grew up in such places to take readers inside old-time chop suey houses. Their stories provide a candid telling of the personal, familial, and cultural significance of these famil-iar cafes. As with his earlier books on Chinese family-owned laundries and grocery stores, the author sheds a fresh and ample light on a subject even more familiar. And once again he does it so well from the inside out.

Mel Brown,
Chinese Heart of Texas: The San Antonio Community 1875-1975.

Sweet And Sour is a powerful historical exploration of an American institu-tion: the family-owned Chinese restaurant. John Jung succeeds in bringing to life the exterior side of such Chinese eateries across the nation--their appearance, their location, and of course, their hybrid, Americanized menu offerings. In addition, by means of a variety of interviews and primary sources, he focuses attention as well on their little-known private side, the daily routines and harsh working conditions that made them run. Jung underlines the contributions of all family members, including children, that were necessary for success.

Greg Robinson,
A Tragedy of Democracy: Japanese Confinement in North America

Sweet, sour, bitter, and pungent,
All must be tasted.
Chinese Proverb

Menu

Foreword

Americans have been eating Chinese food in small towns and big cities alike for more than a century. The longstanding absence of the reading public's interest in Chinese food is mind-boggling. We apparently cannot simply attribute this absence to its lack of interest in the mundane topic of food. McDonald's has attracted much public and scholarly attention, as is evidenced by the numerous publications about the fast food giant. But Chinese food has been around much longer and Chinese restaurants far outnumber McDonald's. In fact, the 40,000 or so Chinese restaurants in the United States are more than McDonald's, Burger King and KFC combined. The absence of major studies of Chinese food in the public domain represents an important and interesting subject of serious sociological inquiry. Scholars can certainly attribute this to the various forms of structural and ideological prejudice against the Chinese. But we must point out that scholars themselves also bear some responsibility: they have not taken enough time to research and write about Chinese food.

As the first decade of the twenty-first century came to a close, the American public finally discovered its Chinese food. The year 2008 witnessed the publication of Jennifer 8 Lee's *The Fortune Cookie Chronicles: Adventures in the World of Chinese Food*, which was followed by Andrew Coe's 2009 book, *Chop Suey: A Cultural History of Chinese Food in the United States*. In many ways, these two books are the first major book-length studies of Chinese food written by Americans for American audiences. Although there have been Ph.D. dissertations, Master's theses, and scholarly articles devoted to the topic over the years, they seldom went beyond the narrow specialized academic readerships.

This is why I was so delighted when I discovered in the summer of 2009 that Professor John Jung was finishing a book on this topic. Professor Jung, a psychologist by training, retired from California State University, Long Beach after a fulfilling career and since then has successfully entered another field, the historical and sociological study of Chinese Americans. While many of us write and publish because we have to, as is revealed by the old saying about academics, "publish or perish," in his retirement, he has become a prolific scholar in his new field, having written several books: *Southern Fried Rice: Life in A Chinese Laundry in the Deep South, Chinese Laundries: Tickets to Survival on Gold Mountain,* and *Chopsticks in The Land of Cotton: Lives of Mississippi Delta Chinese Grocers.*

Professor Jung's latest book, *Sweet and Sour: Life in Chinese Family Restaurants,* tackles the long-neglected topic of Chinese food with a focus on Chinese restaurants. This well-researched, thoughtfully conceptualized monograph brings academic rigor and adds historical depth, as well as the perspectives of an insightful scholar and a second-generation Chinese American, to our understanding of the development of Chinese food in the realm of public consumption in the United States and Canada. It promises to elevate that understanding to a higher level.

The book recognizes the importance of America's Chinese restaurant as a socioeconomic phenomenon. Chinese entered the restaurant business, he notes, because of economic necessity. The restaurant industry provided an important source of employment. The book, in particular, is focused on small family-run restaurants. Such a focus brings attention to the essence of the Chinese restaurant as an economic institution and a vehicle for immigration. The book contains detailed stories about the vital significance of the labor of family members for the survival of the family-based restaurant. The restaurant, in turn, facilitated the immigration of many individuals to the United States and Canada, offering them a means to start their new life in the New World.

The book perceptively covers many significant aspects of Chinese restaurants. One is the change in how Chinese restaurateurs named their establishments, offering insights into the unspoken interaction between them and their customers. Equally interesting are the discussions of the racially diverse clientele of the Chinese restaurant, from which we can valuable glimpses into its importance as a site of cultural encounters.

Through the extensive and fruitful use of a wide range of sources — archival, oral, and visual, Professor Jung vividly reconstructs the development of the American Chinese restaurant. Those interested in further reading or research will benefit from the primary and secondary sources listed in the bibliography and footnotes. Another important and innovative feature of the book is the inclusion of first-hand accounts by "insiders" of their own and family experiences in the Chinese restaurant industry. These are coherently connected to the rest of the narrative of the book. They can also be read separately as family histories.

Through this book, I hope, consumers at the ubiquitous Chinese restaurants can also gain a deeper appreciation of historical forces and human experiences that have shaped the food they now enjoy.

Yong Chen
Professor of History
University of California, Irvine

Preface

Although the title, *Sweet and Sour,* suggests a popular style of Chinese restaurant fare, the focus of this book is *not* on Chinese food, but on the difficult lives of the Chinese immigrants and their families that made their livelihoods operating countless small restaurants during most of the past century often in small remote places all over the U. S. and Canada. These restaurants, which provided the primary, if not the only, experience with Chinese food for most non-Chinese people were a major source of self-employment for earlier generations of Chinese immigrants and their families from villages in the southern China province of Guangdong. *Sweet and Sour: Life in Chinese Family Restaurants* is a study of their experience in this livelihood and its impact on Chinese family relations and interactions. As with my other books on the early Chinese immigrant experience, a primary goal is to help preserve a record of the hard lives of Chinese families that operated small businesses such as laundries, grocery stores, and restaurants and to further an understanding and overdue recognition of their contributions to their communities.

Sweet and Sour serves as an apt metaphor for the often, contradictory experiences of Chinese restaurant families. The long hours of never ending work each day made for harsh lives, which were soured by the hostile reception they often faced as foreigners in a racially prejudiced society. Yet, they persevered, and through painstaking labor enabled their children to have a better education that afforded them better options in life. Sweet was the reward for enduring the sour aspects of their work. As one Chinese from a family restaurant noted, "the title… captures exactly how life was. The *sweet* was how the profits from operating the restaurant added to our quality of life… The *sour* was how we were treated by some of the customers, and all the crap we had to take, not to mention the hard work into the late hours!"[1]

---

[1] e-mail to author from Ralph Young, Sept., 2009.

On a personal note, it was not until I was 15 that I first ate in a Chinese restaurant when my parents moved our family to San Francisco from Macon, Georgia, which at that time had not a single Chinese restaurant. One index of how much social change has occurred is that Macon now has over 20 Chinese restaurants. Although I have since dined in many Chinese restaurants, I never thought about their origins and operations. Writing *Sweet and Sour* has given me a deep appreciation and admiration of those who toiled in this vital economic and cultural enterprise.

I thank many that shared personal experiences, especially those that wrote narratives about their family restaurant lives for *Sweet and Sour*, listed in order of appearance in Chapter 8: Flo Oy Wong, Quong Wong family members, Dora Leung, Joe Chan, Bill Tong, Darren Lee, Karen Tam, Gilroy Chow, Raymond Wong, and P. C. Wu. Their perceptions and accounts provide a vivid behind the scenes view of restaurant operations. Without their contributions, *Sweet and Sour* would be a lifeless recital of historical data rather than an enlightening glimpse into the difficult lives of Chinese families that ran these restaurants. Their moving disclosures tell how their families managed their businesses and how they overcame many obstacles. Their narratives honor their roots and show that these experiences taught them valuable lessons that led to significant benefits for them.

Sylvia Sun Minnick, Mel Brown, Greg Robinson, and Yong Chen, experts on matters historical, generously gave valuable time to provide suggestions, criticism, and encouragement. Long-time friends Rod Wong and Ron Gallimore offered helpful feedback on early drafts. I thank Phyllis, my wife, for enduring the mood swings that many authors, myself included, undergo during the task of writing as well as for numerous discussions that help clarify my thinking about many aspects of the book. Special thanks go to Bill Lee for first whetting my appetite to undertake this important research topic.

JJ
Jan. 2010   Cypress, Ca.

1. Varieties of Chinese Restaurants

The average American knows very little about the Chinese restaurant. The average Chinese knows equally little, perhaps just a little more.   *Louis Chu, 1939, p. I*

Chinese restaurants are one of the most popular ethnic businesses today, found in virtually every city and town across North America, as well as in many other parts of the world including South Africa, Peru, New Zealand, Australia, and Europe.[1] "Chinese restaurant," somehow suggests that they comprise a homogenous group, much like the thousands of outlets for a fast food franchise. However, nothing could be further from the truth as Chinese eating establishments come in a variety of forms, ranging from opulent, luxurious restaurants with many professionally trained chefs that can serve exquisite banquet dishes to hundreds of patrons in large dining halls embellished with elaborate Chinese art decorations to small hole-in-the-wall cafes in facilities with only a handful of Formica top tables and poorly decorated interiors run by single families with little or no initial restaurant experience. While some offer full waiter service, many resemble fast food places or self-service cafeterias. Take-out only and catering services also exist. More recently, there has been an increase in "all you can eat" for one price buffets.

Although there are certainly some common features among Chinese restaurants, the extent to which they vary can be considerable as the following description of two restaurants clearly reveals. The *Imperial Palace*, prominently located in the Chinatown of a large city, is a recently refurbished 400 seat-dining venue with expensive Chinese art decorating the entrance and dining room walls. The dining room tables are decked out with linen tablecloths and napkins and attractive tableware with a Chinese motif. The bi-lingual waiters are neatly attired, and polite, if not downright fawning, in their attentiveness to patrons. A separate spacious dining room on the second floor allows for weddings, birthday parties, and other special occasions.

Attractive to the many tourists seeking a gourmet Chinese meal, the Imperial Palace offers an extensive menu of American-Chinese dishes that appeal to the western palate including their specialties that are reverently described as their "Signature" dishes, and command higher prices. Another menu, written in Chinese, boasts an extensive selection of Chinese dishes that appeals to its large Chinese patronage, but they are not offered on the English menu. A fully stocked bar adjoins the foyer where diners may have cocktails while waiting for a table and a large selection of wines and beers are available on the dinner menu as well.

The capital investment necessary for such a large facility is substantial, and far beyond the resources of a single family. The size of the staff needed by way of managers, cashiers, hostesses, chefs, kitchen assistants, waiters, dishwashers, and cleanup personnel is considerable. A syndicate or partnership with dozens of investors is typically needed to raise the necessary capital.

In contrast, *Canton Gardens*, the hole-in-the-wall café, occupies a small strip mall storefront in a blighted part of a mid-sized town that has a very small Chinese population. At the present time, a young Chinese immigrant family owns and operates the business but at least two other Chinese were prior owners before they retired. The father, a quiet and serious man with limited English speaking ability, stays in the kitchen most of the time where he does the cooking. He rarely enters the dining area where his outgoing wife, with a better command of English, performs the duties of hostess, waitress, and cashier. A young adolescent girl, probably their daughter or a close relative, helps after school and on weekends. Two younger children, a boy and a girl, are also present after school. They take menus and glasses of water to customers; otherwise, they sit in a corner booth where they quietly do their school homework or watch TV.

After the dinner hour rush subsides, the family members find time to sit down to eat their own meals, though in staggered shifts, at a table in a corner of the kitchen where they can keep an eye on the dining room. Then, sometimes with the help of a hired hand, the dishes are washed, the dining room is tidied up, and a menu for the next day is made by 10 p.m., more or less. The restaurant then closes for the evening. Fortunately, the family residence is located in a flat above the restaurant so it does not take long after cleaning the dining area and kitchen each evening for the family to reach their living quarters. This convenient proximity also saves valuable time because early the next morning the food preparations must be started well in advance of the arrival of customers.

Canton Gardens has a steady mostly white, and a few black, customers that enjoy "American-Chinese" fare such as egg rolls, chop suey, orange chicken, sweet and sour pork, and fried rice. Only a handful of their customers order dishes unfamiliar to them with ingredients such as tofu, salted fish, shark fins, sea cucumber, bitter melon, bok choy, or chicken feet.

The dining area is comfortable but nothing fancy and the furnishings are showing signs of age. There was little effort made to try to disguise the fact that this facility previously housed an American coffee shop. In fact, in one part of the dining room there are some incongruous decorations that reflect a western ranch theme. The new owners tried to create a Chinese-y feeling by placing a statue of Buddha near the entrance, which is bordered with a pair of ceramic foo dog statues. Chinese calligraphy adorns the dining room walls, and some Chinese lanterns hang from the ceiling. Behind the cash register is a wall calendar advertising a Chinese grocery supplier graced by a photograph of an attractive, smiling young Chinese woman wearing a tight fitting, silk embroidered Chinese style dress or cheongsam.

The restrooms are small and could use some redecorating. They are functional, but they are marginally maintained, as the short-handed staff is too busy to clean it except at the end of each day. Despite the physical limitations of the premises, *Canton Gardens* manages to survive by offering fresh tasty food in plentiful portions. The food is prepared quickly, the service is sincere, and the prices are low, largely because labor costs are at a minimum by the unsalaried help from all family members.

Actually, neither the *Imperial Palace* nor the *Canton Gardens* just described really exist. The descriptions are only composites of imaginary or fictional Chinese restaurants, one depicting an elegant Chinatown dining venue with authentic Chinese cuisine prepared by highly trained chefs and the other representative of the mom and pop run restaurant located in a suburban or small town setting featuring Americanized Cantonese dishes. They reflect two extremes of the variety of "Chinese restaurants," both of which have had significant impact on the successful acceptance of Chinese food in North America. These descriptions are provided to emphasize the wide variety that exists among "Chinese restaurants."

Some Important Questions

In many respects, it is quite surprising that Chinese food and restaurants eventually came to be so well accepted and regarded by the general public. When one examines the history of Chinese in North America, it is clear that they were not welcomed immigrants. The Chinese, with their strange customs, attire, and language evoked a mixture of intolerant ridicule and curiosity. Their exotic food ingredients such as shark fins, seaweed, lotus roots, and bird nests led Westerners to disparage Chinese cuisine, which was so different from the plain foods traditionally preferred by middle class non-Chinese. Furthermore, popular stereotypes of Chinese eating rats and dogs added to their contempt for Chinese foods.

This growth and prevalence of Chinese restaurants is also somewhat surprising since, except for cities in metropolitan areas with large Chinese populations, most of the patrons are *not* Chinese. Times change, and today virtually everyone has heard of Chinese restaurants even those few that have never eaten in one. Chinese restaurants acquired a new image for serving low-priced delicious meals that were also nutritious and healthy.

Why Did So Many Chinese Open Restaurants?

One question for historical investigation is why Chinese immigrants entered the restaurant business? The rapid growth in the number of Chinese restaurants is surprising because the great majority of the Chinese immigrants in the 19th century, and well into the 20th century were young men who came from rural farming regions of Guangdong province in southeastern China. These men worked in the fields all day and it was their wives and mothers who did the cooking at home. Restaurants did not even exist in many small villages. What conditions led these immigrant men, most of whom were not cooks in China to start operating restaurants in North America as well as in many other countries? Success was not likely given their lack of training and experience in managing restaurants. How many were able to earn a living from running a restaurant and what were the keys for their success?

The Chinese restaurant, like the Chinese laundry before it, assumed a dominant role on the economic, sociological, and psychological lives of early generations of Chinese in North America. To a large extent, these occupational "choices" were indirect consequences of the Chinese Exclusion Act in 1882 that prohibited the further entry of Chinese laborers and their families to the United States. In Canada, a different barrier in the form of a Head Tax was imposed on Chinese in 1885.[1] Ironically, had such severe restrictions on immigration not been imposed, and Chinese had been able to bring their wives and families to North America, there may well have been less growth of Chinese restaurants because the wives of the immigrants would have cooked the family meals at home.

During the economic depression from the late 19th century into the first decade of the 20th century, the Chinese were blamed for the hard times because they were willing to work for low wages. The exclusionary barriers were the culmination of strong resentment toward Chinese. These unfair restrictions prohibiting new immigrants from China and the many extreme acts of violence directed toward those already here adversely affected the Chinese in North America in many spheres of their lives for much of the twentieth century.[2]

Several generations of Chinese immigrants and their descendants from the mid 1800s to the mid 1900s had few work opportunities due to racial discrimination. From the mid to late 1800s, racism had driven the Chinese out of the gold fields and from many occupations for which they had expertise and experience such as farming, fishing, cigar making, and shoe making.

The railroad construction work for which thousands of Chinese immigrant men were recruited by the Central Pacific Railroad in the 1860s was drastically reduced in 1869 with the completion of the transcontinental railroad at Promontory Point near Ogden, Utah. Although many of these Chinese found work on other rail lines under construction, the strong hostility toward Chinese severely restricted their opportunities to compete with whites in the labor market.

Out of sheer necessity, Chinese had to find or develop forms of self-employment because most forms of work were denied to them. Lacking English language skills, having little money, and little experience, one of the few opportunities was in domestic work, typically considered "women's work." Thus, they started their own small businesses such as laundries, farms, grocery stores, and restaurants often in areas where there were few other Chinese. These forms of self-employment proved to be their primary means of economic survival.

Work in the demeaning role of houseboys or domestics perhaps had a "silver lining" for these Chinese in that they acquired greater facility with the English language than Chinese who lived and worked in the confines of Chinatowns. Furthermore, domestic employment provided experiences and skills that would later lead to economic self-sufficiency as some Chinese opened laundries, and later, others started restaurants.[3] As an example, in 1880 there were as many as 44 Chinese identified as cooks in Boise, Idaho in the U. S. Census.[4] They found employment in many hotels, restaurants, and private homes preparing western style food rather than Chinese cuisine, which had not yet gained popularity among whites. Thus, the 1899 menu of one Idaho City restaurant run by a Chinese did not list a single Chinese dish.[5]

In San Francisco, middle and upper class families hired Chinese, in preference to Irish, as domestic servants for washing, cleaning, and cooking. However, they expected western dishes, and not Chinese foods, which they regarded as "odd, smelly, and repulsive."[6] [7]

Raising Capital for Restaurants

Another important question is how were they able to raise sufficient capital needed to open cafes and restaurants? Chinese immigrants were poor and as laborers did not earn much money. Restaurants required more capital and manpower than laundries so it is not surprising that before 1900 the vast majority of self-employed Chinese opened laundries instead.

A rotating credit system known as a *hui* was a common method for Chinese to raise relatively small sums. Each member of a group of immigrants contributed equal amounts to a pool of funds, and they took turns borrowing the combined amount for starting a business.[8] Sometimes, direct loans from relatives or friends might be adequate to start a small café.

Elegant restaurants that had the capacity to serve banquets in large dining rooms required partnerships involving financing from several entrepreneurs because most individuals did not have sufficient funds to open these larger facilities alone. Some of the partners actively participated in the day-to-day operations of the restaurant, which they considered to be a long-term business, but others were "silent partners," investors who would likely sell their share if, and when, they could realize a profit.[9]

It was not uncommon for an immigrant to come over from China as a laborer. After working for several years until he could save enough money, he would become a partner in a restaurant or other business venture. For example, a 1924 newspaper article described how Lee Foo, owner of New York's Far East Restaurant started with $5,000 and four partners. After 16 years, they had expanded to three restaurants with over $100,000 from 40 Chinese investors, including some silent partners in Canton and Hong Kong.[10]

How Chinese Restaurants Evolved

Chinese restaurants changed or evolved over time.[11] Chinese immigrants from Guangdong province started "chow chows" around the mid-1800s to serve familiar Cantonese dishes that fit the tastes of their countrymen. These restaurants were located in "Chinatowns" near large populations of Chinese, their primary source of customers. They held limited appeal to most non-Chinese when they first appeared.

In the transition to the industrialized society of the last half of the 19th century, a restaurant industry grew rapidly as more people lived in cities than in rural areas.[12] However, most whites did not patronize Chinese cafes frequently, if at all. They generally viewed foreign foods as strange and odd. Few had any interest in eating dishes served by Chinese cafes and restaurants.[13]

However, from the late 1890s to the early 1900s, a surprising reversal of fortune took place for Chinese restaurants that will be detailed in subsequent chapters. Even with little or no promotion by the Chinese, their cafes were "discovered" by adventuresome white diners and the ensuing publicity widened their popularity among non-Chinese. Prejudices against Chinese immigrants were still strong, but their cuisine was gaining favor. Restaurants soon became one of the primary forms of self-employment among Chinese. In Chinatowns, newer, larger, and more elegantly decorated dining facilities were built to attract and accommodate the growing demand. Partnerships involving both active and silent investors raised capital for the expensive startup costs of remodeling and refurbishing existing facilities or building new ones and for the expenses for hiring numerous cooks, waiters, kitchen helpers, and other staff.

Even in cities and towns with few Chinese residents, growing awareness and popularity of Chinese cuisine, especially chop suey, attracted interest and curiosity by the 1920s. This improved attitude toward Chinese food led to the growth of smaller Chinese cafes and restaurants in regions where there were few competing Chinese restaurants.[14] Many small restaurants were not, strictly speaking, run by families, but by several male kin or friends working as partners because immigration laws prevented Chinese, unless they were merchants, from bringing their wives and children. Consequently, most of the earliest family-run restaurants involved families of Chinese immigrant men married to women that were American citizens, Chinese or non-Chinese.

During the Great Depression of the 1930s, Chinese restaurants, like most restaurants, struggled. Some failed but the demand for Chinese restaurants revived after the end of World War II. During the late 1950s until the early 1960s, these family-run businesses that featured American-Chinese and Cantonese style cuisine became one of the most popular ethnic foods.

This book will examine the origin and operations of the far more numerous small family-run restaurants, which sprang up virtually everywhere. These, rather than the large banquet halls, are the kinds of Chinese restaurants that are familiar to most people not living near Chinatowns. Family restaurants involved members of one, or a few families, which sometimes also included uncles, brothers, and cousins. These Chinese were generally among the few or only Chinese living in the areas where they were located, a situation that left them culturally and socially isolated for many years living apart. It is important, however, to realize that generalizations about Chinese family restaurants must be qualified as they differed in many aspects during different *historical periods* such as the Depression, World War II, or the Civil Rights era. The *generation* of the owners, in terms of whether they were immigrants or born here, is also an important consideration.[15]

Sweet and Sour seeks to understand the psychological, economic, and sociological status of the families that earned their living from small family restaurants. Work and social interactions within these Chinese families differ from those in large restaurants where the management has formal business training, skill, and experience. Most of the cooks, waiters, busboys, dishwashers, and other employees of large restaurants are not relatives or close friends with each other. Furthermore, located near large Chinese communities, they have many Chinese patrons who want authentic Chinese food, as do some non-Chinese customers. Finally, these restaurants and their staff are part of an extensive community network of Chinese social and cultural ties that sustain them in their business and personal lives. The study of the large Chinatown restaurant is a worthy topic in its own right, but will receive limited discussion in this book because the circumstances and nature of their operations differ markedly from those of family-run restaurants and cafes.

In contrast, the small family-run Chinese restaurant relied on, and generally received, long-term involvement and commitment from all family members and, in many instances, a few hired employees. Owners generally lacked much experience managing a business like a restaurant in which they had to deal with the public. Many lacked proficient English speaking skills, knowledge of the host culture, and social skills for interacting with non-Chinese customers. How did these ubiquitous family-operated Chinese restaurants located in regions where they were among the few, if not the only, Chinese manage to survive?

It is from the diligence and perseverance of pioneering Guangdong immigrants that several generations of Chinese were able to eke out their living by running restaurants. The fruits of their labor provided the financial resources that helped educate their children who could then move beyond the arduous and low-paying restaurant work to pursue careers in professions and white-collar occupations. These Cantonese family-run Chinese restaurants deserve recognition for the significant role they had in introducing Chinese food to non-Chinese and for the contributions they made to the economic and psychological condition of the following generations of Chinese Americans.

Endnotes

[1] "There are some forty thousand Chinese restaurants in the United States – more than the number of McDonald's, Burger Kings, and KFCs combined." Jennifer 8. Lee. *The Fortune Cookie Chronicles: Adventures in the World of Chinese Food* (New York: Hachette Book Group, 2008), 9.

[2] Jean Pflazer. *Driven Out: The Forgotten War against Chinese Americans (New York: Random House, 2007).*

[3] Terry Abraham, "Class, Gender, and Race: Chinese Servants in the North American West." (Paper presented at the Joint Regional Conference Hawai'i/Pacific and Pacific Northwest Association for Asian American Studies, Honolulu, Hawaii, March 26, 1996).

[4] Bureau of the Census, *Manuscript Census* (1870).

[5] Liping Zhu. *A Chinaman's Chance: The Chinese on the Rocky Mountain Mining Frontier* (Boulder, Co.: University Press of Colorado, 1997), 118-119.

[6] Andrew Coe. *Chop Suey: A Cultural History of Chinese Food in the United States* (London: Oxford University Press, 2009), 133-134.

[7] Laundries involved lower initial costs and fewer personnel than restaurants. They provided the primary form of self-employment for Chinese initially who dominated the laundry business until the early 1900s brought more competition from white-owned steam laundries.

[8] Paul C. P. Siu. *The Chinese Laundryman: A Study of Social Isolation, edited by J. K. W. Tchen* (New York: New York University Press, 1987), 92-96.

[9] Jie Zhang. "Transplanting Identity: A Study of Chinese Immigrants and the Chinese Restaurant Business" (Ph.D. diss., Southern Illinois University, 1999), 102.

[10] R. G. Carroll. "Chinese Laundries Gone: Restaurants Are Many." *Los Angeles Times*, May 27 1924, Proquest Historical Newspapers Los Angeles Times (1881-1986), 6.

[11] Zhang, "Transplanting Identity," 67-90. Four periods of Chinese restaurants can be distinguished: gold mining days (1848-1869, anti-Chinese agitation and eastward relocation (1870-1944), post World War II 1945-1965, age of new growth, 1965-present (1999). Three periods of restaurant development were identified In San Francisco: international restaurants (1849-1853), Chinese-only restaurants (1873-1905), and post-earthquake (1906) tourist restaurants. Tonia Chao, "Communicating through Architecture: San Francisco Chinese Restaurants as Cultural Intersections, 1849-1984 (California)" (Ph.D. diss., University of California, Berkeley, 1985), 43-80.

[12] Richard Pillsbury, *From Boarding House to Bistro: American Restaurants Then and Now* (Cambridge, Ma: Unwin Hyman, 1990). Until recent times, most people ate meals in their homes or in rooming houses. As the growth of cities increased over the 19th century, many people no longer worked close to home and had to bring their own meals to their workplace or purchase food from street peddler carts and food stands. The growth of opportunities to sell prepared food and meals led to the opening of lunchrooms, diners, cafes, and restaurants. More travel with overnight stays away from home created a need for food services in taverns, which previously focused on drinking. Similarly, inns, which focused on lodging for travelers, began to provide facilities to sell meals.

[13] Richard Pillsbury. *No Foreign Food: The American Diet in Time and Place* (Boulder, Co.: Westview Press, 1998).

[14] A cursory examination of databases for persons listed on U. S. Census Schedules as born in China or of Chinese race for several American cities with Chinese residents showed that in 1910 the primary Chinese occupation was laundryman, with a handful of cooks (probably in homes rather than cafes). The 1910 Schedules, depending on the city, showed an increase in Chinese listed as waiters and cooks, and the 1920 Schedules showed substantial numbers of restaurant owners, waiters, and cooks while the numbers of laundrymen declined.

[15] In a given era, the second generation generally had more opportunity than the first, or immigrant, generation due to better English skills and knowledge of western customs. Whereas the identity of the immigrant generation was rooted to the country of origin, the second generation had allegiances to both the country from which their parents came and the one where they were born. Their children, the third generation, were

closely identified with their country of birth. Such differences affect the extent to which each generation is governed by values of the country of origin or host country.

Chinese in the restaurant business, like all Chinese, had a difficult existence due to prejudices prior to the end of World War II. Their children, despite more education and assimilation, did not enjoy much greater economic opportunity. Many second- and later generation Chinese from roughly 1925 to 1945 had no better work than to take over the family restaurant when their parents retired. Following the repeal of Chinese Exclusion Act in 1943 in the U. S. (Canada in 1947), the second generation had improved work choices. Even greater prospects arose for the second, and later generations, after the Civil Rights era.

2. *Fan Deems* and Noodle Shops

Strong racial prejudices reduced the chances of Chinese being hired to work in white-owned businesses from the last third of the 19th century well until the middle of the next century. Those that managed to avoid this obstacle still often faced unfair treatment from white employers and co-workers.

Chinese immigrants were of an independent spirit, and preferred to be self-employed rather than work as employees of whites.

> …they decided to continue fulfilling the women's work roles they had assumed during the pioneer era, operating laundries and restaurants. From the Chinese point of view, owning, managing and operating a business was far superior to being employed as domestics by whites. Being owners of laundries, restaurants, etc. accorded them proprietary status. [1]

Restaurants were a viable form of self-employment for Chinese immigrants in areas with large Chinese populations. In comparison to laundries, restaurants were a distant second most common occupation in the late 19th and early 20th century. The 1870 U. S. Census listed 3,653 launderers and laundresses, as the fourth leading occupation among Chinese following miners, laborers, and domestic servants, but only 66 "restaurant keepers" near the bottom of the list. [2] For example, in Chicago, in 1872 there was one Chinese laundry, and the number rose to a peak of 704 by 1928 and by 1942 had dropped to 591. [3][4] In contrast, the first Chinese restaurant in Chicago was listed in 1893, and they increased substantially to 118 by 1915, of which no more than seven were in Chinatown, supporting the growing trend of Chinese food being accepted among non-Chinese.[5]

In 1920, U. S. occupational statistics showed about half of employed Chinese worked as laundry operatives (11,534) as compared to those employed as cooks (6,943), waiters (2,766), and restaurant, café, and lunchroom "keepers" (1,688) or managers.[6] The relative number of Chinese laundries and restaurants reversed over time. By 1930, laundries were declining in number as they faced increasing competition from home washing equipment while restaurant growth continued its upswing aided by more favorable attitudes among non-Chinese toward Chinese people and their foods. Some laundrymen became restaurant owners and workers.

Still, there were regional differences. As late as 1945, Chinese in Philadelphia engaged in laundry work still far outnumbered those in restaurant work by 4:1. The persistence of limited occupational opportunities for Chinese was evident in that only 47 of 547 Chinese in Philadelphia were engaged in occupations other than laundry or restaurant work.[7] St. Louis in 1952 similarly had more laundries, 49, than restaurants, 13. However, by 1980, there was a dramatic reversal, with only 1 laundry compared to 41 restaurants.[8]

Early Chinese Restaurants

The segregated living conditions of Chinatowns, therefore, gave rise to opportunities for men who could cook to provide Chinese meals for sale to other Chinese. These foods were not served in "restaurants" where waiters delivered food that customers, seated at a table, had ordered from a menu offering many selections. In fact, some street cart vendors may have preceded sit down restaurants. The earliest restaurants in Chinatowns were better described as noodle shops, which consisted of a small kitchen and a few tables and served mostly bowls of noodles or rice porridge, or "jook." They were easier to operate, requiring only 1 or 2 workers, offering a limited menu of simple items, and no language barriers with Chinese customers.

Figure 1 Inside a Chinese Fan Deem. From Wing Ching Foo. "The Chinese in New York." Cosmopolitan, June 1888. 300.

Restaurants, or cafes, offered a selection of Chinese dishes that the immigrants would have had back in their villages. Typically, they had three-cornered yellow silk flags with Chinese characters posted by otherwise unadorned storefronts to signify their business.[9] The interiors were decorated simply, if at all, and provided plain tables and tall stools for seating. These *fan deems* or "rice houses," along with noodle shops, were the Chinese equivalent of cafes and diners.

> ... Besides a few small tables, many of these places use lunch counters to serve their customers, generally bachelors and workingmen. For a modest sum, a customer can order a plateful of rice topped with his favorite ingredients: tomato beef, chicken curry, almond chicken, even hambork fan. The humble, everyday fare served at these economical fan deems are basically "home-style" cooking--dishes one would make if eating at home (vs. banquet style dishes). Generally, they were not served at fancier restaurants.[10]

IN A SECOND-CLASS RESTAURANT.

Figure 2 A second class restaurant. From Louis J. Beck, New York's Chinatown (New York: Bohemia Publishing: 1898) 48.

These initial providers of cooked meals served authentic home dishes using ingredients that the immigrants were familiar with from their Guangdong villages as an observer noted in 1898.

> The bills of fare in these places are more limited and the prices lower. The service, as mentioned already, is vastly inferior and the surroundings anything but desirable. The staple dishes served at these places are usually ready cooked. The prices charged are five and ten cents, according to the demand of the guest...A hen coop will be found adjacent to every restaurant kitchen, amply supplied with live chickens, ducks and pigeons, ready for slaughter and cooking as required.[11]

A typical menu included items such as Chop Shu (roast pork), yok bang (minced pork), chee kok (pig's feet, ham dau (salted eggs), lap chong (dry sausages), choy (greens), and of course, fan (rice, a Big Bowl). A bowl of soup is furnished with the foregoing free of charge.[12]

> Small restaurants that focused on Chinese customers offered different dishes, and did not have a regular menu that was printed, but served different dishes on a daily basis written on paper pasted on the wall or written on a mirror or a wooden board so that they can be changed easily.[13]

The atmosphere in *fan deems* was not one that would attract anyone seeking a refined, elegant dining experience. The patrons received basic meals, without attentive and fawning waiters or tables with clean linen tablecloths and napkins.

> The proprietors of the restaurants of Chinatown do not seem to consider that service is any part of their business. Their waiters do not wear white aprons, nor

are they ubiquitous and attentive to the wants of guests. They stand near at hand to receive orders, which are bawled out to the cook in the kitchen at the further end of the building, calling for the exercise of no little lung power. Unless you are familiar with the habit you might fancy he was calling to his partners to come and fight you. When served the waiter leaves you.[14]

Other restaurants of a cheaper character abound, commonly occupying basements. They are less lavishly decorated and furnished. Their tables have no linen, but are otherwise as clean as the average cheap American restaurant. The viands provided are not so peculiar and are served with much less pretention. They are patronized by the laboring classes and outlaws, and quite largely by the lower classes of white people who visit Chinatown for vicious purposes, dissipation, or mere curiosity.[15]

Nonetheless, for the Chinese men, *fan deems* not only served inexpensive cooked native foods, but also provided a public gathering place for them to be with other Chinese. One observer pointed out that Chinese felt comfortable and accepted in the safe confines of the *fan deems*, which offered a refuge from a hostile, white society.

... It provides for the Chinese aliens, therefore, a neighborhood of primary relations, where "no one will stare at him, make fun of him, nor mistreat him... Here he may eat with chopsticks instead of knife and fork, drink tea instead of cold water, wear comfortable dress instead of stiff collar and unmanageable tie, talk and swear in Cantonese dialect and indulge in a cup of *Ng-Ka-Pei* or a game of *Fan-T'au*.[16]

The patrons of these establishments were other Chinese men, consisting mostly of laundrymen from surrounding areas and Chinatown merchants that sold groceries and foods from China.

Fan deems had few non-Chinese patrons. For one matter, most Chinese did not speak or understand much English. Furthermore, attitudes that whites held toward Chinese, and their food, was generally negative, and reflected repugnance and disdain toward unfamiliar foreign food fare.

> In Chinese restaurants, reported one disgusted white observer, 'pale cakes with a waxen look, full of meats, are brought out. They are sausages in disguise. Then giblets of you-never-know-what, maybe gizzards, possibly livers, perhaps toes.[17]

An article in a St. Louis newspaper by Theodore Dreiser, a young writer who later became a famous novelist, described his first encounter with Chinese food in positive terms as "wonderful, awe-inspiring, and yet toothsome." However, a demeaning drawing of a Chinese eating with chopsticks from a bowl that had the head and tail of a rat draped over its edge accompanied the article.[18]

Many American children in the late 19th and early 20th century grew up with similar views about Chinese, "We knew that they lived entirely on a horrible dish called chop sooey (sic) which was composed of rats, mice, cats, and puppy dogs."[19] Such stereotypes about Chinese were often reinforced in magazine and newspaper articles, as in a 1901 drawing of children bringing cats and dogs to a Chinese restaurant, presumably to be cooked, which accompanied one article describing an adventure of eating in Chinatown.[20]

Figure 3 "Peck's Bad Boy" image suggesting that Chinese served dogs and cats.
New York World, 1901, 7.

The Vital Role of Chinatowns

Because of the past virulent racism toward Chinese in many
parts of the west still lingered until after World War II, Chinese
were restricted to living in confined areas that came to known as
"Chinatowns" in San Francisco, Los Angeles, Portland, Tacoma,
and Seattle, as well as in numerous smaller towns such as Sacramento, Stockton, Riverside, and Eureka. These enclaves of Chinese
immigrants provided some measure of safety because these quarters consisted almost entirely of Chinese men. They were almost
all bachelors; those that were married had left their wives and children back in China. It was not until the 1920s that some
semblance of Chinese family life was found in some communities,
the result of more merchants bringing their families over. In addition, more marriages occurred between American-born Chinese
men and women and between Chinese immigrant men with either
American-born Chinese or non-Chinese women.

As already noted, around the early 1900s the most prevalent
occupation of Chinese immigrants was laundry work, an occupa-

tion that required them to open their laundries in neighborhoods remote from Chinatowns to be closer to where their customers lived. On Sundays, typically their only free day, these bachelors congregated in Chinatown for many reasons. Chinatown merchants provided them with Chinese services, merchandise, and foods as well as temples, fraternal organizations, and family associations. They had opportunities to socialize with other Chinese and some engaged in social vices such as smoking opium, gambling, and consorting with prostitutes.

Years before Chinatowns became profitable tourist attractions, non-Chinese visitors ventured there in search of an exotic Oriental experience, souvenirs, curios, and Chinese meals. Chinatowns were self-sustaining ethnic enclaves for Chinese in the area who patronized its merchants and restaurants. Merchants also had a thriving business shipping Chinese products and foods to Chinese living in areas that were far removed from any Chinatown.

As the fascination with Chinese customs, traditions, and rituals increased among non-whites, their forays into Chinatowns expanded the potential for Chinese restaurants to prosper.[21] [22] Ironically, at the same time that exotic aspects of the Chinese were being promoted, many Chinese were becoming increasingly westernized in their lifestyle with increased adoption of white fashions in clothing, American movies, English language, and even in eating meals with knives and forks instead of chopsticks.[23]

Endnotes

[1] Beck, *New York's Chinatown*, 261.
[2] U. S. Census, 1870.
[3] Siu, *Chinese Laundryman*, 26-39.
[4] Chinese restaurants initially had to be located close to a Chinese popula-tion, their primary source of customers. Precisely the opposite situation existed for Chinese laundries. Their customers were primarily non-Chinese, which required that they be located in residential neighborhoods outside of Chinatowns.
[5] Ben Bronson and Chuimei Ho, "1901: The boom in Chinese restau-rants begins." Chinese American Museum of Chicago. http://www.ccamuseum.org/Research-2.html#anchor_90
(accessed Aug. 16, 2009).
[6] Ching Chao Wu, "Chinatowns: A Study of Symbiosis and Assimilation" (Ph.D. diss., University of Chicago, 1928), 87.
[7] David Te-Chao Cheng. Acculturation of the Chinese in the United States: A Philadelphia Study" (Ph.D. diss., University of Pennsylvania, 1945). Foochow, China: Fukien Christian University Press, 1948.
[8] Huping Ling, *Chinese St. Louis: From Enclave to Cultural Community* (Phila-delphia: Temple University Press, 2004), 144.
[9] Chao, "Communicating Through Architecture," 44.
[10] Ibid., 121, 123.
[11] Beck, *New York's Chinatown*, 52.
[12] Ibid.
[13] Cheng, "Acculturation of the Chinese," 98.
[14] Beck, *New York's Chinatown*, 52.
[15] Ibid., 48-49.
[16] Wu, "Chinatowns," 158.
[17] John Mariani, *America Eats Out: An Illustrated History of Restaurants, Tav-erns, Coffee Shops, Speakeasies, and Other Establishments That Have Fed Us for 350 Years* (New York: William Morrow: 1991), 77.
[18] Ling, *Chinese St. Louis*, 46-47.
[19] The writer expressed regret that he too had been guilty of such cruel conduct as a child, but argued that children generally tend to ridicule anyone different from the majority such as foreigners but there was no real antagonism toward Chinese..."It was a purely inborn impulse to devil anyone who was different." Robert Lawson. *At That Time.* (New York: Viking, 1947): 42-45.

[20] "Peck's Bad Boy Takes the Groceryman to Chinatown," *New York World,* 1901, 7.

[21] The tour guides thrived on the curiosity of "slummers" who descended upon Chinatowns to observe the "heathens." The Chinese Consul-General filed a complaint in 1904 against "white tour guides who set up fake opium dens, led tourists up and down stairs many ladders to create the illusion that the Chinese lived many stories underground like gophers, and staged immoral exhibitions in Chinese brothels for tourists." Ruth Hall Whitfield. "Public Opinion and the Chinese question in San Francisco, 1900-1947." (M. A. Thesis, University of California, Berkeley, 1947), 52-53. Cited by Chao, "Communicating Through Architecture," 139.

[22] In the 1920s, elevated sightseeing buses full of rubbernecking tourists descended into Chinatown hoping to see 'slave girls,' gambling dens, and trap doors. Jan Lin. *Reconstructing Chinatown: Ethnic Enclave, Global Change* (Minneapolis: University of Minnesota Press, 1998), 174-175.

[23] Yong Chen. *Chinese San Francisco: 1850-1943. A Trans-pacific Community* (Stanford, Ca.: Stanford University Press, 2000), 196-197.

3. Dining Rooms And Banquet Halls

By the early 1900s Chinatowns in San Francisco, Chicago, and New York had many large eating houses and restaurants, with adequate dining rooms and facilities for serving large gatherings on celebrations of holidays, weddings, and birthdays as well as after solemn occasions such as funerals. These banquet restaurants had more staff, elegant Chinese décor and furnishings, and more extensive menu offerings than *fan deems*. Decorated with expensive artifacts and furnishings imported from China, these facilities served foods native to Guangdong to social gatherings of Chinese men, many of whom were separated from spouses and families left in China either by choice or necessity as well as by immigration restrictions.

> The interiors of these restaurants are ordinarily well decorated with all sorts of colorful objects. Red, which represents the favorite Chinese color, seems to be the popular choice. Hence, red tables, red chairs, red walls, red lanterns. When one enters it gives an impression almost like a Buddhist Temple. Another type of decoration is characterized by the use of the old style furniture and symbols. The "Far East" restaurant is a classical example. Black wood tables and stools inlaid with marble or mother-of-pearl, hanging lanterns, embroidered pictures, etc. suggest the drawing room of an old Chinese house. In other restaurants outside of Chinatown the Chinese atmosphere is diluted and neutralized and even overwhelmingly dominated by the American luncheon room style.[1]

Figure 4 An early 1900s San Francisco banquet hall restaurant.

The large, opulent restaurants capable of providing banquet service were typically housed in three-story buildings that had balconies on the upper two stories, as in Figure 4. This description of the interior of one large San Francisco restaurant, *Woey Sin Low*, that predated the Chinese exclusion years but was destroyed in the 1906 fire and earthquake, clearly distinguishes the different purposes of each floor of the typical three-story restaurant building and descriptions of the elegant and ornate furnishings inside.

The ground floor is used as a provision store; on the second floor are the common dining rooms, and on the third, the grand saloon for parties and first-class customers. It has false archways, with an alcove for musicians, and is furnished with carved and richly polished stools, round or square, and ponderous, and with tables both of mahogany or dark Chinese wood, inlaid with marble, and the stools covered with small mats. This saloon is at times formed into numerous small divisions by screens or trellis-work, ornamented with foliage, birds, and monsters in various colors. Round the walls are lacquered boxes, and cabinets, musical instruments, and bills of fare; the whole presided over by the idol Kwan Sing (sic). This is the place where the grand banquets are given, in honor of prominent men on the inauguration of an establishment, or on the occasion of a windfall. Associates at a factory will meet here once a year and testify their gratitude to a kind employer by a supper, which often costs from two to ten dollars each.[2]

These larger Chinese restaurants with banquet facilities included more comfortable dining facilities with dark colored wooden tables and chairs with Oriental motif and design imported from China to remind Chinese of home. The decor was formal, with dark dining rooms filled with imported scrolls of Chinese poetry, richly carved wooden screens, and altars.

In many restaurants, space in the building that housed the restaurant was allocated to house boarders and restaurant workers. In San Francisco, for example, the second floor of the building housing the *Hang Far Low Restaurant* had lodging for regular boarders while the third floor provided apartments.

Figure 5 Oriental Restaurant, 4-6 Pell St. New York. Lower Floor, Ladies Dining Room and Upper Floor, Main Dining Room ca. 1920.

In 1878, many Chinese restaurants advertised themselves as "cha-ju jiu-yuan" (tea house/room and banquet catering), a term which in Chinese can also refer to a brothel. Not surprisingly, most restaurants were close by to lodging facilities, gambling houses and bordellos.

> Chinese restaurants, like many of their San Francisco contemporaries, including Delmonico's, Marchands, and Maison Doree, mixed dining and amourous pleasures...in general, the function and clientele of all of these late nineteenth century restaurants accurately reflected the social conditions. It was an institution that was created for and catered to the needs of the "bachelor" society...

The restaurant owners did what they could to help their clientele feel at home by surrounding them with imported furnishing and by serving Chinese food.[3]

These restaurants served authentic Chinese food. The menu offerings were familiar to the immigrants, but foreign and generally unappetizing to non-Chinese, as illustrated in a sample of the more expensive menu selections in New York restaurants around 1888.

```
                    BILL OF FARE.
    Two Dollars per Dish:—
Yu Chie—(Shark's Fins).
Wong Ye Tao—(Sturgeon Head).
Yen War—(Bird's Nest).
She Kiao—(Air Bladder of Eels).
Sze Kwa Ap—(Deviled Duck).
Don Bark Gop—(Steamed Squab).
Sut Ye—(Snow Moss).
Shake Ye—(Rock Moss).
Sen Mi—(Angel's Beans).
Hoi Tsam—(Beach de Mare).
Bow Ye—(Holiotis).

    Seventy-five Cents per Dish:—
Por Law Gai Pin—(Fried Chicken, Boneless, with Pine-
    apple).
Chow Gai Pin—(Fried Boned Chicken).
Tao Pin—(Fried Pig's Paunches).

Chow You Ye—(Fried Duck's Web).
Park Gop Song—(Fried Minced Squab).
Chow Loong Har—(Fried Lobster with Vegetable).
Chow Foo Kwar Gai—(Fried Chicken with Balsam
    Pears).
Chow Gai Sue Mean—(Fried Noodles with Boneless
    Chicken).
    Soups—Twenty-five Cents a Dish:—
Sne Kwa Kiang—(Sponge Squash Soup).
Tso You Kiang—(Mushroom Soup).
Chop Suey Kiang—(Giblets and Pork Fried).
Hoy Shum Kiang—(Beach de Mare Soup).
Too Kwar Kiang—(Balsam Pear and Pork Soup).
Ho She Kiang—(Dried Oyster Soup).
```

Figure 6 Menu. Source: Beck "New York's Chinatown," 1898, 49-50.

Although Chinese generally were thrifty and ate plain meals of rice, vegetables, and pork, chicken, or fish, when there were holidays, celebrations, and other gatherings, they spared no expense in having banquet dinners with expensive dishes.

> Commonly, the Chinaman's habits are very economical, but when a feast is decided upon, he is lavish in expenditures, and apparently does not allow the cost of any desired article to trouble him. And it does not require an event of great note to furnish an excuse for a banquet. The anniversary of the opening of a business, the arrival of a much loved friend, or any occasion of but inconsiderable importance is good cause to rejoice over by a little extra eating and drinking. These banquets are usually held in the larger Chinese restaurants and much of what is set before the guests is insipid or offensive to the American taste. Some of the stews and roasts are remarkable for the fine flavor they retain after cooking, and the tea is superior to any that is prepared by other than heathen hands. Beef and potatoes are seldom offered at a Chinese feast. The Chinese look upon the use of cattle for food as a very great sin, as they are valuable beasts of burden. There is also a tradition among them to the effect that "The killers of beef shall endure punishment in Hades after death and should they be born again, they will return as cattle." To have potatoes for dinner is considered a sign of hardship and a mark of extreme poverty.[4]

A few Chinatown restaurants, as in Philadelphia, were among the first to offer take out and delivery by filling food orders for parties and for the gamblers of Chinatown.

> Instead of coming to the restaurants to get their food, the restaurants have to send the food to the customers in the gambling houses or the places where the parties are

held, This, the Cantonese call "guoy mai" or outside sale. One small restaurant 1 know is more or less monopolizing this business for other restaurants are too busy to take care of it. Every gambling house has to have at least two meals a day, lunch and supper, provided for its customers. The order varies from $3.50 to $5.00. For such an order one does not have to specify any particular dishes, The menu will consist of whatever the cook can prepare during that day for that sum of money. The restaurant always provides enough rice for at least ten persons with this kind of order.[5]

Owners and employees of successful restaurants earned more than either the average laundryman or the storekeeper. At the *Jong Far Low Restaurant* in Philadelphia, employees earned $40 or $35 a month plus board in 1906.[6] Lee York, with experience working in both a Chinese restaurant and a Chinese store, felt that his earnings were definitely higher at $60 a month plus $15 in tips working at the *Yen Kom Low Restaurant* in 1911.[7]

The compensation for cooks, of course, depended on their expertise and experience, with some already trained in China while others learned "on the job" only after coming to the United States.

A Chinese cook of the first class employed in these restaurants is paid $80 a month and his board. But he must be adept at his business, trained to it in China and thoroughly familiar with all dishes peculiar to his native land. Cooks of the second class receive $60 a month. They may have acquired their trade since coming to this country, but must be proficient in it, and perfectly familiar with Chinese dishes and condiments. Other cooks earn from $33 to $40 a month, which is probably all they are worth. They may never have seen the inside of a kitchen before coming to America. And know little of the preparation of choice Chinese dishes. But they can fry a piece of pork, boil or stew a chicken, and prepare table greens, and that is about all that is required of them in the cheap restaurants.[8]

In contrast, however, in 1912, Chin King still earned only $7 to $10 a week, but this amount was no worse than the amounts that his laundering and store-keeping kinsmen could make.[9]

Conflicting Opinions About Chinese Restaurants

Although the popular press depicted Chinatowns as "dens of iniquity," this notoriety did little to deter upper as well as working-class whites from venturing into the dark alleys of the mysterious Oriental enclaves. If anything, these sinister images only added to their allure for the adventuresome.

> Young intellectuals called Bohemians regarded visits to Chinatown to taste immigrant Chinese culture as a form of rebellion against conservative middle class values. In particular, Chinese restaurants were an attractive venue for them to be exposed to gustatory and olfactory experiences of China at the same time they fulfilled their appetites for cultural sight seeing.[10]

The ambiance of Chinese restaurants was dreadful, in the eyes of John Huber Greusel, but it only served to enhance the adventure for youthful "slummers" of the Gay Nineties, as he described it in an article, "Some Oddities of Chinatown," in the July 1, 1893 issue of the magazine *Once A Week*:

> Through a narrow hall and up dirty stairs brings one to the Chinese Delmonico's restaurant. A good dinner consists of nine courses, served on bare wooden tables and eaten with chopsticks. The meal begins with sweets, half a dozen bits of sugared ginger - heaped on a small

eggshell compote; the ginger is dyed a brilliant scarlet. In rapid succession follow dried nuts, candied apricots, and other delicacies...Some of the patrons have before them huge bowls of steaming rice which they eat by bringing the dish to their lips and then literally shoveling the food into the open mouth...As the dinner proceeds, some of the natives kick off their slippers, their bare stockings peering through the rungs of their stools. The odor of fuming cigarettes fills the air; an incessant babble prevails; every few moments you will see a Chinese pick up a bone or a bit of refuse food and deliberately send it flying under the table to the dirty floor! A greedy cat munches away under one of the tables. Were it not for the red banners on the walls, the eating house would be as bare as a barn; and assuredly, it is as uninviting as a pig sty. Yet the visitors to Chinatown love it dearly, and laugh and chatter there in a corner; the ladies, especially, on their first visit, cannot prevent themselves going into ecstasies over the tiny teacups. Thus, today, the "slummers" eat, drink, and are merry in their new experience with strange dishes."[11]

In contrast to the negative comments about early Chinese restaurants, a highly positive 1853 account of a dinner at one restaurant (called Hong-Fa-Lo in the article) by a white journalist invited to a 10 to 12 course meal of exotic dishes appeared in the *San Francisco Times*. He exclaimed, "We have dined at many a crack restaurant where it would be a decided improvement to copy from our Chinese friends."[12]

A writer in 1903 commented positively about Chinese restaurants and pointed out that:

The American who enters one of these restaurants for the first time may be surprised that the way to the table leads through the kitchen...The idea is to give the patron evidence that everything is done in a cleanly manner... In

Chinatown good cooking is a part of religion__ the cook is a priest.[13]

In Washington, D. C., it was observed that among the smart set, eating in Chinese restaurants had become rather fashionable.

> ...a visit to a Chinese restaurant is looked upon as an excursion into Bohemia, a taste of slumming, as it were. In Washington there is hardly a night that the Chinese restaurants are not patronized at some hour of the night by fashionably dressed women with escorts in evening attire. Members of the legation are regular patrons and may be seen almost any night at one or another of the restaurants.[14]

The popularity of Chinese restaurants was not hampered by what the reporter, using western criteria, regarded as their abysmal interior dining quarters.

> The interior of a Chinese restaurant, indeed, is a rather forbidding place at first glance. No soft music floats on flower-scented air and the waiters are not attired in evening clothes...back of the rear room is the kitchen with the door standing wide open, and the mingled odor of many Chinese dishes makes the air of the dining rooms heavy with its smell. The tables are cheap oak affairs, and are devoid of any covering. The floor is laid with a cheap linoleum or oilcloth.[15]

He also reported that during the early evening, the patrons of Chinese restaurants are of a "poorer class of persons, some of whom eat all their meals there." But around 10 p.m. the class of patrons dramatically shifts for the better, in his opinion. They come in search of chop suey despite the unpleasant surroundings of Chinese restaurants.

It is at this hour that Government clerks and many
newspapermen drop in for a plate of chop suey. This,
too, is the time when the young man introduces his
sweetheart to Chinese cooking. It is not unusual to see a
Government clerk and his best girl seated at a table at
about this time of the evening __ he assuming the air of
a man of the world, while she sits embarrassed and
shrinking, half afraid and ashamed to face so many men
in so strange a place. With the mien of a veteran the
young man orders "chop suey for two," and then, turning to his girl, explains that chop suey is a dish "fit for
the gods," and he is "sure she will like it." When the
chop suey comes, steaming hot, the young woman is
more than likely to doubt her escort's enthusiastic asser-
tion that she will like it, and it is not with any great
amount of avidity that she takes the first mouthful..."[16]

Some white middle-class Americans found Chinatowns were a

source of excitement where they hoped to observe, from a safe dis-

tance, of course, the depravity of opium fiends, slave girls, and

gambling.

Frequently accompanied by paid white tour guides,
who led their charges safely through the streets, tourists
visited "joss houses," or temples, attended Chinese
plays, shopped in curio stores, and in the process,
turned Chinatowns into popular sightseeing destinations.
During the first decades of the twentieth century,
Chinatowns saw even more fervent boundary crossing,
as thousands of Americans continued to seek in Chinese
immigrant communities, novelty, relaxation, titillation,
and excitement. Tourists brought with them dollars and
dreams, and as entrepreneurs hoped, took home souvenirs and memories.[17]

"THE CALL OF THE WILD."

Figure 7 Young slummers going to Chinatown for chop suey. Source: New York Sun, Nov. 29, 1908, 2.

Other reports were more positive and offered some praise although with an air of condescension.

> ...most of these places are really what they are supposed to be, eating houses, carried on under Chinese management. The cooks are invariably true Celestials, and in only a few cases are the proprietors Americans. The food is prepared, therefore, according to the most approved methods of the Middle Kingdom, with the result that in cheapness and savoriness (if you like it) it can easily outclass similar places run by American cooks. The Chinese is a master of the art of making palatable dishes out of next to nothing, or, rather, a little of everything...Moreover, in spite of appearances, the food is prepared in an extremely cleanly manner. No one is debarred from entering the kitchen, and a visit thither sends one back with renewed appetite to the untidy eating room.[18]

The journalist described the atmosphere in Chinese eating houses as highly conducive to an informal meal among the uninhibited denizens that frequent such lowly establishments.

There is also a free and easy atmosphere about the Chinese eating house which attracts many would-be "Bohemians," as well as a goodly share of a class below the lowest grades of the city's many graded Bohemia. Visitors loll about and talk and laugh loudly. When the waiter is wanted some one emits a shrill yell which brings an answering whoop from the kitchen, followed sooner or later by a little Chinese at a dog trot. Anyone who feels like it may stroll into the kitchen and try a little pidgin English on the cook. The proprietor will teach anybody to use the chopsticks and roar with laughter over the failures of the novice. Everybody does as he or she pleases within certain very elastic bounds.[19]

Restaurant Expansion In Tourist Trade

Chinese were quick to capitalize on this economic opportunity, especially since they were prohibited from most other gainful means of employment. They courted business from tourists and the curious with remodeled restaurants designed with a stereotypical Oriental motif both inside and outside. Chinese dishes were modified to appeal to Western tastes.

> By 1900, the increasingly powerful Chinatown merchant class initiated a campaign to "clean up Chinatown" by suppressing the local vice industry, and shop owners and theater proprietors began renovating their facilities for a white clientele. Restaurateurs refurbished their establishments with gaudy lanterns, colorful wall decorations, and bright red facades, to match stereotypical white fantasies of "Oriental" decor, and scrubbed their floors and kitchens meticulously, lest rumors of poor sanitation arise. New dishes, too, were created for the Visitors "pineapple chicken" and "stuffed chicken wings," among others but even these, for many tourists, still seemed too foreign.[20]

Chinese cafes began to thrive. By 1903 more than a hundred chop suey restaurants could be found in New York City between 14th and 45th streets, from Third to Eighth avenues. When Longacre Square (now Times Square), became the theater district, the after theater crowd flocked to Chinese restaurants that were decorated with "pseudo-Oriental glitter-colored lanterns, silk and bamboo hangings, and polished wood tables. The floors were carpeted and the waiters were dressed in clean uniforms."[21]

One newspaper article viewed the growth of the Chinese restaurant business in New York City with some scorn, wondering how such unattractive facilities could attract so many non-Chinese customers:

> In the last year or two a surprisingly large number of Chinese restaurants have made their appearance in uptown districts. The tawdry outward decorations of red and blue lights and huge Chinese characters are in every case the same. The same, too, are the unattractive entrances and the general dilapidation of the establishment. Nothing about them seems attractive and yet these places thrive and their number increases with astonishing rapidity...Twenty-five cents worth of some kinds of chop suey, served with rice, will make a toothsome dish for two people. Tea is served free of charge and the quantity is not limited...Negroes are in disproportionately large numbers.[22]

Chinese restaurants in New York welcomed black customers, who found it almost impossible to eat in restaurants outside their segregated neighborhoods, but since most New Yorkers refused to eat in a room with blacks, some chop suey places had only black customers.

Issues regarding service for blacks in Chinese restaurants arose in different cities periodically. A newspaper article in 1904 accused some Chinese restaurants in Chicago of denying service to black customers.[23] In New York, blacks reportedly feared going to Chinatown, but they patronized chop suey places located uptown.[24] A Chinese restaurant owner in Los Angeles was sued for denying service to a black on three separate occasions in 1916.[25] In places like San Antonio and St. Louis where segregation was the norm before the civil rights activism of the 1960s, some Chinese ran popular chop suey joints in black neighborhoods and also employed black waiters.[26] [27]

In 1906 the great San Francisco earthquake and fire destroyed most of Chinatown, including many of its dinghy cafes. The leaders of the Chinese community in San Francisco realized that this disaster provided an opportunity to rebuild Chinatown from the ground up and to design it to appeal to western images of the Orient. New restaurants occupied buildings constructed in the shape of pagodas. Chinese art was a prominent part of the design and decoration of serving dishes, teacups, bowls, furniture, and dining rooms. Chinese decorations adorned the exteriors and interiors, and cultural symbols representing yin and yang and double happiness emphasized an Oriental theme to capitalize on the fascination that non-Chinese had for the exotic, foreign, mysterious far east.

By the beginning of the twentieth century, Chinese food was more familiar to whites than previously and they dined more frequently at Chinese restaurants according to one Chicago newspaper.[28] Another newspaper article asserted, "IF the signs of the time are not misleading, Chicago's appetite, like the nation itself, is expanding far toward the east."[29]

Between the 1900s and 1920s, the Chinese restaurant industry experienced rapid expansion. Attracted by the growing popularity of chop suey and physical improvements in many Chinatowns following the example set in San Francisco, Chinese American merchants refashioned their image, and advertised the "new" Chinatown as clean and safe, and with less vice to attract more non-Chinese to visit Chinatowns and eat in Chinese restaurants.

The number of Chinese restaurant workers rose from 164 to 11,438 between 1870 and 1920, even though the number of Chinese employed overall declined during the period. In many cities, the number of Chinese restaurants greatly increased in number.[30]

In 1906, Chicago's *King Joy Lo Restaurant* opened with spectacular and elaborate decorations, art deco dining rooms, and featured live music and dance floors. Advertising for the opening of Chin Foin's *Mandarin Inn* in 1911 proclaimed:

> At tonight's opening there will be free souvenirs for all__ there will be Chinese singing by the celebrated Chinese duo Don-Tin-Yaw and Chau-Shu-Yin __ there will be music by a world-traveled and world-famous orchestra__ there will be a first view of Chinese mural decorations by Chinese artists__ pictures of the famous "moon bridge" and a scene from the "Forbidden City."
> …The entrance admits immediately to the main floor, from which three stairways lead to side and rear balconies, while in a front entresol the orchestra and singers will entertain. The floors are softly carpeted instead of being harshly mosaic. The scene will be luxurious and magnificent in the extreme, but the prices will be ex-

tremely moderate for a menu of such exalted excellence and marvelous variety in both the Chinese and American dishes.

...The new *Mandarin Inn Café* has a seating capacity of 350, and has high hopes of keeping that seating capacity taxed to its utmost by reason of the very superior excellence of its cuisine and service, the novelty of its Mandarin dishes, and its superior service by a corps of finely trained waiters.

…The menu includes a limitless variety of Chinese and American dishes and the choicest vintages of European, American and Chinese wines, liquors and cordials. A welcome and a souvenir await all comers tonight.

Eat at the Mandarin Tonight at 6:30 and Always Thereafter.[31]

Figure 8 Part of Mandarin Inn ad. Proquest Historical Chicago Daily Tribune, Aug. 16, 1911, 11.

The popularity of Chinese restaurants was evident in the east as well. By 1924 New York had over 250 Chinese restaurants. The

larger ones were housed in elaborate dining rooms with silk embroidered wall panels and teakwood tables with ornate inlaid mother-of-
peak designs. Many provided live bands and dance floors for patrons,
which were not unique to Chinese restaurants but offered in many
first class dining establishments during the early 20th century. However, most Chinese restaurants were "simply uniquely decorated
places where heaping dishes of chow mein or chop suey with bowls
of rice, cups of steaming hot tea, almond cake, kumquats, water
chestnuts, and lychee nuts can be procured."[32]

Figure 9 Chin Lee Restaurant, Times Square, New York.

Chin Lee opened a restaurant bearing his name in New York
near Times Square, with $120,000 from 250 partners.[33] Serving
American Chinese food, this facility could seat almost 1,000 diners on
the second and third floors. A live band and dance floor attracted
customers in search of food and social recreation. The Mayor of New

York sent congratulations when his restaurant opened.

Before he achieved success with a series of restaurants, Lee had been a cook and restaurant worker. In 1913 he opened his first restaurant in Lawrence, Massachusetts, A year later, he sold it at a profit and opened another one in Boston. Shortly afterwards, Chin Lee opened restaurants in downtown Providence, Rhode Island and then in Buffalo, New York, before the one in Times Square.[34]

However, the age of extravagant Chinese dining halls was short-lived. Start-up costs and operating expenses rapidly increased as labor unions pressed for higher wages for waiters at the same time the Great Depression was starting. After repeal of Prohibition in 1933, larger Chinese restaurants began in 1936 to add cocktail lounges and bars. The added revenue from alcohol beverage sales helped them survive for a few more years. Meanwhile white entrepreneurs opened popular lavish nightclubs with floorshows featuring big name entertainers that proved to be formidable competition for larger Chinese restaurants.

The continuation of the Great Depression into the 1940s forced many Chinese, as well as other, restaurants out of business. Tax delinquencies closed down other restaurants such as Chin Lee's in 1949.[35] Some cooks and waiters from larger Chinese restaurants invested their savings to start their own small family-run restaurants. Ironically, it was the improved reputation of large restaurants that paved the way for the acceptance of small restaurants in towns and cities across the country, which previously had no Chinese restaurants. By the end of World War II, smaller Chinese restaurants that were more plainly decorated and better suited to middle class incomes and tastes fared better than many larger Chinatown banquet halls.[36] The food tasted good and the prices were low but the physical surroundings inside often left much to be improved.[37] Such restaurants were able to survive because they relied heavily on family labor instead of salaried workers.[38]

Almost All Male Customers

For many decades, men were the primary customers, as Figure 10 shows in a San Francisco Chinatown restaurant in 1946. There were very few Chinese women in Chinatown, whether they were born here or were immigrants from China. It was not appropriate in that era for women to dine in public in any restaurant.

Figure 10 Serving male diners, Hang Far Low, San Francisco, c. 1940s. Courtesy, San Francisco History Center, San Francisco Public Library.

Eventually some Chinatown restaurants set aside a section, or entire floor for women and for groups that included women. Many restaurants installed closed booths to protect their privacy.

Historical Changes in Chinese Restaurant Names

Changes in the characteristics of Chinese restaurant names occurred over time provide a barometer of the acceptance of the restaurants in the larger society. The earliest *fan deems* served only Chinese patrons so it was fitting that they used Chinese names, written in Chinese characters on their storefronts, for their businesses. As they attracted more non-Chinese customers, the restaurant owners accommodated them by transliterating their Chinese names, leading to names like *King Ying Low, Sun Heung Hung, Ting Yat Sak, and Tao Tao.*

However, these names often consisted of syllables that were difficult for non-Chinese to pronounce or remember. To further accommodate non-Chinese customers, western equivalents of Chinese restaurant names such as *Far East, Pekin, Golden Palace,* and *Lotus Gardens* became popular. Names that evoked images of the exotic Orient appealed to Westerners' romantic images of China. A different strategy was to use restaurant names such as *Republic, Liberty,* or *Mayflower* to convey identification with America.

Some restaurant names reflected expressions of owners' hopes for a profitable business as in the name, *Ho Sai Gai,* which translates to "prosperity" and the name, *Ho Ho,* meaning "very good." The transliterated versions of some popular Chinese restaurant names such as *Hung Far Low* in Portland or *Hang Far Low* in San Francisco evoked unintended amusement among non-Chinese.[39] From the imagery evoked by the name, non-Chinese visualized physical dimensions of male sexual anatomy. However, the Chinese ideograms for this restaurant name, a popular one that was found in many cities across the country, have a quite different meaning, as its English translation is "Apricot Blossom Building or Red Flower Tower."

Eventually, as non-Chinese customers became better acquainted with Chinese names and more tolerant toward Chinese culture, it became fashionable after 1950 to return to Chinese names like *Tat Yat Lo* or *Joy Ying Lo,* indicated in Figure 11.

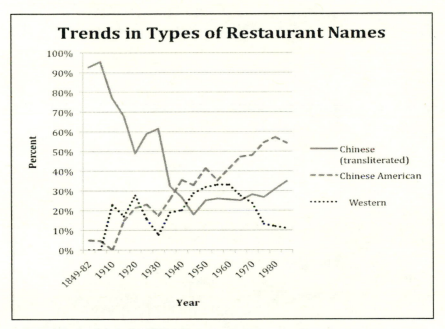

Figure 11 Types of Restaurant Name Trends. Based on Chao, 1985 data.

Upscale restaurants often used English names such as *Panda Gardens*, *Lotus Pavilion*, and *Golden Dragon* that evoked images associated with Chinese symbols and culture. Chinese also began to use "numerical names" of unfathomable origin to non-Chinese such as *Cafe*

888 or *Restaurant 369*. These names were selected on the Chinese belief that certain numbers like 8 or 3 are lucky whereas others like 4, which in Chinese sounds like the word for death, are considered undesirable as part of a restaurant name.

Endnotes

[1] Cheng, "Acculturation of the Chinese," 93.

[2] Hubert Howe Bancroft, *History of California*, vol. 6 (San Francisco: A. L. Bancroft, 1888).

[3] Chao, "Communicating Through Architecture," 77-78.

[4] Alexander McLeod. *Pigtails and Gold Dust* (Caldwell, Idaho: Caxton Printers, 1948), 131-132.

[5] Ibid., 93-94.

[6] Philadelphia 412-C, Jong Nong, D. L., Case Files of Chinese Immigrants.

[7] Philadelphia 1918-C, Lee York, D. M., Case Files of Chinese Immigrants.

[8] Beck, *New York's Chinatown*, 52.

[9] Philadelphia 1875-C, Arrested, Chin Tong, Eric, PA., Case Files of Chinese Immigrants. Philadelphia "146-C, Lee Poy, D. L," Case Files of Chinese Immigrants, 186.

[10] Beck, *New York's Chinatown*, 52.

[11] Grace M. Mayer. *Once Upon a City: New York from 1890 to 1910* (New York: Macmillan, 1958), 417-418.

[12] "A Chinese Dinner," *Pittsfield Sun*, Sept. 22, 1853.

[13] Ibid., 418-419.

[14] "Chinatown "Slumming" Parties Are Now the Fad." *Washington Times*, March 29, 1903, 6.

[15] Ibid.

[16] Ibid.

[17] Samantha Barbas. "I'll Take Chop Suey: Restaurants as Agents of Culinary and Cultural Change." *Journal of Popular Culture*, 2003, 36, 4, 669-686.

[18] "Chinese Restaurants: Those Uptown Becoming Increasingly Popular With "Bohemian" Classes." *New York Tribune Illustrated Supplement*, Feb. 3, 1901, B6.

[19] Ibid.

[20] Ibid.

[21] Arthur Bonner. *Alas, What Brings Thee Hither: the Chinese in New York: 1800-1950* (Madison, N.J.: Fairleigh Dickinson University Press, 1996), 105.

[22] Ibid.

[23] "No Chop Suey for Black Men." *Atlanta Constitution,* Apr. 14, 1904. Proquest Historical Newspapers Atlanta Constitution, 3.

[24] "Chop Suey Resorts" *New York Times,* Nov. 15, 1903. ProQuest Historical Newspapers New York Times (1857 – Current file), 20.

[25] "Not Lunch, But War." *Los Angeles Times,* May 30, 1916. ProQuest Historical Newspapers Los Angeles Times (1881 – 1985), II2.

[26] e-mail to Author from Robert Louie, Sept. 14, 2009. In our San Antonio restaurant in the 1950s, "Nobody ever explained to us why we didn't serve them. Only that we were told that we would not and when we told them they didn't seem to be upset about it. They just left."

[27] Ling, *Chinese St. Louis,* 49. Letter from Richard Ho.

[28] "Chinese Restaurants Increasing in Popularity," *Chicago Daily Tribune, Jan 26, 1902.* Proquest Historical Newspapers Chicago Tribune (1849-1986), A7.

[29] "Chicago's Appetite Is Becoming Cultivated to Chinese Dish of Mystery," *Chicago Daily Tribune,* Jul 19, 1903. Proquest Historical Newspapers Chicago Tribune (1849-1986).

[30] Cheng, "Acculturation of the Chinese,"

[31] Display Ad 9 –No title. *Chicago Tribune.* Aug. 16, 1911. Proquest Historical Newspapers Chicago Tribune (1849-1986), 11.

[32] Carroll, "Chinese Laundries Gone."

[33] Ibid.

[34] Grace Lee Boggs. *Living for change: An autobiography* (Minneapolis: University of Minnesota Press, 1998), 4-9.

[35] Ibid., 14.

[36] "Chinese Restaurants Move Down-Market, 1910s-1960s." http://www.ccamuseum.org (accessed: August 1, 2009).

[37] ...You reached it down a flight of stairs. The fan in the bathroom was coated with grease and asbestos. The urinals stank. The floor was linoleum. You sat in a booth, or at a flimsy table, which, in the suburbs, would have been reserved for a child's birthday party. Poker-faced waiters--all middle-aged men--took your orders. The tea was pure Lipton's, plunked down in plain metal pots. Only the table settings attempted decoration. The chopsticks came in sleeves with printed directions for use, whose simplicity was negated by the fact that they did not actually explain how to use them... Richard Brookhiser. "Eats from the East." *National Review,* Sept. 25, 2006.

[38] Chu, "The Chinese Restaurants in New York," 33-35.

[39] The Portland sign is in the top left corner of the back cover.

4. Chop Suey Mania

Although the earliest Chinese restaurants opened to serve Chinese immigrants with familiar dishes from their native land, they soon attracted adventuresome non-Chinese customers seeking new taste experiences. Insofar as most non-Chinese had little or no first-hand acquaintance with Chinese food ingredients or the Chinese style of cooking, Chinese were surprised by this new source of patronage, especially in view of the overall societal hostility toward them. Chinese restaurant owners had not tried to promote their cuisine to outsiders. Instead, it was the curiosity of non-Chinese that led to their increased patronage and fascination with Chinese food, an expansion that soon exploded when a well-publicized "Chinese" dish was "invented."

The Chop Suey Craze

Around the end of the nineteenth century, some Chinatown restaurants began serving a new stir-fried dish, chop suey, consisting of a mixture of bean sprouts, celery, onions, water chestnuts, green peppers, combined with small pieces of either pork or chicken. Soy sauce provided another flavor that was novel to Americans.

Many non-Chinese readily developed a taste for the dish although others held a deep-seated fear and suspicion of any foods of the Chinese. As one observer, Lucien Adkins, in Beck's 1898 history of New York Chinatown noted, the reluctance might have stemmed from popular derogatory

stereotypes of Chinese formed during childhood. This preju-
dicial misconception prompted cautious hesitation on their
part when confronted with a plate of chop suey.

> Take a friend to Chinatown for the first time and
> watch his face when the savory chop-suey
> arrives. He looks suspiciously at the mixture.
> He is certain it has rats in it, for the population
> superstition that the Chinese eat rats is in-bred.
> He remembers his schoolboy history, with the
> picture of a Chinaman carrying around a cage of
> rats for sale.[1]

Even when the newcomer is pressured into trying
chop suey, he still seems rather dubious despite his claims
that he likes it.

> He quickly puts aside the chopsticks, which are
> evidently possessed of the devil, and goes at the
> stuff with a fork. It is a heroic effort, but it is
> not sustained. The novice gets a mouthful or
> two, turns pale, all the time declaring that it is
> "great." However, a miraculous transformation
> takes place once the skeptic recognizes the
> delights of this concoction and he becomes a
> devotee of the once dreaded "chop suey." It is a
> long time before he can be persuaded to go
> again, but he is sure to surrender eventually to
> the enchanting decoction, and soon there are
> times when the knowing hunger for chop-suey,
> and for nothing else, draws him to dingy
> Chinatown, alone and solitary, if he can find no
> one to accompany him. For awhile he half
> believes there must be "dope" in the stuff. He is
> now certain that there are no rats in it. He is a
> confirmed chop-suey eater.[2]

From the early part of the twentieth century, chop suey came to be synonymous with Chinese food in the eyes of non-Chinese for several decades. Chinese were quick to recognize how marketable chop suey was, and even though they held the concoction in low regard, Chinese restaurants, large and small, across the land soon responded to the great demand and served it to its devotees.

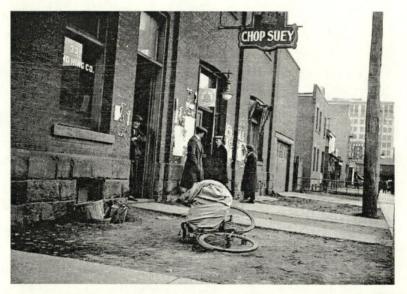

Figure 12 Chinese "bachelors" hanging out at a chop suey joint, Toronto, 1923. Credit: John Boyd/ Library and Archives Canada/PA 086020

Overnight, chop suey single-handedly made Chinese food a popular choice for non-Chinese.[3] Chop suey joints or chop suey houses became common terms referring to all Chinese restaurants. Chinese responded by displaying "Chop Suey" on their store signs, often more prominently than the name of the restaurant itself. Chop suey storefront signs appeared even outside of Chinatown as part of many urban landscapes.

Origins of Chop Suey

How and when did "chop suey" originate and why did non-Chinese consider it as the stereotypical Chinese food? And why might it be the case that this dish, so disparaged with contempt by many Chinese, ironically was a key factor in the success that Chinese restaurants had among non-Chinese?

Several accounts were proposed about the origin of chop suey. Two of the more interesting and plausible theories follow. In one version popularly held on the east coast, Chinese in New York invented chop suey in conjunction with a big feast held in honor of a visit in 1896 from the Chinese Viceroy, Li Hung Chang.[4]

> To show his special skill and inventiveness the cook prepared one special dish for the Viceroy who enjoyed it immensely. Being a new combination of his, the cook, when asked for the name of the dish, shyly answered, "Chop suey," being unable to think of some other name for it. And it soon became the fashionable dish among both Chinese and Americans. The name "chop suey" has ever since gone far and wide, hand in hand with the popularity of Vice Li Hung Chang!

This account has not been documented and may simply be apocryphal. In fact, the Oxford University English dictionary had a definition for "chop suey" years before Li Hung Chang's visit, which discredits the view that this occasion led to the creation of the dish. Nonetheless many Chinese restaurants capitalized on this popular view and for many years promoted the dish on their menus by listing it as *"Li Hung Chang Chop Suey"* to imply they were serving the authentic concoction. Whether true or not, the story elevated the status of chop suey and generated curiosity that drove throngs of non-Chinese to Chinese restaurants to see what the fuss was about.

A quite different view existed in the west where a former Chinese ambassador, Dr. Wu Ting-fang, suggested that:

> "The discovery of gold in California brought thousands of Chinese coolies to San Francisco, and soon the Chinese colony in the city was large enough to support a couple of Cantonese restaurants. One night, a crowd of miners decided to see what these pig-tailed yellow men ate. When they got to the restaurants, the regular customers had finished. The proprietor was ready to close. But the miners demanded food, so he dumped together all the food his Chinese patrons had left, put a dash of Chinese sauce on top and served it to his unwelcome guests. They did not know what he meant when he told them that they were eating "chop suey" or "beggar hash." At any rate they liked it so well they came back for more, and in that chance way the great chop suey industry was established. Many more Chinese fortunes have been from it than were ever made from gold mining, and for generations thousands of Chinese have laughed because every dish of chop suey served is a culinary joke at the expense of the foreigner. Chop suey restaurants are to be found in big cities all over the world __except for China. [5]

This may also be a tall tale without firm documentation even if it has a ring of plausibility. Even if it were only a myth, it was popular among Chinese as it allowed them to enjoy a small measure of revenge over their white tormentors by "pulling the wool over their eyes." Thus, while the legend on the east coast connects chop suey with a specific event, the banquet for a notable Chinese dignitary, the legend that stems from the west involves a fable in the form of an insider joke of wherein Chinese turn the tables by duping unsuspecting white bullies.

A simpler explanation than these two accounts is that a Chinese cook may often had nothing much food at the end of the day but leftover odds and ends that Chinese called *tsap seui*, which Americans heard as "chop suey."[6] The truth may never be known but this fact remains clear. Chop suey, a dish that the Chinese did not savor, came to be viewed by non-Chinese as the epitome of Chinese food to such an extent that almost every Chinese restaurant offered it to attract business. Most restaurants offered more than one chop suey dish since it could be combined with pork, chicken, lobster, shrimp, or other meats.

In parts of New England, many lunch counters, drugstores, five-and-dimes, and amusement parks offered a variant known as the *chop suey sandwich* as early as the 1920s. Its heyday was in the 1930s and 1940s, and it was also popular in the New York City area.

> The Chow Mein part is easy enough to describe,
> a mixture of minced meat (pork), celery, onions
> and bean sprouts in gravy over deep fried noo-
> dles. The Chow Mein is placed between a
> hamburger bun or sliced white bread.[7]

Adapting to Tastes of Non-Chinese Diners

Larger Chinese restaurants began to see the potential for including more American or Western menu offerings to accommodate non-Chinese patrons such as tourists, the adventuresome, and those already familiar with Chinese cuisine.

An example of the extreme extent to which some Chinese restaurants adapted their offerings to meet the taste of non-Chinese is the lunch menu at Philadelphia's *Cathay Tea Garden* for Dec. 2, 1920, which offered mostly American food and only two Chinese dishes, *chop suey* and *chow mein*, each for 65 cents.[8]

Almost two decades later, most Chinese restaurants still followed this approach. The *New Hankow,* which was located outside of New York's Chinatown still served a lunch menu shown in Figure 13 that featured American favorites such pork chops, Virginia ham, and roast beef prime ribs along with a small selection of "Chinese" dishes limited to popular items like chop suey, chow mein, and egg foo yung.

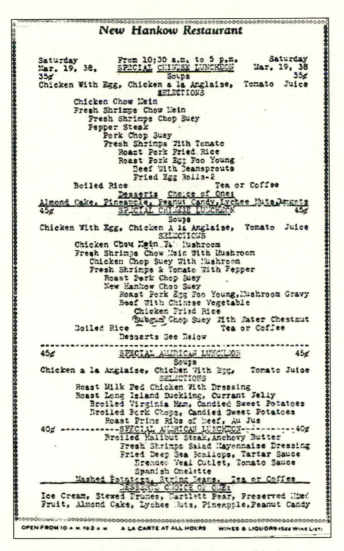

Figure 13 Menu of New Hankow, New York.

A Dish As American As Chop Suey

Chop suey was so popular during the 1920s, that even non-Chinese restaurants saw the need to offer the dish on their menus although some of them harbored doubts about eating Chinese food, as expressed in one newspaper article that grudgingly admitted, "Chinese vegetables are a bit queer, but we seem to like 'em." [9]

However, not only did the non-Chinese restaurants lack recipes for the dish but many of its key ingredients such as bean sprouts and soy sauce were not readily available from white restaurant suppliers.

> One American restaurateur lamented:

> I operate a medium size restaurant and recently I have received a number of calls for chop suey," wrote one proprietor to a restaurant industry trade publication. As neither myself nor my chef have any experience in preparing the dish, we ask you to help us out and send us a good recipe for chop suey. [10]

Across the nation, customers were suddenly requesting chop suey, and cooks at non-Chinese restaurants, not knowing how to prepare the dish, went in frantic search of recipes. [11]

> During the early 1920s, the pages of National Restaurant News, The American Restaurant, and other food service journals were filled with similar requests.

A "conspiracy theory" suggested that some Chinese capitalized on the sudden popularity of Chinese food with non-Chinese by opening several restaurants that would be more profitable due to economies of scale and scope. In 1903 the *Chicago Daily Tribune* reported on a plan toward single ownership and control over Chicago's Chinese restaurants. It alleged, without citing any concrete evidence, that Chinese had formed a "chop suey trust" to exploit the enthusiasm among non-Chinese patrons for the concoction and predicted eventual higher prices in Chinese restaurants.

> Twenty-five of the thirty-five Chinese restaurants in the city have been absorbed by a Chinese company. The others are holding out for better offers, but the trust has threatened to cut rates and drive out competitors who refuse its terms. Time was when Chicago could boast of but two chop suey cafes, on in State street, the other in South Clark street. Now Clark street has a dozen, and scarcely a principal street but has its Chinese cafes. Most of them are presided over by chefs and waiters from the Chinese colony in South Clark street.[12]

Another newspaper article in 1920 reported that the Chicago Council questioned "bewildered Orientals" about high prices for chop suey.[13] An observation in the New Yorker Magazine in 1928 speculated that the chop suey houses were being controlled by:

> "syndicates of Chinese importers and bankers, and their success is due to several factors. In the first place, larger floor space and popular prices. Again, the trick of supplying a dance band and all the trimmings at an approximate price of four dollars a couple. Furthermore, Chinese food is not perishable, there is a minimum of wastage, and costs are cheap...The kitchen, in fact, is where the Chinese syndicates first got their hold. Last year the frequent openings of new night clubs were for a time largely the result of Chinese financing. The syndicates bought up the kitchen

concessions in many of the "white" clubs. They
paid a handsome sum in advance and large royal-
ties on the gross intake, so that the actual
proprietors were able to open and keep going the
first few weeks on this money. Many of the Oc-
cidentals opened and closed so rapidly that the
ventures didn't pay anyone, but where the clubs
continued the profits to the kitchen men were
great."[14]

One news article elaborated on some of the advantages
that a trust had. For example, it could:

buy exotic ingredients in bulk – contracting for the
production of ingredients such as bean sprouts that
could be grown in the United States, arranging for
the importation of ingredients such as shark fin
that were available only in China. It could standard-
ize the format of Chinese restaurant menus and
centralize their printing. It could set up a system
for the training of chefs and the selection of new
restaurant sites. It could regulate competition to
prevent too many Chinese restaurants from select-
ing any particular location. Under such an
organization the cost of provisioning *each individual
restaurant* could be lower.[15]

Americans Claim Chinese Foods

American-Chinese offerings like chop suey, egg rolls,
chow mein, and fortune cookies achieved such popularity that
enterprising white businessmen in major cities saw opportunities to open their own "Chinese" restaurants. In New York, a
popular American restaurant hired a Chinese chef so it could
offer Chinese dishes. [16]

In 1924, a university student, Wally Smith, along with

his Korean-born partner, lhan New, bottled and canned bean sprouts, soy sauce, "brown sauce," and a vegetable mix, which they marketed as chop suey under their *La Choy* brand to the public, restaurants, hotels, and other food service institutions.[17]

Chop Suey in the American Home

During the early twentieth century, middle-class cookbooks emphasized recipes that best be described as "creamy, meaty, and sweet." Nutritionists with conservative food preferences promoted the traditional New England menu consisting of such foods as baked beans, brown bread, boiled vegetables, and beef stew. Middle-class white American cooking typically centered on heavy, starchy, and plain, if not bland, recipes that avoided spices, sharp flavors, and any "foreign" or non-European ingredients.

In contrast, recipes for Chinese dishes that appeared in mainstream cookbooks and women's magazines of the 1920s marked a significant departure from established western culinary preferences and patterns. These new recipes called for rare and unfamiliar ingredients such as bean sprouts, ginger root, soy sauce, and water chestnuts.[18] It was not easy to find these ingredients and even when they were found, many devotees of the dish felt that American-made Chop Suey still failed to match the 'real thing.' Numerous attempts to learn how to make chop suey from Chinese cooks proved futile. Such frustration led to one commentator to lament that perhaps

Chinese could not share the recipe because they communicated poorly in English.

> Chinese cooks have been hired by families, but they never seemed to be able to impart the secret of the dish to others. Chop suey receipts (sic) have been published in books and periodicals. When these have been interpreted to Chinese cooks they smiled knowingly.[19]

A different view was that Chinese cooks simply did not want to divulge chop suey secrets. Any recipes from a Chinese were not to be trusted because the "inscrutable Chinese generally omit one vital ingredient so that the resulting dish never matches the taste of chop suey from a Chinese restaurant."[20] Both explanations fit the pernicious negative stereotype of Orientals as inscrutable, deceptive, and untrustworthy.

Many middle-class housewives of the 1920s were, in fact, using soy sauce, bean sprouts, water chestnuts, and chow mein noodles from can goods to prepare "Chinese" meals at home. Chop suey and chow mein were frequently the centerpieces of elaborate luncheon parties and "theme dinners." Restaurants, magazines, and cookbooks, however, continued to classify chop suey as Chinese, and during the 1930s, many families who ate chop suey for dinner seem to have genuinely believed that they were "eating ethnic."[21]

In the 1940s, an Italian-American marketed frozen and canned chop suey and chow mein because chop suey had been served in Army mess halls during the war. He used a Chinese-sounding brand name, *Chun King,* to connote authenticity.[22]

Chinese Restaurants, 1925-1945

The "Chop Suey craze" helped introduce Chinese food to non-Chinese, which led to rapid growth of the Chinese restaurant business over the twentieth century. As it became the dominant source of employment for Chinese Americans by the 1920s, a concern of paramount importance was how to market Chinese restaurants to continue its success and expand their appeal.

To attract the patronage of the non-Chinese population, Chinese entrepreneurs designed the exterior appearance of the restaurants as well as the interior decor, physical arrangement of space, and furnishings with cultural symbols calculated to present 'messages' to patrons that they could enter the exotic world of the Orient without ever leaving home. Through their advertising and presentation, restaurants "emphasize a stereotype of Chinese culture, by virtue of how they market 'authentic' Chinese cuisine, how they decorate and furnish the places where that cuisine is eaten, and in how they dress the employees that serve that cuisine."[23] Since most non-Chinese were unfamiliar with Chinese meals, some menus even provided guidance and suggestions about how much and what types of dishes to order.[24]

> Restaurateurs were no longer looking homeward, they were looking to American themes.

The red doors, green tiles, golden letters and silver couplets, paired stone lions and golden dragons, carved figurines and flowering plants, palace lanterns, precious ceramics and delicate embroideries were used not to help the old Chinese "bachelors" feel at home, but rather, to present a public image of the "exotic."[25]

In hindsight, it is somewhat surprising that chop suey was such a sensation a century ago especially in light of its low status today. It must not be forgotten though, that it was the public excitement at the turn of the century about chop suey, a dish unheard of in China, which opened these opportunities in the first place. Although it subsequently was discredited and faded into obscurity, chop suey deserves some credit for making Cantonese Chinese food universally popular for decades.[26]

To current tastes, the dish is a brownish, over-cooked stew, strangely flavorless, with no redeeming qualities, and redolent of bad school cafeterias and dingy, failing Chinese restaurants. Any redemption is only possible through nostalgia; perhaps a forkful of the dish evokes memories of Sunday evening family meals down at the corner Chinese American eatery. To American diners of a century ago, chop suey was the dish of the moment, both sophisticated and enjoyed by everyman. They liked chop suey because it was cheap, filling, and exotic, but there was something more. Chop suey *satisfied,* not just filling stomachs but giving a deeper feeling of gratification.[27]

The success of chop suey was a double-edged sword. It increased non-Chinese interest in Chinese food, even if focused on a dish of questionable status among Chinese. Chop suey proved to be an economic boon for Chinese restaurants and other stores selling Chinese products ranging from foods to curios and art. Such increased positive contacts of the general population with Chinese helped improve attitudes toward Chinese beginning around the 1950s.

However, many whites still would not accept Chinese Americans in many social settings or business dealings, but had little trouble with them in subservient roles such as restaurant waiters or cooks with the exception of fears in the early part of the past century that Chinese men mingling with white women would lead to sexual encounters among them.[28] Moreover, success in restaurants burdened Chinese with domestic stereotypes of cooks and waiters, impeding opportunities for Chinese to enter higher status occupations and professions until long after World War II.

Endnotes

[1] Beck, *New York's Chinatown*, 296.

[2] Ibid., 297.

[3] Coe, *Chop Suey*, 166-179.

[4] Renqiu Yu. "Chop Suey: From Chinese Food to Chinese American food." *Chinese America: History and Perspectives,* (1987): 87-99; Haiming Liu. "Chop Suey As Imagined Authentic Chinese Food: The Culinary Identity of Chinese Restaurants in the United States." *Journal of Transnational American Studies* (2009) 1, 1-24.

[5] J. S. Tow. *The Real Chinese in New York* (The Academy Press 1923), 91. Carl Crow. "Sharks Fins and Ancient Eggs." Harper's Sept. 1937: 422-429.

[6] Chop suey, *tsap seui* in Cantonese, existed in Toishan before it became wildly popular in North America. E. N. Anderson *Food of China* (New Haven: Yale University Press, 1988), 212-213.

[7] Imogene Lim. "Chinese Cuisine Meets the American Palate: The Chow Mein Sandwich." In *Chinese Cuisine/American Palate: An Anthology*, edited by Jacqueline M. Newman and Roberta Halporn (New York: Center for Thanatology Research and Education, 2004), 134.

[8] Cheng, "Acculturation of the Chinese," 98.

[9] Colman, F. "The Makin's of Chop Suey." (1929, Dec. 15) *Los Angeles Times* G5. Proquest Historical Newspapers Los Angeles Times (1881-1986), 6.

[10] Emory Hancock,. "Making the Small Town Restaurant Pay." National Restaurant News Jan. 1925: 26. Cited by Barbas, "I'll Take Chop Suey," 677.

[11] "Food Bureau." Cafeteria Management Jan. 1928: 18. Cited by Barbas, "I'll Take Chop Suey," 677.

[12] "Chop Suey Trust Octopus has Tentacles in Chicago." *Chicago Daily Tribune* (1903, July 15). Proquest Historical Chicago Tribune (1849-1986), 3.

[13] *"Investigates High Cost of Chop Suey." Boston Daily Globe, Nov. 18 1920.* Proquest Historical Newspapers Boston Globe (1872-1924), 17.

[14] "The Talk of the Town (1928, March 28). Yellow lights." *The New Yorker,* 13.

[15] Susan B. Carter. "Celestial Suppers: The Political Economy of America's Chop Suey Craze, 1900-1930." Cliometrics Conference, Gettysburg College, June 5, 2009, 27.

[16] "Growing Popularity of Chop Suey." *San Francisco Chronicle (1869-Current File)* Dec 31, 1912. ProQuest Historical Newspapers The San Francisco Chronicle (1865-1922), 6.

[17] Barbas, "I'll Take Chop Suey," 677.

[18] Ibid., 680.

[19] "Chop Suey Resorts," 20.

[20] "Growing Popularity of Chop Suey."

[21] Barbas, "I'll Take Chop Suey," 682.

[22] Ibid., 681.

[23] Wu, "Improvising Chinese Cuisine Overseas," 61.

[24] Chen, *Chinese San Francisco,* 198.

[25] Chen Ben-Chang. *Mei-guo Hua Qiao Can Guan Gung Ye*, Taipei, Taiwan: Far East Book Co., 1971, 317. Cited by Chao, "Communicating Through Architecture," 120.

[26] A striking example of the popularity of Chinese food is the logic of Bill Fitch, a professional basketball coach who concluded, *"I always figure if you don't like Chinese food, there's something wrong with you."* Dave Anderson "Chemistry, Chinese Food And No. 1" *New York Times* June 28, 1990. D23

[27] Coe, *Chop Suey*, 175-176.

[28] "Chinese Mix Sin with Chop Suey." *Chicago Daily Tribune, Mar 27 1910.* Proquest Historical Newspapers Chicago Tribune (1849-1986), 3. "Girls Drink Beer at All Hours in Chop Suey Houses." *Chicago Daily Tribune, May 16 1914.* Proquest Historical Newspapers Chicago Tribune (1849-1986), 1. "Red-Haired Waitress to Marry a Chinaman." *Boston Daily Globe, Oct. 3, 1923.* Proquest Historical Newspapers Boston Globe (1872-1924), *6.*

5. Some Chinese Restaurant Pioneers

An historical description of Chinese restaurant characteristics, operations, and locations is inadequate for the understanding of the lives of those who operated them. Tracing the journeys of individuals from Guangdong that worked in Chinese restaurants throughout the U. S. and Canada can provide insights into the difficulties and hardships they endured. Examining the lives of several earlier Chinese in the restaurant business provides details of how they came over from Guangdong, how they entered this occupation, how their restaurant involvement changed over the years, and how their activities contributed to the public acceptance of Chinese restaurants. Many aspects of their experiences reflect similar ones of most Chinese restaurant owners.

There was, with minor variation, a standard "script or template" for Chinese immigration to North America in the late 19th and early 20th century. It consisted of young men, often the eldest son, coming to seek work. They came to be known as "paper sons" because many used false identity papers to claim they were sons of merchants, a class that was still allowed to enter the United States after the enactment of the 1882 Chinese Exclusion Act. These men were single, or if married, had temporarily left their wives and any children behind with plans to return after striking it big on Gum Saan or Gold Mountain. Meanwhile, they sent remittances from their meager earnings to provide for their families.

After a few years, those bachelors that could afford the passage returned to their village to marry through an arrangement with a matchmaker someone they had never previously met. Within the first year or two, the men would leave the village to return alone to their employment in the U. S. and Canada as immigration laws denied laborers the opportunity to bring their wives. In addition, pragmatic and cultural reasons limited Chinese from bringing their wives. It would cost money to bring the wife, and she would be a financial burden. In China, she and her children would increase the likelihood that her husband would eventually return instead of remaining in North America. Those who were fortunate made short return visits every few years to visit their families and to father more children.

Chinese immigrants eventually wanted to bring their oldest sons to help them in their work as soon as they reached early adolescence regardless of whether their business was a laundry, grocery store, or restaurant. However, under the Chinese exclusion law, being classified as laborers, they were not allowed to bring family members over. To circumvent this barrier, they had to first acquire merchant status, which they could obtain by investing about $1,000 as a partner in a business. Then, they sought and purchased identity papers of someone whose age and physical features resembled those of their sons. The price was somewhere around $1,000, which was a substantial amount for those days. In addition, the son assuming the false identity had to memorize many details of the person they were pretending to be such as family relationships, characteristics of their house, and physical features of their village. Boys as young as 10 years of age came under these conditions. These "paper sons" faced stringent interrogation by immigration officers upon their arrival and were deported if they failed this examination. Those who passed were permitted to enter the country, but had to use their paper names instead of their true surnames.

Some Early Restaurateurs
Moy Ju Hee, Minneapolis, Mn.[1]

Moy Ju Hee, born in 1865 in Gum Ping village in the Taishan area of Guangdong Province, came to the United States as a merchant when he was 21, leaving his wife, Hom Shee, and daughter Moy Foon Hai, in the village. He first managed *Hong Yen Hong*, a Chinese drug store in San Francisco. Before long he headed to the midwest where he worked with relatives in Oshkosh, Wisconsin.

His first wife died at a young age, so he returned to China to remarry. The next year he returned to the U.S. bringing his second wife and two children, but his children were denied entry at Port Townsend, Washington, and he had to send them all back. He returned to China in 1894 and 1896 for extended visits to see his wife and daughter. Moy had four children two girls, Moy Quai Fong and Moy Son Woon, and two boys, Moy Hong Yik and Moy Tai Heung.

In 1901 Moy moved from Oshkosh to St. Paul to manage *Hui Xian Low*, advertised as a "high-class Chinese Chop House." The following year, Moy Hee established a retail shop, Wing Wah Chong Merchandise Company in St. Paul, with eight other Moy relatives as partners. They sold silks, embroidered goods, rice, pottery, canned goods, groceries, toys, as well as supplies for Chinese laundries. In addition to starting his own retail shop, in 1903 Moy Hee established two restaurants, *Kwong Tung Low* in St. Paul and *Shanghai Low* in Minneapolis. A 1904 *Minneapolis Journal* article praised the latter, managed by his cousin Moy S. James, as a "first-class Chinese restaurant, catering only to the best class of patronage and run strictly on business principles."

Using his merchant status to obtain certificates of identity, he was finally able to bring his wife, Wong Shee to the U. S. in 1904. She soon adopted an American name, Judith Moy, and before long became actively involved in social, church, and business activities in the community.

Moy established a Chinese Nationalist League of America office to support the new republic of Sun Yat Sen in China and served as president of the local chapter. The group urged Americanization among the Chinese. In 1921, Moy established the Chinese public school in St. Paul. Local newspapers recognized and commended Moy's success as a business and community leader.

Chin F. Foin, Chicago, Ill.[2]

Chin F. Foin came to Chicago in 1895 after entering the U.S in 1892 as a merchant with family ties to a trading company. By 1905, Chin was selected to be the manager of *King Yen Lo's Oriental Restaurant*, an upscale restaurant located above a saloon run by a corrupt alderman outside the Levee, a down-and-out part of town. By 1912, Chin and his four brothers expanded their business beyond their South Clark Street Chinatown restaurant to a total of

five Chinese upscale restaurants including the *King Joy Lo* and the
Mandarin Inn. King Joy Lo opened in 1906 with funds from both local white investors and the Chinese Empire Reform Party, or
Banhuanghui, which made a substantial financial investment with the
goal of using profits to support their political agenda in China.[3] Its
leaders appointed Chin Foin as the manager. This association of
Chin with elite Chinese reformers enhanced the acceptance of the
opulent restaurant.[4]

Centrally located downtown, *King Joy Lo* attracted "hundreds of well dressed men and women," with "quaint Oriental
decorations" that included exquisite Chinese art, a central fountain,
and grand chandelier on the main floor. With live orchestra per-
formances nightly, the restaurant immediately earned a citywide
reputation as one of the "unique wonders of the city."

However, the public's positive image of Chin was formed
without knowledge that investors in China had charged that Chin
Foin was a poor manager who failed to generate profits.[5] Never-
theless, under his management Chin Foin and the restaurants
improved the status of Chinese cuisine. "Americanized" and upper-class Chinese businessmen such as Chin Foin were viewed as
financial successes with no apparent links to the businesses associated with the vices of gambling, prostitution, and opium smoking
that were prevalent in Chinatowns across the country. Whites ad-
mired Chin as a "model minority," a reputation that ironically came
from the exotic atmosphere he created in his restaurants to attract
non-Chinese patrons.

Chicago newspapers held Chin in high regard because of his economic success and acceptance of Western material upper-class culture. In contrast, Chicago newspapers condemned the dark side of the Chinatown on South Clark Street, publicizing and condemning its illegal businesses, corruption, and tong wars. Chin's reputation helped counter the negative images of Chinese.[6]

Mar Tung Jing, Wichita, Ks.[7]

Using identity papers of Jee See Wing purchased by his father, an import-export merchant, Mar Tung Jing arrived in San Francisco in 1922, leaving his wife and newborn son behind in their Guangdong village. Mar first worked as a laborer or in a restaurant in San Francisco for two years before six other Chinese, also from his Mar village clan, persuaded him to join them to buy and work at the *Pan-American Café*, a Chinese restaurant in Wichita, Kansas. Opened in 1917, the *Pan-American* thrived for many years serving the area's oilmen and cattlemen. Mar and two others bought the café from the original Chinese owners who retired and returned to China. Mar served as the cook for Chinese dishes, which comprised about a third of the menu offerings while the majority of dishes were American food.

Whereas Chinese restaurants in Chinatowns were entirely staffed by Chinese men, the waitresses at the Pan-American were Caucasians, because at that time there were no Chinese women in Wichita. Using white waitresses made it easier for white customers to place orders, but the waitresses then had to shout aloud the orders to Chinese cooks who did not read English.

Figure 14 Pan American Cafe, Wichita, ca. 1930s, Courtesy Wayne Wong.

The *Pan-American Cafe* seated 118 customers, required a sizeable staff of salaried cooks, waiters, dishwashers, and kitchen aides. Providing meals and inexpensive sleeping quarters supplemented wages and tips for 12 Chinese workers in partitioned sections on the second and third floors above the restaurant. Their living conditions were marginal, as there were only two toilets, and no showers or bathtubs.

The café opened 24 hours everyday of the week to meet the demand. The restaurant workers had two long shifts of 12 hours each, one starting at 8 a.m. and one starting at 8 p.m. Mar's earnings from the successful restaurant supported his wife and the son he had before he immigrated as well as three more children he fathered during three subsequent return visits to the village between 1928 and 1935.

Just as his father had done for him in 1922, Mar arranged in 1935 for his first son, then 13 years old, to come to Wichita to work in the restaurant. He arrived in Seattle using the paper name, Wong Hung Yin, although he soon adopted an American name, Wayne. After a few days to recover from the trip across the ocean and the immigration interrogation in Seattle, Wayne arrived in Wichita late one evening. After a sound night of sleep, he received a simple breakfast the next morning before his father welcomed him to Gum Saan by introducing him to the restaurant life, handing him a clean white apron. "Here," he said gruffly, "wash these bean sprouts." After he completed this task, his no-nonsense father "shoved a tub at me and ordered me to start bussing dishes."[8] This was just the beginning, as every day after attending school Wayne did his school homework until 5 p. m. Then he helped in the restaurant until about 8:30 bussing dishes, cleaning, and resetting tables before he resumed his school work until 11 p.m.

Not wanting to spend his life working in restaurants, Wayne saw an opportunity to receive training in the Signal Corps so he enlisted in the Army in 1942 and served for three years. After he was discharged, he made a visit to China to see his parents. There he met an attractive young woman, Kim, and soon they married. As a G.I., he was allowed to bring Kim to Wichita as a war bride in 1947.

Wayne returned to work at the *Pan-American* for several years serving as the night chef with long 12-hour night shifts, but it was still a struggle to support his growing family on his salary. He worked in other restaurant jobs before becoming the kitchen manager and cook of the *T-Bone Supper Club* for 16 years.

After their children grew up, his wife wanted to work and urged him to buy a restaurant, the *Georgie Porgie Pie Shoppe*, in a new suburban part of Wichita in 1972. The menu was the basic American cafe fare including, soups, sandwiches, buckwheat pancakes, meatloaf, and fried chicken, but each day it also offered a different popular Chinese-American dish. Wayne worked the dining room while Kim did the kitchen duties. They received help from their children, but in 1973 the two oldest, Linda and Wilma, moved from Wichita leaving only Edward, the youngest, to help. However, Wayne made some successful commercial real estate investments, and by 1991, he sold the *Georgie Porgie Pie Shoppe* and retired.

Frank Fat, Sacramento, Ca. [9]

Shortly after Dong Sai Fat was born in Toishan in 1904, his father left for the U. S. as a paper son to earn money for his family. In Canton, Dong worked in a restaurant for two years for only room and board. When he was 16 in 1919, his father purchased a paper identity of Wong Bing Yuen for him to immigrate to the U. S. where he would later adopt as his American name, Frank Fat.

His uncle emigrated earlier and was running a restaurant in Sacramento, California. He could not afford to hire Frank but provided him with board and a place to sleep in the basement in return for working in the restaurant. Frank also took a few odd jobs including picking fruit in orchards but the earnings were meager so he soon left with a cousin to work in a laundry in Akron, Ohio. There, Frank managed to contact his father, then employed as a restaurant cook in nearby Cleveland. He moved there and worked for a while side by side with his father. Frank's father, unwisely, decided to open his own restaurant in Youngstown, Ohio, but it was a failure. His father left for China for a period before returning to Sacramento.

At age 20, Frank returned to his Guangdong village to marry in an arranged match. He remained for over a year and fathered a son. Then Frank joined an older cousin, who was a retired merchant, in a venture in Canton. There, with the aid of loans from his cousin, he led an active and carefree social life. However, when his cousin suddenly died, Frank decided to return to the U. S. alone in 1926 to earn money to repay his loans and to provide for his wife and son whom he left behind.

This was the period of the Great Depression so it was difficult to earn a living. Frank worked in a succession of jobs as a waiter in Chinese restaurants in Grand Rapids, Michigan, and Chicago, Illinois, until 1930. Then he moved to join his uncle in Sacramento who had just remodeled the *Hong King Lum Restaurant*, and even added a dance floor. Located near the state capitol building, it did a brisk business with all the state politicians and lobbyists. It was in this setting that Frank, with his charming and outgoing personality, became a very successful businessman.

In 1939, an old restaurant in a run-down area of downtown Sacramento was for sale. Frank felt confident that he could make it into a successful enterprise. Although his friends were skeptical, he felt this place, located two blocks from the State Capital, was better located than *Hong King Lum* and he made the decision to start his restaurant there. His family's meager savings combined with a business loan enabled him to buy and remodel the restaurant, which he renamed *Frank Fat's*.

> Putting in 16 hours daily alongside his 12 employees, Frank gradually established the business. He served a full lunch for 35 cents, dinner for 85 cents and gave ladies fresh gardenias on Friday nights. Frank installed a window between the dining area and the kitchen so patrons could see the sanitary meal preparations themselves, effectively squelching the common rumors of dirty Chinese restaurant kitchens. After eight months *Frank Fat's* was turning a profit and attracting a clientele from the Capitol and other businesses. Therefore Capitol denizens did, lured mostly by Frank's unfailing graciousness and willingness to accommodate his clientele. After hours, lawmakers and lobbyists could forget the differences of the day and indulge in drinking and gambling.[10]

Combined with his hosting skills and friendships that he had cultivated for years at *Hong King Lum*, his restaurant prospered, and *Frank Fat's* became a gathering place for influential state legislators, lobbyists, and other government employees to dine and conduct business. After 32 years, Frank retired in 1971, but his sons and their families continued operations and the restaurant remains a success and popular dining spot in the region.

Chung Gim Suey, Los Angeles, Ca. [11]

Chung Gim Suey was born as Zhang Bao Shen in 1922 in Hoiping, Guangdong, also the birthplace of his father. Only a decade earlier, his father, Zhang Yang Shou, married to wife #1, had emigrated as a "single man" to the U. S. in 1912 using the paper name, Chung Moi. He first worked in San Francisco for a dry goods and food products store of which his father, living in Boston, was a silent partner. In 1917, he moved to Cambridge, Ma. to serve as manager for two years at the *Imperial Restaurant* where his father was also a silent partner. After he managed to raise $500, Chung Moi became a partner and manager at the *Royal Restaurant*, which opened with capital of $15,490 raised from 42 silent and 5 active partners. This first-class restaurant in Boston's Chinatown seated 100. It served American and Chinese food, with $6,000 in monthly receipts for which he earned $90 a month.

In 1921 Zhang Yang Shou returned to China for a brief visit and married in an arranged match to Huang Qin Chun, wife #2. Shortly after Zhang Bao Shen was born, Chung Moi left his family behind and returned to Cambridge in 1923 where he became a partner in the *Imperial Restaurant* for $700. This first-class restaurant could seat 170 customers and had capital of $13,000 raised from 33 silent and 7 active partners. It served Chinese and American dishes, especially chop suey, with $4,000 in monthly sales for which he earned $100 a month as manager.

By 1932, his son, Zhang Bao Shen, was 9 years old. Chung Moi decided it was time to bring him to America. A village relative gave him false papers bearing the name, Chong Gim Suey, which enabled him to immigrate to the U. S. for a good education and a higher income. Gim Suey memorized the biographical information associated with his paper identity and successfully gained entry. However, father and son struggled to make ends meet, even though they lived in quarters above the restaurant to save money. Like many businesses, the *Imperial Restaurant* did not do well during the Great Depression, so Chung decided to sell his share in 1936 and move to southern California. There he worked as a waiter at the *Yet Quong Low Restaurant*, a chop suey joint, in the "Little Tokyo" district of Los Angeles, founded in 1913 by several Chinese from Chung's village. After school, Gim Suey worked as a busboy in the *Yet Quong Low*, where father and son used a storage room in the back for sleeping quarters.

Educated in the U. S., Gim Suey had greater employment opportunities than his father. Upon completing high school in 1941 in Los Angeles, Gim Suey studied aeronautical engineering at the Curtiss Wright Technical Institute in Glendale, Ca., until 1943, when he found employment in San Francisco as an airplane mechanic working on the *China Clipper* for Pan American Airways System.

Nonetheless, after work, and on weekends, Gim Suey still found it necessary to work as a waiter because employment in engineering was still limited for Chinese. After the war, he became a partner (and waiter) from 1946-1950 at Eddie Pond's *Kubla Khan Theater Restaurant*, which included a nightclub and bar. They served Chinese (Cantonese style) and American dishes. Located at the entrance to San Francisco Chinatown from downtown, the *Kubla Khan* occupied the building that previously housed the *Mandarin Cafe*, which went out of business during the Great Depression.

Figure 15 Gim Suey Chong (rt) with fellow waiters at Kubla Khan. Courtesy, Chong Family.

Featuring an all-Chinese revue with a mixture of vaudeville and burlesque acts, the *Kubla Khan* along with the *Forbidden City* and the *Chinese Sky Room,* two better known Chinatown nightclubs, pioneered opportunities for Chinese entertainers to perform western style songs and dances as white nightclubs never booked Chinese performers. The Chinese venues attracted primarily non-Chinese audiences, a reflection of their curiosity about "Orientals" as well as a growing acceptance of Chinese participation in main-stream society.

But business declined eventually by the early 1950s, as the novelty wore out and competition with other clubs, non-Chinese as well as Chinese, increased. Gim Suey sold his share of the *Kubla Khan* and returned to Los Angeles to live with his father in the "New Chinatown" district near City Hall.

Gim Suey worked as a quality assurance inspector for the Lockheed Aircraft Corporation from 1950 to 1979, but on week-ends he served as a waiter for 24 years at the *Far East Café* operated by five Zhang village cousins that had moved from Mason City, Iowa, where they had a hand laundry to run this restaurant in "Lit-tle Tokyo." *Far East Café* was known in the Nikkei community for its "China-Meshi" cuisine, a Japanese version of Cantonese food.

Richard C. Wing, Hanford, Ca.

As a political activist during the Taiping Rebellion against the regime in China, Gong Ting Shu found it necessary to flee Guangdong to escape reprisal. In about 1883, he immigrated to Hanford in the middle of California's rich farming region. At that time Hanford's China Alley was the center of one of the state's largest Chinatowns, populated by some of the 15,000 Chinese rail-road workers left unemployed after they finished laying a spur of the Southern Pacific Railroad.

Gong, whose American name was Henry Wing, opened a restaurant in Hanford named *Mee Jen Low* (English translation: Beautiful and Precious Restaurant) selling noodles at 5 cents a bowl. This family-run restaurant occupied only the upstairs part of the building located in the center of China Alley, the Chinese business street. After Gong Ting Shu died in 1923, his son, Gong Chow Wing, continued running the family business but in the 1930s he closed the *Mee Jan Low* to open a new restaurant, *Chinese Pagoda*, which also relied on family involvement.[12]

Richard Wing, born in 1921, and the fifth of his seven children, was called to the Army in 1944. Unable to complete basic training for health reasons, Richard was assigned to temporary KP duty. One day, Richard received a completely unexpected order to report to Washington, D. C. where he learned he was to be assigned as a personal cook to General George C. Marshall, the U. S. Army Chief of Staff.[13]

During World War II, General Marshall was an important leader in Europe operations but in 1944, he was sent to China to head a diplomatic mission, which accounts for why he sought a Chinese cook to accompany him. After the war, Richard Wing served from 1945-1947 as a chef for General Marshall, who in 1947 was appointed Secretary of State. Through his association with General Marshall, Richard had the rare opportunity to visit many world capitals including London, Paris, Moscow, Warsaw, Shanghai, and Chungking. As a chef for General Marshall, his skills impressed world leaders.[14] Richard benefited from these experiences during as well as after the war as he learned about other cultures and their cuisines.

After the war, he spent a brief time convalescing from an
illness acquired during the war. He then attended the University of
Southern California to obtain a degree in International Relations.
In 1956, the Wing family asked him to return to run *China Pagoda*
and help rebuild Chinese Alley.   In 1958 he opened a new restaurant, the *Imperial Dynasty*, next door to *Chinese Pagoda,* run by his
brother until it closed in the early 1980s.[15] Richard developed and
promoted a revolutionary and distinct cuisine. His creativity as a
chef led to original dishes that were a fusion of Chinese and
French cooking, known as "chinoise" cuisine and established his
reputation. The restaurant received awards and recognition from
major culinary organizations for its *chinoise* cuisine, which was
ahead of its time. Wing's reputation as a chef attracted world leaders and dignitaries to dine at the *Imperial Dynasty*.[16]

Figure 16 Chinese Pagoda (left) and Imperial Dynasty (right) China Alley,
Hanford, Ca. Courtesy, Loren Madsen.

In spite of international acclaim, the *Imperial Dynasty*, in many respects, still had the imprint of a family-run restaurant. As many as 22 family members including his mother, siblings, children, and grandchildren worked in different roles in the restaurant. After almost 50 years of operation, however, the *Imperial Dynasty* closed its doors in 2006 with the retirement of both Richard and his sister, Harriet, who managed the restaurant for many years.

Song Wong Bourbeau, Santa Rosa, Ca.[17]

If she was not the very first Chinese woman to own and operate a Chinese restaurant, Song Wong Bourbeau was certainly among the pioneers. Song Wong's grandfather, Poy Jam Kee, born in 1857 in China, opened the *Jam Kee Restaurant* in 1877 in partnership with his brother whose paper name was Moon Young. It started with only two tables and was the first Chinese restaurant in Santa Rosa, located about 60 miles north of San Francisco. His son, Tom Wing Wong, also born in China, came to work for a San Francisco Chinatown manufacturer of shoes. Next, he became a labor contractor and recruited work crews from China to Sonoma County for farmers and others needing laborers. He also had a boarding house that rented rooms to Chinese laborers. In addition, Tom Wing Wong played other vital roles in the small Chinatown, serving as caretaker for the Chinese temple, managing the operation of a Chinese lottery, and acting as a lawyer for the Chinese community. Due to his prominence in Chinatown affairs, he was regarded as the unofficial "Mayor of the Chinatown."

Tom had three earlier wives that had all died young in

China. He had an arranged marriage with a fourth wife, Lun Moon, who was born in San Francisco. She was the only Chinese woman living in Santa Rosa and she cooked the meals for the boarding house laborers. Song Wong, their daughter born in 1909, was the only Chinese girl in town. She faced taunts routinely from other children due to the racism of the times against Chinese. Tom Wing had to walk her to and from school everyday, because she was often threatened or accosted by other children.

When Tom Wing Wong died suddenly in 1918 during the great influenza epidemic, Song Wong, only 9 years old, and her mother went to work to help her grandfather Poy operate the restaurant.

> We raised all of our own food, chickens and rabbits and pigeons and as well as vegetables in the yard behind the restaurant. If we wanted something we just went out in the backyard and got it, we had our own garden. Then we had an apple dryer. And we use to dry apples and sulfur them and send them to market.[18]

Song attended Santa Rosa College and then Stanford University. In the late 1920s, Song Wong secretly married a high school classmate, Charles Bourbeau, despite the California antimiscegenation law that prohibited marriage between white people and "Mongolians," a law that was not repealed until 1948.

By the 1930s, Santa Rosa's Chinatown population, which had risen to as high as 200, dwindled to only about 30 elderly men. Chinatown had been dying for years, and urban renewal in 1966 was the final nail in the coffin that saw most of the remaining Chinese laundries and grocery stores in the area close, leaving only a few Chinese restaurants that survived by serving mainly non-Chinese customers.

After grandfather Poy died in 1956, Song Wong inherited the restaurant. Song Wong and Charles Bourbeau continued to run the *Jam Kee Restaurant* for three more decades, even though it had been torched once. The restaurant occupied several different locations in downtown Santa Rosa until it finally closed in 1988 after Charles died.

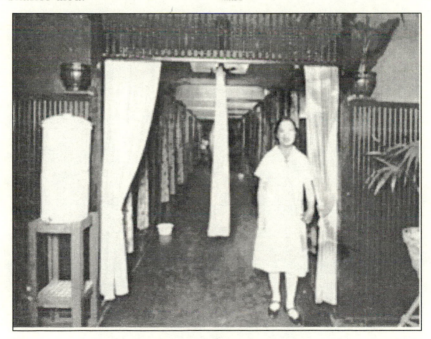

Figure 17 Song Wong Bourbeau at her Jam Kee Restaurant, Santa Rosa, Ca., Courtesy, Sonoma County Museum.

Song Wong was a pioneer as a Chinese woman owner of a restaurant, named "Business Woman of the Year" in 1971, and she was also civic-minded. She interpreted for lawyers with Chinese clients and tutored Chinese preparing for U.S. citizenship. In 1989-1990 Song received recognition by Santa Rosa's American Legion Auxiliary as a nominee for Woman of the Year. When Song died at age 86 in 1996, she left a large collection of valuable Chinese artifacts to the Sonoma County Museum.

Conclusions

The stories of these Chinese restaurant pioneers were similar in many ways to those of many other Chinese immigrants whether they were in the restaurant, grocery, or laundry business. First, they worked long hours for low wages, but somehow scrimped and saved enough money until they could start a restaurant either alone or with partners. Many managed to send money back to their villages to support their wives and children there. Some were able to make periodic return visits for brief periods to their families, father more children, and eventually send for their families.

If they held an immigration status of merchant, they petitioned to bring their families to this country. If they could only bring some of their family, a preference was for sons as soon as they were around 10 years old because they could provide help in operating a business. If they were classified as laborers, and not legally bring their children over, they purchased papers that falsely identified them as children of merchants to make them eligible to immigrate.

Many Chinese immigrants worked as laborers or in other businesses before settling in restaurant work. Many relocated several times around the country seeking better opportunities. They received work, lodging, and financial assistance from relatives and acquaintances from their villages. Not all restaurant owners were successful, or not to the extent achieved by the examples in this chapter. Still, most of them managed to earn a living, raise a family, and provide their children the means to enjoy better lives.

The objective of most Chinese restaurant owners was to earn a living by providing meals to diners. In addition, a few remarkable owners, through their success with their business, also had a major impact on fostering positive images of Chinese and their food. These five men, Moy Ju Hee, Chin Foin, Frank Fat, Gim Suey Chong, and Richard Wing, and one woman, Song Wong Bourbeau, each in their own way, made significant contributions toward enhancing the reputation and image of Chinese restaurants and cuisine among non-Chinese.

Endnotes

[1] Sherri Gebert Fuller. "Mirrored Identities: The Moys of St. Paul." *Minnesota History*, 57, no. 4 (2000): 162-181.
[2] Chinese Food and Politics in Chicago, 1905-07.
http://ccamuseum.org/Food.html#anchor_150 (accessed June 1, 2009).
[3] Shih-Shan Henry Tsai, "The Emergence of Early Chinese Nationalist Organizations in America." *AmerAsia Journal* (1982), 8:2 121-143; Adam McKeown. *Chinese Migrant Networks and Cultural Change: Peru, Chicago, and Hawaii 1900-1936* (Chicago: University of Chicago Press, 2001).
[4] The Chinese Reform Party's Commercial Corporation made a large investment in the King Joy Lo Restaurant. Chin persuaded Tom Leung and other leaders of Los Angeles' Chinese Reform Association to invest

in a Chicago restaurant to raise money to support political reform in China.

[5] Jane Leung Larsen. "New Source Materials on Kang Youwei and Bao-haunghui." *Chinese America: History and Perspectives,* 7 (1993): 151-198.

[6] Phonsia Nie. Chinese in Chicago's "Levee:" Chinatown before 1912 (Master's Thesis, Northwestern University, 2009).

[7] Wayne Hung Wong. *American Paper Son, A Chinese immigrant in the Midwest* (Urbana, Il, University of Illinois Press, 2006).

[8] Ibid., 38.

[9] Peter C. Y. Leung and Eileen Leung, "Mr. Frank Fat, A Legendary Restaurateur in Sacramento," In: *150 Years of the Chinese Presence in California* (Sacramento, Ca.: Sacramento Chinese Cultural Foundation and Asian American Studies, University of California, Davis, 2001).

[10] Ibid., 107.

[11] Raymond Chong. "Gim Suey Chong: From Hoyping to Gum Saan." *Gum Saan Journal,* 31 (2009): 19-52.

[12] Charles Hillinger. "The Chinatown a Chef Saved" *Los Angeles Times* May 29, 1975. ProQuest Historical Newspapers Los Angeles Times (1881 - 1986), OC1.

[13] Susie Ling. "Dreamer in the Kitchen: Richard Wing." *Gum Saan Journal,* 2007, 30, 21-32.

[14] Richard C. Wing "General George Marshall and I." *Gum Saan Journal,* 30, (2007): 33-44.

[15] Camille Wing, Personal communication, Dec. 14, 2009.

[16] Cassandra Queen. "The Last Days of A Dynasty." *Valley Voice Newspaper Archive,* Jan 18, 2006. http://www.valleyvoicenewspaper.com/vvarc/2006/january182006.htm (accessed Aug. 20, 2009).

[17] Sue Doherty. "Sonoma Stories And The Song Wong Bourbeau Collection: A Model For An Exhibition And A Public Outreach Program— An Innovative Approach To CRM" (Master's Thesis, Sonoma State University, 2005), *http://worldcat.org/oclc/67553433* (accessed July, 2009).

[18] Ibid., 182.

6. Moving Beyond Chinatowns

Around the end of the 19th century, increasing numbers of Chinese began leaving the Pacific and Atlantic coast regions to relocate in the middle of the country. Similar remigration occurred for Chinese in Canada away from the west coast. A major reason for this dispersal of Chinese during the 1880s and 1890s was the escalation of threats to their physical safety. During this period, numerous violent actions toward Chinese occurred throughout these regions aimed at expelling them. Many Chinese died from mob violence and many of their businesses, temples, and homes were burned to the ground. Chinese were literally 'driven out' or purged from entire cities as they fled for their lives.[1] They tended to disperse into communities where there were few other Chinese, contrary to the adage that there is "safety in numbers." In 1920, census records showed only one Chinese living in 10.4 percent of U. S. counties and only from 2 to 20 Chinese residing in another 20.3 percent of U. S. counties.[2]

During this time, Chinese were expelled from many occupations including fishing, farming, mining, and manufacturing. Consequently, many Chinese turned to self-employment as merchants or in providing domestic services. During the late 1800s and early 1900s, as previously noted, the primary form of self-employment among Chinese involved laundry work, but a shift toward the restaurant business began around 1910. By 1920, among recent arrivals, 30.5 percent of Chinese immigrants were still engaged in laundry work, exceeding the 15.6 percent in restaurant work. But a clear reversal occurred by 1930 with only 21.2 percent in laundry work as compared to 30.5 percent in restaurant work.[3]

Chinese faced fewer barriers in domestic work like meal preparation in the frontier west. Some Chinese with prior experience as cooks for mining companies, railroad construction companies, and private homes, opened restaurants to meet the need for cooked meals for the many single men, both Chinese and non-Chinese. Other Chinese immigrants acquired experience with cooking American or western-style foods after leaving China. Some gained experience working as cooks on ships or cooking food for sale to white gold miners. Other Chinese working as houseboys for white families learned how to cook western foods as well as how to launder clothing. These culinary experiences prepared them well for the cooking part of running a restaurant,

As already noted, few Chinese immigrants had families here due to exclusionary laws. Consequently, most early Chinese restaurant operations did not involve family participation. Additional legislation in 1924 imposed a quota system that further curtailed Chinese immigration. Even American-born Chinese that married Chinese women from Guangdong villages were not allowed to bring them to the U. S. Some relief occurred in 1930 with legislation that permitted admission of wives from China, provided they had married before 1924.

Chinese Family Growth

The Chinese exclusion law was finally repealed in 1943 in the U. S. and in 1947 in Canada. Actually, the repeal in the U. S.

was mainly symbolic as it admitted only a total of 105 immigrants of Chinese descent worldwide each year. Other laws had far more significance for the growth of the Chinese population and family reunification. The War Brides Act in 1945[4] and the G. I. Fiancées Act in the following year admitted alien dependents of World War II veterans without quota limits, allowing over 6,000 Chinese women to enter the U. S. between 1945 and 1948, which enabled the reestablishment of family life that had been long absent in Chinese American communities.[5] As their children grew up, they provided help for Chinese with businesses such as laundries, grocery stores, and restaurants that improved their income.

A rising trend of eating-out following the war favored the growth of small family-run Chinese restaurants. Dining out was not the norm for most Americans prior to the war years; it was cultivated by the restaurant industry as a leisure activity. With increased affluence, the appetite for restaurant dining increased.[6] As more women began to work outside the home, there were fewer home-cooked meals, and an increase in dining out. Chinese restaurants, like all others, benefited from this rising tide, and they were found all across the U.S. and Canada by the 1950s. These small restaurants depended on the labor of the entire family, children included. If they had more success than they could handle, they would hire a few workers. They preferred to hire other Chinese with whom they could communicate with more readily. They often hired Chinese exchange students on a part-time basis to work after school or during their summer vacations.[7] However, in regions with few

Chinese, they hired white women as waitresses and minority group members as kitchen help and dishwashers.

Some ambitious Chinese opened larger restaurants that required more capital than a single family could save or obtain through the traditional association rotating credit mechanisms of the past. Formation of partnerships of investors and bank loans were necessary to meet the high startup costs for large restaurants. Although these more elaborately furnished and decorated restaurants could afford to hire the larger staff of managers, cooks, waiters, and kitchen helpers necessary to accommodate banquets and larger groups from 100 to 300, there was no guarantee that they would be more profitable than family-run restaurants.[8] Some fancy new restaurants offering authentic food failed due to high overhead costs and the tendency of some of their professional cooks to quit and open their own smaller restaurants.[9] Furthermore, they often had to compete against large restaurants by offering low prices that reduced profitability.

Partners of large restaurants sometimes bickered over business decisions. In some instances, a partner might turn out to be a swindler and abscond with funds.[10] Waiters had conflicts among themselves as well as with managers. Similarly, cooks sometimes fought with each other, with managers, and with waiters. Employees, aside from top cooks, were poorly paid and sometimes badly treated by authoritarian managers. Not surprisingly, some disgruntled employees wasted or even stole food and supplies.[11]

Small family-run restaurants were not without their own

problems. Family members could also have conflicts with each other. But most owners felt they could trust their family members to be generally more cooperative, reliable, and honest than hired employees. Furthermore, using family members offered more flexibility. They changed their work hours to adjust to the level of business more readily than large restaurants that had to quickly hire or dismiss employees to meet business demands.[12]

Chinese versus Western Food Preparation and Service

> "*...a Chinese chop suey restaurant sporting a flashy neon sign that screamed "serving American and Chinese cuisine," but the dishes they served were nothing like the food we ate at home"*
> *Marie Rose Wong, Sweet Cakes, Long Journey p. xiii*

In towns and regions without sufficient numbers of Chinese patrons, Chinese restaurants had to make adjustments in many ways to serve non-white patrons to accommodate to Western eating preferences. For example, Chinese ate meals with chopsticks whereas non-Chinese used forks.[13] Diners also needed knives to cut the large pieces of food in many Western dishes, which were unnecessary for Chinese dishes that had bite-sized pieces. Chinese ate family-style meals, where everyone in the group shares several common dishes. This format depended on each person not taking too large a serving of any dish, so that everyone could have a fair portion. In contrast, non-Chinese preferred to have individuals order their own entrées.

Chinese always consumed rice with their meals whereas non-Chinese usually preferred bread and butter.[14] Even the sequence of serving dishes was modified. Soup was served first in conformity with western customs whereas in China, soup was the last part of a meal, as it was believed it would aid the digestion of the richer main courses.

Chinese restaurants with many non-Chinese customers adapted their recipes for Chinese dishes to appeal to their tastes, preparing sweeter and deep-fried batter dishes in heavy sauces instead of the stir-fried, steamed, and braised dishes with light sauces that were typical in Cantonese cuisine.[15]

In Chinese cooking, the cook slices and chops meats and vegetables into small thin pieces, which are then cooked rapidly at a very high temperature in a wok. The bowl shaped wok is versatile and better suited for the Chinese-style of stir-fry cooking than the flat western cookware. Stir-frying maintains the crispness and tasty flavor of fresh ingredients, which Chinese prefer. The technique is a major reason why Chinese dishes need only a short time between ordering and being served.

In contrast, American dishes involve whole or large pieces of meat and vegetables, which require long cooking times when they are baked or boiled. They must be cooked well before they are served, often sitting around for a long time before they are ordered. Canned vegetables are often used because of their convenience. When fresh vegetables are used they are often boiled until they are soggy and lose their bright color and taste.

Finally, unlike with traditional western meals, Chinese do not serve sweets or desserts at the end. A satisfactory substitute for dessert in Chinese American restaurants was the fortune cookie, an item invented in America that is absent in restaurants in China. The appeal lies more in the 'fortune,' a supposedly wise Chinese saying, printed on a slip of paper tucked inside the cookie than in the taste of the concoction itself.[16]

West

San Francisco, the port where the majority of Chinese immigrants entered the U. S., as already noted in earlier chapters, had Chinese restaurants starting as early as the 1850s, and they quickly grew in number and size. Other towns in the west with sizable Chinese populations such as Portland and Seattle also had restaurants that served dishes favored by Chinese. Chinese restaurants sprang up in towns of all sizes located along the major rail routes such as the Union Pacific, Central Pacific, Northern Pacific, and Southern Pacific Railroads. Thus, in California, they appeared in places like Stockton and Sacramento and Truckee, Carlin, Elko, Wells, Toano, and Montello in Nevada. Chinese opened restaurants in Nevada mining camps near towns north of the transcontinental routes such as Cornucopia, Mountain City, Gold Creek, and Contact.[17]

Even in towns with only a few Chinese, there were always one or two Chinese restaurants along with a few Chinese laundries. In Idaho, many Chinese with cooking experience opened restaurants to feed the many Chinese attracted to the area by gold finds in the late 1800s. Around 1900 every town of any size In Idaho had at least one Chinese café.[18]

When the transcontinental railroad was completed in Utah in 1869, many Chinese railroad construction workers were stranded in the area. Some of them remained to settle there and in nearby regions. They recognized opportunities to engage in domestic work like washing clothes and cooking meals. For example, Chinese who drifted into Prescott, Arizona, like those moving to other towns in the region during the 1870s, noted that the:

> ...resident Euro-American population, in a ratio of five males to one female, routinely got hungry and dirty but had no inclination to tend to these needs. Recognizing that cooking and washing required little specialized skill and only a minimal command of English, these migrants, like other Chinese throughout the mountain West, formed small-scale food and laundry service industries that were to flourish for the entire lifetime of the local Chinese community.[19]

Similar circumstances further to the east led Chinese to open restaurants starting in the 1870s in cities near the Rocky Mountains like Ogden, Salt Lake City, and Denver, toward the north in Laramie, Evanston, and Cheyenne, and toward the southwest in Phoenix, Albuquerque, San Antonio, and Houston.

Central

In Deadwood, South Dakota, Chinese opened restaurants in the late 1800s that served mostly dishes popular with westerners. With low prices and fast service, they were successful enterprises on the frontier.

> Most of the Chinese eating houses bore American names such as "Sacramento Restaurant," "Philadelphia Café," "Lincoln Restaurant," "Bodega Café,"

"Elegant Restaurant," "OK Café," "Club Restaurant," "Empire Café," "Drakes Chinese Noodle," and "Paris Café." Some operated as if they were part of a white-owned establishment; for example, Sam Wols Chung's Restaurant was located on the first floor of the Bullock Hotel in Deadwood. Except for a few exotic items like rice wine and chicken rice soup on the menu, the Chinese-owned restaurants mainly served familiar western dishes, including roast beef, T-bone steak, rabbit stew, French bread, and apple pie. Each meal usually cost only twenty-five cents, with a five-dollar discount plan that covered twenty-one meals. The restaurants were often open from early morning to late evening to accommodate their customers. The Empire Café was advertised in various issues of the local newspaper as a place with "everything new," "neat and clean," "best of Service," and "cuisine unexcelled." The Club Restaurant claimed that it had the "best table in city." Reasonable prices, fine cuisine, and prompt service assured these restaurants a stream of loyal customers.[20]

In the late 19 century Chinese in St. Louis opened restaurants, merchandise stores, and grocery stores to provide services to Chinese in Hop Alley, the Chinese section of St. Louis. The number of restaurants increased from 1900 to 1950. In contrast, Chinese laundries, mostly located in white residential neighborhoods, dwindled in number until they disappeared completely by the 1960s. After the liberalized 1965 immigration law, a new wave of Chinese immigrants came to St. Louis from regions other than Guangdong. The number of restaurants increased rapidly but the type of cuisine shifted away from Cantonese toward northern styles.[21]

Chicago, a city with immigrants from many countries, had a reputation of more ethnic tolerance. It was especially attractive to Chinese fleeing the violence and hostility toward them in western states. Not surprisingly, it had many Chinese restaurants, as previously noted. The first one listed was in the 1893 city directory. By 1902 it listed 17 restaurants, and in 1907 it showed 57. As they spread beyond Chinatown to other parts of the city, the number rose to 122 by 1917.[22]

Figure 18 American Moderne interior of Kin Chu Restaurant, Minneapolis, 1930s. Courtesy, Norton & Peel, Minnesota Historical Society.

Other large cities in the region like Milwaukee and Minneapolis were also attractive places for Chinese to open restaurants even though their Chinese populations were smaller. The important role of the Moys in opening restaurants in Minneapolis and St. Paul was cited in Chapter 5. There, by the 1930s as elsewhere, Chinese relied less on Oriental motifs and created interiors in their restaurants to fit American styles, as illustrated by the *Kin Chu Restaurant* in Figure 18.[23]

East

In New York City's Chinatown, with its large Chinese community of merchants, grocers, and laundrymen, had some of the earliest Chinese restaurants. Around 1900 Chinese restaurants began opening outside of Chinatown throughout the city, and as noted in Chapter 3, quickly increased to over several hundred. However, this growth made survival in the competitive restaurant business very difficult.[24] Many restaurants lasted only a few years. In Philadelphia, for example, eight of the 12 Chinese restaurants operating in 1912 were out of business in 1915.[25] The four surviving restaurants operated for at least another decade.[26]

Around the end of the 19th century, New England cities like Lowell, Massachusetts and Providence, Rhode Island, prospered from textile mills and manufacturing. In 1907, a Chinese restaurant opened in Lowell, with others following there and in many other towns. But, their growth stalled when industry in the region declined over the 1920s as many mills moved to the South attracted by cheaper labor costs.

The first Chinese restaurant in Portland, Maine opened in 1880, and a second one, the *Oriental*, opened a decade later.[27] Chinese restaurants were often located in parts of town frequented by sailors, soldiers, longshoremen, fisherman, and laborers. Disturbances and fights occurred among patrons after drinking too much, which harmed business Trouble also developed when some customers harassed and taunted Chinese proprietors.

Prosperity during the shipbuilding boom during World War I led to an expansion of Chinese restaurants with the infusion of capital from a syndicate of Chinese investors. The *Empire*, and other restaurants, that opened in 1916 were popular deluxe dining establishments with a band and dance floor.

During World War II, the local economy boomed and the Chinese restaurants prospered with several new restaurants. Following the war, however, the downtown section declined and the restaurants began to close or move to the shopping malls and suburbs.

South

Although few Chinese immigrants settled in southeastern states, Chinese restaurants could be found scattered over the region by the 1940s. The best known Chinese restaurant in the southern states was the *Joy Young Restaurant* in Birmingham, Alabama, which several partners from Guangdong opened in the 1930s, featuring a band and dance floor.[28]

Other Chinese restaurants opened from Richmond and Norfolk in Virginia all the way to Memphis, Tennessee and Greenville, Mississippi. Most served many popular American dishes like pork chops, fried chicken, and steak with only a few American-Chinese dishes like chop suey, chow mein, and egg foo yung.

Figure 19 Fort Gordon soldiers and officials dine at Joy Young Restaurant, Augusta, Ga. ca. 1950. Courtesy, June Law.

One of the largest Chinese communities in the South during the 1930s, Augusta, Georgia, had four Chinese restaurants. A *Joy Young Restaurant* was located there as well as in Savannah, Memphis, and Petersburg, Virginia, but these were not part of a chain. *Joy Young* was a popular name choice that was well suited for a restaurant as in Chinese it referred to "a place where good persons are gathered in harmony."

Rural New England

Not surprisingly, most Chinese restaurants were located in towns and cities where eating out is a popular activity for a large portion of the population. In contrast, in rural and farming areas, people generally prepared their own meals at home and less frequently dined in restaurants. Nonetheless, Chinese restaurants and cafes were found in many remote areas, which differed in many respects from those found in cities, especially those with Chinatowns, according to interviews with a small sample of owners, their children, and employees of several of these cafes. [29]

Chinese family restaurants in rural Vermont and New Hampshire served customers that are essentially entirely non-Chinese. The owners generally had prior experience working in restaurants elsewhere before acquiring these restaurants, which date back to the 1960s. Most of the owners entered this occupation because they had poor English skills or were undocumented immigrants.

Owners chose to locate their businesses in rural New England where they felt there would be less competition, lower rent, and better opportunities to create a new market for Chinese food. Those coming from the New York City area were often motivated to escape the control of the Chinese mafia that extorted protection money from many merchants and storeowners. The slower pace of life and the prospect of a better environment for their children to grow up in were attractive features.

However, the work was demanding and required long hours each day. Employee turnover was high, since there was social and cultural isolation for Chinese living so far from a Chinese community. Some employees lived as far away as Boston or New York, and would commute to work in the rural restaurants for a few days each week and then return to the Chinatowns for the rest of the week so they could maintain social and cultural ties.

Rural Western Canada

Across the northern border, nearly every rural town in the prairie provinces of western Canada had at least one, or two, Chinese family-run cafes.[30]   In the smaller towns, with populations of around 500, it was hardly surprising that most of the customers were local people who were not Chinese and hence, the menu was primarily western food, with only one or two Chinese dishes such as chop suey.[31]   Cafés in these towns, whether run by Chinese or non-Chinese, served as local hangouts where residents gathered to socialize and take work breaks. They typically had a counter and a few Formica top tables in a plain dining area, with a few decorations to provide a Chinese accent.[32]

Chinese relocating from other parts of Canada to escape racism or to find better opportunities chose small prairie towns along the main railroad line. For example, in 1944 Dennis Wong left Vancouver and, with some relatives, purchased a café in Prince Albert in northern Saskatchewan. By 1956, Dennis and his wife, Mary, saved enough to sell their share of the café, and with several relatives, opened the smaller *Lotus Café*, which prospered for the next 30 years, serving both Chinese and Canadian dishes.

Figure 20 A Chinese cafe, Stoughton, Sk., Canada. Courtesy, Joan Champ.

New immigrants that obtained an apprenticeship in the food service business after their arrival opened many cafes in these remote areas, especially if they had relatives there already. Although few of their wives had prior training or experience in this type of business, they shared in the operation. Men were the primary cooks, with wives involved in cutting up vegetables, wrapping wontons and dumplings, and preparing simple dishes and sandwiches. They also served as the cashier, general manager and/or waitress.

Many turned to kinship as sources of financial loans and training to get started but their location in small remote towns provided few co-ethnic connections for long-term help. Failure was not uncommon because many did not have business experience or training in balancing finances, achieving product quality, or marketing. However, these immigrants showed resilience and persistence as many that closed their restaurant in one small town would open again in a different town until they eventually achieved some measure of success.

Figure 21 A café owner's son socializing with a customer. Wakaw, Sk., Canada. Courtesy, Joan Champ.

Despite the distances between Chinese in these remote areas of cultural isolation, Chinese restaurant operators formed an active social network. Most closed every Monday or Tuesday to replenish the stock, and to visit with other Chinese in the region.

The experiences of one Canadian Chinese restaurant owner provide a typical example of owners in the region.[33] Richard, identified here only by his first name, was born in 1944 in a village in the New Territories near Hong Kong. He immigrated to London, England in 1960 to work in a Chinese restaurant operated by someone from his village. A decade later in 1970, he returned to Hong Kong for an arranged marriage. Richard then went back alone to work in London until his wife could join him in the next year. They moved to Canada in 1976 to join his older brother who worked in a Chinese restaurant. When his brother moved to Calgary to take another position, Richard and his family followed, and with the financial aid of his brother, purchased a Chinese restaurant in a nearby rural township.

Due to the lack of other Chinese in the area, all the hired staff (wait staff, cashier, dishwasher, janitor) consisted of local young non-Chinese. Supplies and goods had to be ordered from the nearest cities. The menu consisted of western food (soup, sandwiches, steak, pies and coffee) and a small selection of Chinese items. Richard's cooking skill, management experience, and English proficiency gained from working for 15 years in London greatly aided his restaurant success in rural Alberta.

Unlike Chinese restaurant workers in rural New England who were close enough to Boston and New York to be able to return often to visit Chinatowns, Chinese Canadians on the prairie were too separated from each other to enjoy the social and cultural bonds possible in a densely populated Chinese community. Chinese cultural services and goods, dim sum, and weekend Chinese school for the children were only available in cities like Calgary,

Winnipeg, or Regina. Nonetheless, Richard and his wife, had cultural ties that extended well beyond the rural area where they settled as they retained attachments to their place of birth, Hong Kong, returning regularly to visit relatives and friends. They also still maintained their contacts in London formed during the years when they worked there.

Conclusion

By the end of the 1950s, a shift occurred in the central role of Chinatowns for Chinese immigrants. With more assimilation and improved white attitudes toward Chinese, they were no longer confined to living in the crowded and often dilapidated neighborhoods surrounding Chinatowns. A sociological analysis showed that Chinese had increasingly moved toward the suburbs where many opened small family-run restaurants.

> Many Americans no longer 'slum' in Chinatowns, because the mystery of the ghettos has faded with the cessation of *tong* wars and opium dens. Crooked alleys and secret panels have disappeared. More and restaurants have moved to downtown locations. Often, the dishes found in these establishments are more truly Cantonese style than those cooked in Chinatown.
>
> Chinese restaurants in downtown locations had their greatest appeal during the First World War, the era of America's flamboyant and 'flapperish' abandonment. These restaurants, forerunners of American nightclubs, combined dinners with dancing, and were among the most elaborate in big cities. The music was supplied by a well-known band, thus also attracting many patrons who may have come for the music and dancing but who preferred American food. The

cuisine in Chinese restaurants in downtown areas is both American and Chinese.

The growth of American nightclubs, taverns, bars and lounges dealt a heavy blow to these restaurants. The depression of the 1930's contributed to the change, as luxuries such as music and dancing had to be eliminated. To compensate for the loss of musical attractions, Chinese restaurants charge lower prices, serve ample portions of food, and concentrate upon promoting the dishes they know how to prepare. [34]

Chinese restaurants fell out of favor with the rise of Communist China to power in 1949 and its role against the U. S. in the Korean War. However, they experienced new growth in the 1970s after President Nixon's diplomatic visit in 1972 to China improved relationships and generated interest in Chinese foods and other aspects of Chinese culture. Clearly, the fate of Chinese restaurants in the west is strongly affected by the quality of diplomatic relationships with China.

Endnotes

[1] Pflazer, *Driven Out.*
[2] Susan Carter. "Celestial Suppers," 20.
[3] "Chop Suey vs. Shirts," *Wall Street Journal,* June 9, 1924, 2. Proquest Historical Newspapers The Wall Street Journal (1889-1990).
[4] Canada passed a similar act in 1947 when it repealed its Chinese Exclusion Act.
[5] Other laws that helped renew growth of Chinese families were the Displaced Persons Act of 1948 and the Refugee Relief Act of 1953.
[6] Pillsbury, *No Foreign Food.*
[7] Ling, *St. Louis Chinese,* 147-149.

[8] Tzu-Ching Lu. "Ethnic Enterprise in the Kansas City Metropolitan Area: The Chinese Restaurant Business (Volumes I and II)" (Ph.D. diss., 1990, University of Kansas), 275.

[9] Wu, "Improving Chinese Cuisine Overseas," 65

[10] Lu, "Ethnic Enterprise," 273.

[11] Ibid., 267.

[12] Ibid., 245-246.

[13] Li Li, "Cultural and Intercultural Functions of Chinese Restaurants in the Mountain West: "An Insider's Perspective,"" *Western Folklore*, 61, no. 3/4 (2002).

[14] This difference might explain why non-Chinese, but not Chinese, say they feel hungry a short time after eating a Chinese meal.

[15] Li, "Cultural and Intercultural,"

[16] Lee, *Fortune Cookie Chronicles*,

[17] Chan, "The Chinese in Nevada," 98.

[18] Fern Cobel Trull, History of Chinese in Idaho, 1864-1910 (M. A. Thesis, University of Oregon, 1946).

[19] Florence C. Lister and Robert H. Lister. "Chinese Sojourners in Territorial Prescott." *Journal of the Southwest*, 1989, 31, 1, 1989, 15.

[20] Liping Zhu. "Ethnic Oasis: Chinese Immigrants in the Frontier Black Hills," *South Dakota History*, 2003, 33, 4, 302.

[21] Ling, *St. Louis Chinese*, 44-45.

[22] Zhang, "Transplanting Identity," 131-165.

[23] This style did not persist as Chinese restaurants returned to more traditionally Chinese décor by the 1960s.

[24] Jin Donzheng. "The Sojourners' Story: Philadelphia's Chinese Immigrants, 1900-1925"(Ph.D. diss., Temple University, 1997), 186-187.

[25] Bovd's Philadelphia Business Directory, 1912, 1915.

[26] Boyd's Philadelphia Business Directory, 1925.

[27]Gary W. Libby, "Historical Notes on Chinese Restaurants in Portland, Maine." *Chinese America: History & Perspectives* (2006): 47-56

[28] http://www.bhamwiki.com/w/Joy_Young_Restaurant (accessed June 1, 2009).

[29] Clara Veniard. "Immigrant rural entrepreneurs: Chinese restaurants in rural New Hampshire and Vermont." Geography Honors Thesis, Dartmouth College, 2001. Advisor: Richard Wright.

[30] Cheuk Kwan. *Chinese Restaurants*. 2004. http:// www.chineserestaurants.tv (accessed June 1, 2009).

[31] I made an unexpected personal discovery during the research on these rural cafes when I suddenly recalled that my mother had a niece in Nor-

quay, a rural town in Saskatchewan. We had never met them or even knew how they earned their living. Reading about so many Chinese running cafes in the region made me realize that these relatives may well have run a café. They had left the town after they closed their family café sometime in the 1980s, but after phone calls to about 5 different contacts, I was able to confirm my hunch when I located some of her children, my distant cousins, now living in Regina and Calgary.

[32] An excellent description of the *Lotus Café* in Prince Albert, SK., can be found in a loving memoir, complete with recipes, by a daughter of restaurant parents. Janice Wong. *Chow: From China to Canada: Memories of Family and Food* (Vancouver, B. C.: Whitecap, 2005).

[33] P. L. Josephine Smart, "Ethnic Entrepreneurship, Transmigration, and Social Integration: An Ethnographic Study of Chinese Restaurant Owners in Rural Western Canada." *Urban Anthropology and Studies of Cultural Systems and World Economic Development*, Sept. 22, 2003.

[34] Rose Hum Lee, *The Chinese in the United States of America* (Hong Kong: Hong Kong University Press, 1960): 262.

7. Family Restaurant Operations

Every Chinese family restaurant has a somewhat unique exterior and interior appearance, unlike the sameness found in franchise or chain restaurants. In spite of these differences among Chinese restaurants, they all still manage to evoke a "Chinese" feel. The quintessential Chinese family café might well be represented by this following description of the *Diamond Grill* in British Columbia, except for its unusually shaped twin counters.

> *The CAFE ITSELF IS A LONG, NARROW ROOM*
>
> with two horseshoe counters and the soda fountain up front, and then three rows of booths. The two outside rows along the walls, about a dozen booths, can seat six tightly, which is how the kids from school jam into them. There's another row of smaller booths down the middle that only seat two apiece. At the back, under a large framed Chinese dragon embroidered on white silk and breathing fire, is a large circular booth that can seat about ten, fifteen if you use chairs.[1]

The narrator believed that the horseshoe shape design of these counters must have been intended to bring luck, judging from "the big smile his grandpa had whenever he slapped his lottery book down on them."[2]

> Each counter has three chrome fence-units with special slots for the menus; here's where we set out the napkin dispenser, salt and pepper, and a sugar jar with a shiny chrome screw-on pouring lid. With the two juke boxes on each counter, there's quite a bit

of chrome to keep polished on those counters. Behind and under the counters we keep the sauces (HP, steak sauce, Tabasco, ketchup, and, in the mornings, the pancake syrup dispensers which also have screw-on chrome pouring lids), cutlery trays, and extra saucers, ashtrays, and other odds and ends. A singular omnipotence and authority is available when serving from within the centre of these corrals.

These two counters have been designed for maximum use of a small space and are laid out to form one continuous unit running past the soda fountain and up to the till. The only door in this Arborite feedlot is really a gate between the first counter seat and the glass display case of the till and can only be opened by those who know how to operate the very modern latch, hidden so you have to finger it from the bottom.[3]

Figure 22 Economy Café, Oakland, Ca. Courtesy, Dave Glass.

Improvised Exteriors

Some Chinese restaurants occupied stores that were previously occupied by American restaurants but the Chinese proprietors did not do much to hide or disguise these past histories. If the previous occupant was a failed Kentucky Fried Chicken or Taco Bell franchise, its origins could still easily be recognized despite any embellishments such as a pagoda added to make it look "Chinese." Often located in a low rent section of town, the quirky appearance of Chinese family restaurants was not a deterrent to most customers as long as the food was tasty, plentiful, and offered at low prices.

Figure 23 Lam's Gardens, Sainte Genevieve, Mo. Courtesy, Rich Marino.

Figure 24 (lt) Egg Roll King, Lincoln, Ne.. Courtesy, Jeff Jung.
Figure 25 (rt) Lotus Garden, Knoxville, Tn., Author.

Figure 26(lt.) Peking Garden, Wheeling, Wv. Courtesy, arch.army.flickr.com.
Figure 27 (rt) Chop Suey & Deli, St. Louis, Mo. Courtesy, Marjie Kennedy.

Figure 28 Panda Wok, Greenville, N. H. Courtesy, Andrew Riedl

Idiosyncratic Interiors

Not having much capital, furnishing or remodeling of the interior dining space of family restaurants was often austere. Many dining rooms were crammed with a few tables and booths along the walls as in Figure 29. Decorations were meager and haphazard.

Figure 29 King Ying Low Restaurant, Des Moines, Ia. Courtesy, Maggie Suits.

Family restaurants provided inexpensive, but tasty and abundant, freshly prepared foods for a non-Chinese clientele and did not worry about having culturally appropriate decorations. A wall hanging of a clipper sailing ship may be incongruous with Chinese food, but it was better than nothing to cover a wall as in Figure 30. In contrast, Figure 31 shows that some restaurants went to the other extreme with abundant and assorted decorations.

Figure 30 Panda Garden, Memphis, Tn. Courtesy, Adam Remsen.

Figure 31 House of China, LaCrosse, Wi. Courtesy, Indigo Som.

Location

Many Chinese family restaurants located outside of Chinatowns like the Moon Café and *Golden Star Café* in San Antonio (See Figure 32) were in low rent districts surrounded by bars, liquor stores, and pawnshops. Their low prices still attracted customers despite their undesirable settings.

Restaurants in or near Chinatowns generated substantial business for Chinese grocery stores. Some restaurants located in regions with limited access to Chinese grocery supplies had to produce their own food, raising chickens and vegetables in the back yard, for example. In some areas, Chinese restaurants obtained a variety of vegetables from Chinese farmers, including Chinese vegetables that American markets did not carry.[4]

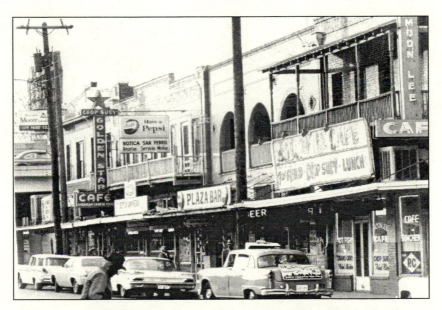

Figure 32 Golden Star Café, San Antonio, Tx. Courtesy, Lim family.

Operating A Restaurant

Running a restaurant involves much more than meets the eye of customers. After looking at a menu, customers place their orders, wait a short while, receive and eat their meals, pay the check and leave. Behind the scenes, operation of a restaurant involves many tasks. Restaurant work began well before the first customer each day. Before the restaurant opens its doors, there is much preparation needed to meet the anticipated customer orders for the day. The amount of raw ingredients used in cooking such as meats, vegetables, rice, bread, seasonings and spices, and other cooking supplies must be estimated accurately and ordered from markets, grocers, and other supply vendors in a timely fashion.[5]

Work is quite hectic for the restaurant staff during lunch and dinner hours because most restaurant customers come within the same short time period for breakfast, lunch, or dinner, and each wants quick service and a tasty meal. The wait staff must take orders accurately, and the cook(s) must prepare the orders quickly. After these meal hours, there are many hours with few customers during which the staff still has much to do. After the last diner leaves, they must clean the premises, wash and put away dishes, pots, and pans, plan the next day's menu, and count the day's receipts.

Restaurants of different size had different staffing needs and roles for family members in their operation. A minimum of two persons is needed to run even the smallest restaurant, one in front to take orders, serve food, and receive payment and one back in the kitchen preparing food, cooking meals, and washing dishes. In reality, of course, two people are not enough even in a small cafe, especially during peak hours when several waiters, kitchen helpers, and cooks are needed to meet the rush.

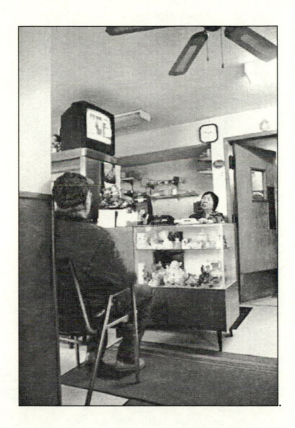

Figure 33 Maryam Tsang at the front counter of the Sunshine Restaurant, Straffordville, Ont., Canada. Courtesy, Connie Tsang.

For the small family restaurant to be profitable, the contributions of all family members helped reduce the expense of hiring employees. Depending on their age, children might seat customers and bring them menus. Older children could take orders and serve the meals as well as bus dishes. Adult relatives in the extended family such as aunts, uncles, cousins, parents might assist with cooking, cleaning, and dish washing in exchange for room and board and perhaps, a small monetary amount.

Figure 34 Hei Shou and Maryam Tsang working together in their Sunshine Restaurant, Straffordville, Ont., Canada. Courtesy, Connie Tsang.

Although all relatives may not have had the best skills, their labor was "free" and contributed to the family's financial success. In return for their labor, children received meals and housing and some spending money, but not a salary. These savings in labor costs helped these restaurants keep their prices low, a factor that helped them stay afloat and compete against larger restaurants with many hired employees.

Figure 35 Toy Gong Lee cooking in the Minnie Gong Lee Restaurant, Stockton, Ca.. Courtesy, Katherine Gong Meissner.

While children may not have always liked the obligations to help in the business, and would have preferred more free time to play or socialize, their contributions were vital as they could determine whether or not the business was profitable. The parents did not offer their children a choice in the matter; their expectations were that all members of the family had to help and feel a responsibility to contribute to the success of their family's business. If, despite their efforts, the family members were not sufficient in skill or number to perform all the necessary tasks, hired hands would be added to wait tables, cook, or help in the kitchen. [67]

Figure 36 Son Chuck, Lee Yee holding Eileen, with wife Thew Yee work at the Joy Young Restaurant, Augusta, Ga. 1948. Courtesy, June Law.

Figure 37 George at order/pickup counter of Chen's Noodle House, which he runs with help from his wife and mother in Austin, Tx. Courtesy, Mel Brown.

Work breaks were essential as restaurant work required workers to be on their feet for many hours rushing about taking orders, serving meals, bussing dishes, preparing, and cooking food over hot flaming woks in a crowded and stuffy kitchen. They needed time to eat a meal or snack, sit down and relax, socialize with co-workers, and for some, have a chance to smoke a cigarette or two.

Figure 38 Workers take a lunch and smoke break behind a Vancouver, Canada restaurant. Courtesy, Randolph Eustace-Walden.

Menu Selections

Although they were Chinese in name, owner, and staff, those restaurants with mostly non-Chinese customers served mostly American or western dishes, with only a few Chinese-like dishes such as chop suey, chow mein, and sweet and sour dishes.

> *'Sweet and sour pork' was their staple, naturally, batter musket balls encasing a tiny core of meat, laced with a scarlet sauce that had an interesting effect on the customer's urine the next day.*
>
> Timothy Mo, *Sour Sweet, p.105*

Menu offerings vary across regions and also change over time to match customer tastes.[8] For example, the 1950s menu of the *Vermont Cafe* in San Antonio offered a mix of western, Mexican, and Chinese fare. Steaks and chops as well as enchiladas and tamales and hamburgers and a variety of sandwiches were on the same menu as chop suey, fried rice, and egg foo yung.

Figure 39 Vermont Café Menu, San Antonio, Tx. ca. 1950s. Courtesy, Mamie Lew.

The daily specials offered at one remotely located Canadian Chinese café, the *Diamond Grill*, similarly focused on non-Chinese dishes.

> The list of specials is always the same except the first on the list will change each day. Hot roast beef sandwich on Monday, sausages with gravy and mashed potatoes on Tuesday, beef stew on Wednesday, pork chops on Thursday, some kind of fish on Friday, maybe Salisbury steak on Saturday, and prime rib of beef, roast pork, or roast turkey on Sunday. I'm partial to Shu's chicken pot pie but he doesn't make it that often. Each of these specials comes with soup, bread, coffee or tea, and dessert of Jell-O, deep apple pie, custard, or, on Sunday, a dish of ice cream.
> Below the daily specials are the entrees. Various steaks, mixed grill, breaded veal cutlets (with a light but spicy tomato sauce, uhm!), fish and chips, half-a-dozen fried oysters, and so forth. At the bottom of the page, the desserts, soft drinks, tea, coffee, and so forth.[9]

Menu offerings also varied for restaurants of different size. Small family restaurants focused on efficiency, low price, and informality. Their menus offered fewer entrees, usually the familiar standard items like Mongolian Beef, sweet and sour pork or chicken, noodles, and egg rolls. In contrast, larger Chinese restaurants with a large Chinese customer base provided a more extensive and varied menu with many authentic and creative dishes as well as the American-Chinese fare found in most Chinese eateries. This menu attracted non-Chinese diners with a more adventurous palate.

TYPING THE MENU

Nellie Wong

Not a day goes by
When Ma, in her blue waitress uniform,
Stops me reading *The Oakland Tribune*
To dictate, precisely at 3:30 P.M.
The next day's menu

All right, Ma says, in English,
Tomorrow we'll serve
Baked spaghetti
Beef stew with potatoes and carrots
Fried breast of lamb and
Boiled ox tongue with Spanish sauce

My mouth waters
As she decides the next day's specials
Ma doesn't need to say
Breaded veal cutlets
Fried oysters or
Prime Rib of Beef
Because they were always
On the menu every day
Though I can write in shorthand
I scribble the specials in longhand
And step down into Bah Bah's office
And insert a piece of paper
Into the old Royal typewriter
I type tomorrow's menu
Watching the purple letters spring up
Like soldiers marching in unison
Filling the paper such plums and grapes

For our daily lives
I proofread, carefully,
The typed menu, making sure
I type the correct specials
That Ma dictated
Making sure that each item
Is spelled correctly
Just from memory
Because Spell Check
Was a futuristic ploy

With the labor of my fingers
My eyes, my back, staring
At the list of items
That ranged from halibut steak
For 50 cents
To prime rib of beef
For 95 cents
Knowing that my fingers
Helped to support the family
My secretarial skills a blip
Of the family business
Known as The Great China Restaurant
Ai Joong Wah
At 723 Webster Street
In Chinatown, Oakland, California
When my sisters and I labored
Without wage
But survived with tips
And *ngow ngook fahn*
Beef over rice
Served us by Bock Gung
The head cook
When Ma and Bah Bah
Weren't looking

When World War II filled
The Great China with customers
Pink of Milen's Jewelers
Mr. Carlson of Carlson's Confectionery
Johnny, the boxer, and his girlfriend Lucille
With her ruby red lips and white teeth

Thlon doy
Single men
Families
Pensioners
Workers from gas stations
The parachute factory
And herb and poultry stores
Tenants from The Aloha Hotel
Gypsies with their love
For bowls of steamed rice overflowing with gravy
Typing the menu
A job I didn't apply for
But became mine
In between making coffee
Milkshakes and lettuce and tomato salads
Anxious for tips that filled
The glasses kept beneath
The Formica counter
Understanding, even then,
That money grew not on trees
But through our labor
Typing the menu
Drying silverware
Stringing string beans
Refilling granulated sugar jars
Washing the coffee urn on tip toes
Sweeping
Mopping
Bah Bah inventorying and planning
The next day's supplies
Vegetable oil
Flour

50 pound sacks of rice
Flank steak
Jello
The Great China Restaurant
Our second home
Sandwiched between
Regular school and Chinese school
Our days of wonder
Questions
Fatigue
Anticipation and
Simmering American dreams.

© 2004 Nellie Wong. Courtesy, Nellie Wong.

Figure 40 At the Great China. Courtesy, Flo Oy Wong.

Authentic Versus Americanized Chinese Dishes

I just love Chinese food. My favourite dish is number 27.

Clement Attlee, 1950s British Prime Minister

Some culinary arbiters disparage the dishes served by most Chinese restaurants that serve mostly non-Chinese, labeling them as "American-Chinese" rather than authentic Chinese food.[10] Such critics of Chinese family restaurant food imply that dishes with origins in the home country are inherently better. This claim would seem to be a form of culinary snobbery. The fact that popular Chinatown restaurants serving both Chinese and non-Chinese patrons often have separate menus in English and in Chinese aroused one critic to suspect that Chinese were "restricting" the best food for Chinese customers while serving the presumably inferior westernized dishes to non-Chinese, possibly as a form of retaliation for immigration barriers against Chinese. A simpler and more plausible explanation is that the dishes that restaurants offer only on a menu written in Chinese are those that they feel certain that non-Chinese would not like.[11]

If, by authentic, one is referring to Chinese food that is served in China, the allegation has some validity. However, not all authentic dishes are appetizing to non-Chinese. Some authentic dishes would either look, smell, or taste strange to them. Most non-Chinese, for example, would reject authentic Chinese dishes that involve organs or body parts such as ox tail, pig tongue, or pig stomach. And, had they wanted authentic dishes, the cook may not have been able to comply, as many of the sauces, spices, and other ingredients such as fresh Chinese vegetables would have been unavailable in most parts of the country.

Moreover, some dishes that are not "authentic" have been especially successful. A prime example is *General Tso's chicken*, a dish of battered chicken pieces served in a sweet and sour chili sauce that appealed to Western preferences for sweet dishes. This popular dish is regarded as an example of the cuisine of the Chinese province of Hunan, but it is largely unknown there. This finding should come as no surprise since the dish was actually created in New York in the early 1970s by Peng Chuang-Kuei, a prominent chef for the Nationalist government who had fled to Taiwan when the Communists took control of China in 1949. Interestingly, in 1990 Peng returned to China to open a restaurant that included General Tso's chicken, but it was a failure as the Chinese considered the Americanized dish, "too sweet." [12]

Another striking instance where an "inauthentic" Chinese dish can succeed is the version of cashew chicken created in Springfield, Missouri, in 1955. It consists of deep-fried chicken chunks served in a brown slurry made from soy sauce, oyster sauce, and stock, topped with green onions and halved cashews. Virtually every Chinese restaurant, and many non-Chinese eateries, in the region offers Springfield style cashew chicken, a concoction unheard of in other parts of the country but a defining exemplar of

Chinese food throughout Missouri.[13]

Another insinuation is that Chinese cooks in America did not know how to prepare authentic Chinese dishes. Inasmuch as most cooks in early Chinese restaurants were from rural areas, it would have been remarkable if they *did* cook authentic food. Coming from villages and living on the edge of famine in Guangdong, the hard lives of these "adaptable and ingenious" peasants "taught them how to make something palatable out of virtually nothing. This experience stood them well in frontier kitchens."[14]

> Immigrants who are self-taught cooks improvise both cooking materials and how they present dishes, to satisfy the imagination of a Chinese eating culture comprising both Chinese migrants and host (non-Chinese) populations.[15]

Moreover, the fact that many overseas Chinese cooks were *not* trained as cooks in China is largely irrelevant for even if these cooks did know how to make authentic Chinese dishes, few non-Chinese customers would either know the difference or even want authentic dishes. For example, a study found that most non-Chinese patrons interviewed in several Chinese restaurants in Athens, Georgia, did express a preference for authentic Chinese dishes, which is not surprising since the desire to experience an exotic or "different" cuisine is part of the reason for choosing an ethnic restaurant in the first place. But when asked how authentic "they thought the food was at the Chinese restaurants they patronized, many were uncertain and claimed they did not pay much attention, and they rejected foods that were defined as "unpleasant" and well outside of their experience."[16] Food that tasted good was more important to most patrons than whether it was authentic. For decades, the American-Chinese dishes served in Chinese restaurants were "Chinese" enough to satisfy most local tastes.

Chinese cooks were well aware of the discrepancy between what non-Chinese say they want to eat and what they actually will eat. Accordingly, cooks made changes in their food preparation and presentation to accommodate the tastes of non-Chinese patrons without completely destroying their beliefs that they were eating the "real thing." One chef explained the cultural reasons why steamed fish was *not* on the menu. First, because it is lightly spiced, it requires fresh fish, which is not always available. Next, Chinese serve fish whole, complete with head and tail, not as the fillets Americans prefer. Thirdly, Americans like strong flavor and would find lightly flavored steamed fish "too fishy."[17] [18]

To succeed, Chinese restaurants located in communities with few Chinese had to adjust their cooking styles to suit the taste and expectations of their non-Chinese customers who were generally reluctant to try authentic dishes prepared with Chinese ingredients unfamiliar to them. Before Chinese restaurants gained their widespread popularity, it was difficult to persuade non-Chinese patrons to order Chinese dishes. Some restaurants printed reassurances to customers on their menus that their high quality ingredients were delicious, nutritious, and easily digested.

All four restaurants in the Athens study adjusted to their customer tastes by using "American vegetables" such as carrots, snow peas, green peppers, broccoli, and mushrooms, which most of them prefer to Chinese vegetables. An additional reason for the change was that locally available American vegetables cost less than Chinese vegetables, allowing the restaurant to charge a lower price. This cost factor was not a trivial one, as some customers were attracted more by low prices than by authenticity. And for many diners, a satisfying taste experience was more important than either price or authenticity.[19] [20]

Chinese restaurants made a different type of cooking adjustment in response to health concerns of Western diners. In the late 1960s, suspicion grew that monosodium glutamate (MSG), a flavor-enhancing additive widely used then in Chinese restaurants, produced headaches, dizziness, chest pains, and other adverse effects for a small percentage of diners. Dubbed as the "Chinese restaurant syndrome," the label was unfair as MSG is also present in many American food products.[21] Chinese restaurants quickly stopped using MSG in their dishes even though subsequent research has failed to support the commonly accepted belief that it was unsafe.[22]

Occupational Risks

All Chinese, irrespective of their occupation, were adversely affected by the virulent racism of the 19th century that did not diminish appreciably until midway through the 20th century, but some forms were specific to those working in restaurants. For example, on one occasion a Chinese restaurant customer hid a few of the emptied dishes after he finished eating their contents, and then refused to pay the check, arguing that the total was too high.

> When my sister who had served them spotted and pointed out the hidden dishes, one of their group threatened her. I had my sister come into the kitchen, but the customer followed her. I had her get behind me, turned up the fire on the wok, and warned the fellow if he came any closer, I'd toss hot oil on him. He backed off, paid the bill in full, and left. A threat to call the cops who cruised the area usually resolved less serious problems.[23]

If the food did not satisfy them or service was not prompt, some customers could be extremely rude, reject dishes they ordered by mistake, refuse to pay the check, threaten violence, or actually inflict physical harm to persons or property. While these hostile behaviors also occurred in non-Chinese restaurants, anti-Chinese feelings may have increased their prevalence and intensity in Chinese restaurants.

Small cafes, open late at night in dangerous neighborhoods, with few staff on hand were vulnerable to robbery, and in extreme cases, even homicide. Take-out delivery boys, and men, were also at risk as they were subject to robbery, or violence, even death.[24]

> Because our restaurant was near the railroad tracks, our clientele was not from the best crowds, and we got a lot of riff-raff, especially after the bars closed on Fridays and Saturdays. Those were the busiest of times, but it was also when we'd get more problem customers; the bars closed at 2 a.m. so we stayed open on those days till 3:30 a.m. to pick up their business. We often had drunk customers from bars in the neighborhood that would hurl racial slurs of

"Chink," "Chinee," and "Chinaman" at us and generally make other customers uncomfortable.[25]

Some Important Factors for Success

What factors made the difference between restaurants that succeeded and failed? Having good cooks was, of course, very important, but that alone was no guarantee of success. The personal charm and *likeableness* of the restaurant personnel that interacted with customers could make or break a restaurant. In addition, the fate of a restaurant could be affected by its physical location as well as the number and quality of competing restaurants, Chinese or otherwise, in the neighborhood.

Whereas a restaurant owner could decide on choice of location, type of decor, and menu offerings, many other factors such as the overall economy or amount of competition clearly were beyond his control. During hard economic times, people are less likely to eat out or spend much money. Owners also had no influence on the changing tastes of diners that affect their choice of where to eat.

Example of Three Restaurants in Midland, Texas

The fate of three restaurants located in Midland, Texas, a medium size oil town will be described to illustrate how several different factors affected how well three different Chinese restaurants in the same community fared over time.[26]

The *Blue Star Inn*, with a capacity of 80-100 seats, opened in 1952 as the first Chinese restaurant in Midland, Texas, a small oil industry town. The owners were three Chinese immigrant partners, fluent in English and with prior experience working in and owning Chinese restaurants in other parts of the U. S. This background led them to believe that this region was a wide open market for Chinese food.

Joe Chung, more personable and outgoing than his partners, worked the counter and served as host. The other partners, Joe Jot and Richard Yee worked as cooks. Family members helped out by waiting on customers and doing minor kitchen chores to cut labor costs. The restaurant was an instant success and was profitable for many years. However, by the 1980s, one of the owners had died and the other two were ready to retire, selling their shares to younger relatives.

Unfortunately, the timing was not good for the new generation of owners. Due to a depressed oil industry, business dropped. At the same time, competition increased from Chinese fast food restaurants, Chinese restaurants offering new cuisine, and national chain non-Chinese restaurants. Attempts to reverse the tide by introduction of new dishes, serving cocktails, and renovating the dining room failed, and the *Blue Star Inn* was forced to cut back on expenses, laying off chefs and kitchen help. It barely survived, but the Blue Star Inn was still operating in 2009 after more than 45 years because the owners reduced their operating expenses. Furthermore, since they owned the building that the restaurant occupied, they did not have to pay rent.

The *Blue Star Inn* featured both American and Chinese dishes that were popular in the 1950s, but failed to adjust promptly to changing tastes. When it opened in 1952, it had the advantage of a central location, a size large enough to accommodate parties, and a prosperous economy. Over the years, however, the development of new shopping centers and highways made their location less favorable. Its fate was similar to that of hundreds of other family owned and operated Chinese restaurants all over the country.

A second restaurant, *Hunan Garden*, also a small family style Chinese restaurant opened in 1991 by Michael Chen who had worked as a cook in his father's Chicago restaurant. After saving enough, he opened a restaurant in Dallas before he and his wife, Lisa, purchased and renamed a Midland restaurant from another Chinese for $50,000, with personal savings and a loan from his father-in-law. *Hunan Garden* offered a limited buffet as well as family dinners. It provided delivery and catering. Located in a shopping plaza near a major shopping mall with ready access to the interstate highway rather than in the older central part of town, it was very profitable during its first three years, clearing $6,000 on sales of $30,000 each month on average. However, by 1994, earnings declined by about a third. In the late 1990s, more pressure came from a boom in the opening of national chain restaurants as well from the opening of a super buffet style Chinese eatery at the same time that population growth in the area declined. Added to these adverse factors, their store rent increased substantially. Business stabilized but mainly because the owners put in longer hours at work, and used family members in the operation to save on the expenses of wages and benefits. It created a website to aggressively compete against its rivals.

Taste of China, opened in 2003, posed a major threat to full service Chinese family restaurants. Its buffet format offered immediate self-service, with unlimited amounts of a wide selection of already cooked dishes from steam tables for a fixed price. Customers did not have to be seated by a hostess, select dishes from a menu, give orders to a waitperson, and then wait to be served.

Four unrelated Chinese, all with prior cooking experience in other Chinese restaurants, formed a partnership to open *Taste of China*. Each invested from $50,000 to $60,000, raised from selling existing restaurants or from family loans. Sales volume is high in a buffet style restaurant, but the food costs and labor expenses of several cooks and kitchen staff are also high. Sales averaged $110,000 to $120,000 monthly but labor costs for 15 to 20 employees ran $20,000 to $30,000 a month.

Such high startup costs prevent single families from opening this type of restaurant. Buffet owners are often investors or speculators seeking to turn a quick profit by selling the restaurant as soon as it is profitable, rather than running it with a long-term involvement. These more complex businesses are not feasible for single families, which generally lack the training and experience to manage the intricate financial and entrepreneurial aspects needed for successful operation.

The comparison of these three Chinese restaurants in Midland holds lessons that could easily apply to the market in other regions of the country. Many factors, some of which are beyond the control of restaurant owners, strongly affect the financial outcomes of restaurants. The single family-owned Chinese restaurant, especially those that have not changed to keep up with changing tastes, is no longer viable in today's marketplace. As their loyal older customers die out, customers from the younger generation will not likely take their place, as they will generally seek innovative restaurants. Similarly, when the last remaining Chinese family restaurant owners retire over the next decade, few of their younger family members will want to take over the operation.

Chinese restaurants, which have steadfastly resisted franchises and chains in the past, may eventually fall in line with these newer business models. Franchises offer standardization, economies of scale for food and supplies, promotion and advertising, and national branding identities. But at what cost to the operators? Will loss of independence hurt their business? And how will it affect the culinary experience of diners? Will the food served inevitably become mediocre, uniform, and bland?

Endnotes

[1] Fred Wah. *Diamond Grill* (Edmonton, Alberta: NeWest, 1996), 119.

[2] Ibid., 33.

[3] Ibid., 33.

[4] In the 1940s, Jim Wong traded home grown Chinese vegetables for meat and fish at Chinese restaurants like the *King Ying* in Des Moines (bottom left row on the back cover). Marie Rose Wong, *Sweet Cakes, Long Journey: The Chinatowns of Portland, Oregon* (Seattle, University of Washington Press, 2004), xiv-xv.

[5] Small restaurant owners often went early in the morning to pick up food supplies as some distributors would not deliver small orders. Personal communication, Wellman Chin, Jan. 9, 2010.

[6] By western standards, these requirements would be illegal child labor, although the work was for their families. But a British ethnography of Chinese family-run takeaways, or take-out kitchens, found most children readily helped in the family business. Miri Song, *Helping Out: Children's Labor in Ethnic Businesses* (Philadelphia: Temple University Press, 1999).

[7] Two insightful memoirs about lives of restaurant children: Eleanor Wong Telemaque, *It's Crazy to Stay Chinese in Minnesota.* (Nashville, Tn: Nelson, 1978), M. Elaine Mar, *Paper Daughter: A Memoir* (New York: Harper Collins, 1999).

[8] An intriguing analysis of rural Chinese Canadian restaurant menu items found the few Chinese dishes offered were the same across restaurants over many years in contrast to the western dishes and suggest that such items as chop suey came to define "Chineseness." Lily Cho. "On Eating Chinese: Diasporic Agency and the Chinese Canadian Restaurant Menu." In *Reading Chinese Transnationalisms: Society, Literature, Film, edited by* Maria Ng and Philip Holden. Hong Kong: Hong Kong University Press, 2006: 37-62.

[9] Wah, *Diamond Grill*, 149.

[10] Shun Lu and Gary Alan Fine. "The Presentation of Ethnic Authenticity: Chinese Food as a Social Accomplishment." *Sociological Quarterly,* 1995, 36, 3, 538.

[11] Imogene Lim. "Chinese Restaurants As Cultural Lessons." *Food and Flavor,* 1997, 13-14.

[12] Fuchsia Dunlop. "Hunan Resources" New York Times, Feb. 4, 2007.

[13] Chinese restaurants in the Springfield area were not successful until the creation of this version of cashew chicken that suited local tastes.

John T. Edge. "He Made Missouri A Chinese Province." http://www.johntedge.com/cashew-chicken (accessed Oct. 10, 2009).

[14] Lee, "The Chinese in America," 81.

[15] Wu, "Improvising Chinese Cuisine Overseas,"

[16] Lu and Fine, "The Presentation of Ethnic Authenticity," 544.

[17] Ibid., 541.

[18] A New York Chinese restaurant chef instructed to prepare several popular Cantonese dishes for either white executives or Chinese diners cooked the same dishes differently, confirming that chefs serve western patrons what they believe non-Chinese prefer. Joanne Lee. "What is real Chinese food?" Flavor and Fortune, 1995, 2 (3), 17 and 21.

[19] Lu and Fine, "The Presentation of Ethnic Authenticity," 540.

[20] In fact, examination of evaluations of a sample of Chinese restaurants posted on various websites shows that some diners prefer the "American-Chinese" Cantonese dishes that they grew up eating rather than newer cuisines.

[21] American Restaurant Syndrome? (accessed Nov. 22, 2009) http://www.msgtruth.org/whywe.htm

[22] Patricia J. Taliaferro. Monosodium Glutamate and the Chinese Restaurant Syndrome: A Review of Food Additive Safety. *Journal of Environmental Health*, 1995. 57, 10: 8-13.

[23] e-mail Sept. 27, 2009 from Ralph Young, whose family had a restaurant in Santa Rosa, Ca. in the 1950s.

[24] Five robbery attacks, four fatal, of Chinese food deliverymen occurred between 2000 and 2005 in New York City, "Chinese Food Murders." *New York Daily News,* March 14, 2005. Posted at: http://www.asian-nation.org/headlines/2005/03/chinese-food-murders (accessed Nov. 1, 2009). Another fatal attack was reported recently in New England. "Chinese food deliveryman dead; Lawrence police suspect foul play." *North Andover Eagle Tribune,* Aug. 1, 2009.

A realistic, award-winning film, *Take Out,* portrays a single day in the difficult life of one undocumented Chinese deliveryman in New York. http://takeoutthemovie.com/home.htm (accessed Nov. 1, 2009)

[25] e-mail Sept. 27, 2009 from Ralph Young,

[26] Andy Lui. "Small Business in the United States: A Field Study of Three Chinese Restaurants in Midland, Texas" (Master's Thesis, Oklahoma State University, 2006).

8. Insider Perspectives

Up to this point, Chinese family restaurants have been examined only in terms of their origins, physical features, menu offerings, daily operations, and the people who operated them. The emphasis has been on objective information. Important as this approach is, it cannot yield much insight into the daily work activities of these families and what impact their experiences had on them over their lives.

Of course, interviews and narratives about restaurant experiences are subjective in nature, and susceptible to distortion, both deliberate and unintended. Often no independent criteria exist to assess accuracy of recollections. Nonetheless, memories and emotional feelings are important ingredients of life experiences and offer insider perspectives, which outsiders who never get beyond the kitchen door cannot fully comprehend. The narratives in this chapter by 10 people from Chinese family restaurants provide rich insights. No claim is made that they speak for everyone from a family restaurant. The willingness of these individuals to reflect on and share their stories makes these respondents a selective sample. Still, their perceptions provide glimpses that further our understanding and appreciation of Chinese family restaurant life as well as raise other questions for investigation.[1]

---

[1] These narratives reflect experiences from about 1950-2000, but some of their restaurants opened a decade or more earlier.

West

Ai Joong Wah, Oakland, California

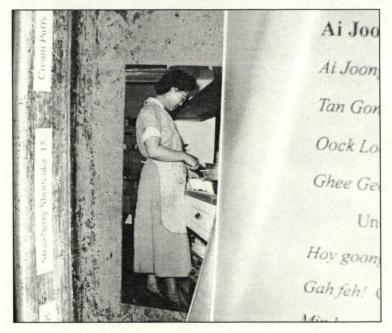

Figure 41 Illustration, Ai Joong Wah detail , 2008, mixed media Courtesy, Flo Oy Wong.

F lo Oy Wong *is an artist who works at the intersection of art and history. From 1980 to the early 1990s she was inspired to draw images of her family working at their restaurant, Ai Joong Wah. This work, the Oakland Chinatown Series, graphite pencil drawings based on snapshots that she took with a Brownie camera, show her family at work*[2].

---

[2] *These images led to her essay, There's More to Being Chinese in America Than Chop Suey: Narrative Drawing as Criticism in Oakland Chinatown, published in Pluralistic Approaches To Art Criticism. Editors: Kristin G. Congdon, Doug Blandy, Bowling Green Press.*

In 2008, Flo Oy was invited to exhibit in a visual arts show, The Distaff Toolkit, shown throughout the United States, for which she created a piece, Ai Joong Wah. Using a cookie sheet, the soup ladle, and a pencil engraved with Great China Restaurant that she collected at the restaurant's closing, her installation visually narrated her experiences at Ai Joong Wah, the restaurant that gave her an identity and was the place where her parents, Gee Seow Hong and Gee Suey Ting, labored to provide a better life for Flo Oy and her siblings in the United States.

Oy, mought cha!

Oy, mought cha!

Oy, wipe forks!

When I heard those words as a young child at my family's Oakland Chinatown restaurant, *Ai Joong Wah*, *Great China Restaurant*, I ran hastily into the kitchen. *Lo Wong Bok*, our dishwasher, lifted a colander from the sink. Clouds of steam billowed. The scalding water dimpled his reddish pink hands. The colander was layered with crisscrossed forks, knives, spoons, and other utensils. I didn't answer *Lo Wong Bok*. We always worked together in silence as if spoken words would interfere with the task at hand. He was a quintessential *slon doy*, a bachelor who like many other Chinese men in America, immigrated to the U. S. alone, leaving their wives and families home in villages in China.

In the dining area of *Ai Joong Wah* behind the salmon-colored Formica counter top I wiped and stacked the washed utensils. I put forks on top of other forks. Sometimes the tines got caught in other tines. I put spoons on top of spoons until they filled the segmented slot to the top. Once in a while I ran back to the kitchen with a crust-ladened utensil that needed to be washed again. All this I did in continued silence.

I worked at *Ai Joong Wah* where we served fair to middlin' Chinese food and some rather tasty American food – beef stew, prime rib, roast pork, liver and onions, veal cutlets, fried halibut, chicken fried steak, Spanish ox tongue, baked spaghetti, and meat loaf. My 5 sisters, only brother, and I toiled there in some capacity throughout our school years, from elementary to high school. In my case, I continued to work at *Ai Joong Wah*, which we called the *store*, when I was a student at the University of California, Berkeley. My siblings and I shared work schedules. There was always someone to cover another's work assignment if one of us had dates or other activities to attend. After some of my older sisters were married they returned to help out, quite often with their young children in tow.

Our jobs? We served countless bowls of soup from the steam table to waiting customers. We wrapped won tons, our fingers deftly folding the soft won tin *pay* around bits of pork, green onions, water chestnuts, into a shape resembling a tiny hill. We set out pans of cold iceberg lettuce to make salads, made jello for dessert, stacked loaves of doughy Kilpatrick bread in the blue and white checkered bags on top of the refrigerator. After each of us had learned to type we all took turns typing and printing the daily menu. At the end of each day one of us would wash the coffee urn. We poured hot water into the urn and brushed away the old coffee grinds inside of the tubes.

Each of us waited on tables. If customers came while we were eating we'd jump up to wait on them. As a result of this practice I ate fast because I didn't want my food to be cold or to find that something I wanted to eat would be gone.

While working during my high school years I wore an apron on top of my Lanz dress (a favorite of the fashionable Oakland High School girls at that time), which I had purchased with tips. My husband, Ed, who was my boyfriend then, took a photo of me in the dress. Many years later, I did a graphite pencil drawing of this photo for my *Oakland Chinatown Series*. To this day it remains one of my favorite *Oakland Chinatown* drawings.

Our family members divided responsibilities between our house and *Ai Joong Wah*. We did little maintenance at our Chinatown residence and at our later house in the Lake Merritt region of Oakland we had more home jobs. My sister, Nellie, did the ironing. I was supposed to dust but seldom did. I was too busy working at the restaurant. Whenever something needed to be done at home my father hired a handyman to do repairs.

Our entire lives for 18 years centered on *Ai Joong Wah*, which was our anchor, our center, our womb. Even though we slept at our Chinatown house on Harrison Street (as a young child I played with my friends there while my parents worked) and the new house near Oakland High School the restaurant remained the core of our family life. It was as if all of us were tethered there from dawn to dark.

Origins of *Ai Joong Wah*

My father, Gee Seow Hong, an only child born in 1896 in the village of *Loong On* (formerly *Goon Do Hong*) in the Toisan area of Guangzhou, had other jobs prior to opening *Ai Joong Wah* in 1943. He came to the U. S. in 1912 at the age of 17 to join two village uncles who taught him how to *jop yeck*, prescribe Chinese herbs and medicine. After marrying my mother, his second wife (his first wife had died in China while he was in the U. S.) in 1926 he returned to this country to work in order to send money home to his family.

While my father lived in Oakland Chinatown (in 1933, my father lived at 723 Webster Street, site of *Ai Joong Wah*, with two of my older sisters when they came from China to join him) he also worked in the neighboring cities of Berkeley and Alameda. At one time he sold produce from a grocery truck. He ran a grocery store with a Chinese fast food take out section in Berkeley. He was a low level partner in an Oakland Chinatown lottery that led to a non-fatal shooting in April of 1940. During the early part of World War II he worked with my oldest sister, Li Hong, at the Alameda shipyard. His first restaurant venture was as a partner at *Harry's Café*. When that partnership faltered my father opened *Ai Joong Wah* next door to *Harry's Café*. The broken partnership led to years of animosity between the Louies, owners of *Harry's Café*, and my parents. My siblings and I befriended the Louie brothers without our parents' blessings. One of the brothers, Daniel, taught me how to fold a brassiere from a paper napkin. Making the paper bra *a la Daniel* is a cherished memory to this day.

My mother, Gee Suey Ting, was my father's helpmate. She had immigrated to this country in 1933 with my 3 older sisters as my father's paper sister due to the impact of the 1882 Chinese Exclusion Law. The statute forbade the entry of Chinese laborers, their wives, and children to the United States of America. My mother coached (from a book that my father sent her with our altered family history) my sisters so that they could pass their Angel Island Immigration Station interrogation in 1933. She claimed to be his *paper sister* and as such lived in this country under a false identity for many years. Before she ran *Ai Joong Wah* with my father she peeled shrimp for pennies a day and sewed parachutes during World War II. She kept the family together when my father was non-fatally shot by a *paper brother*. After the shooting she bravely pursued the assailant who was eventually captured a few blocks away from our house on Harrison Street.

"Loy 'Mee Gwok' yew heck foo, Come to America eat bitter," she used to say to me when I was a child. Life in America was such a struggle for her and my father during their early immigrant years together.

My parents, Gee Seow Hong and Gee Suey Ting, opened *Ai Joong Wah* in 1943 during World War II with borrowed money from a village uncle who made his money from gambling. For 18 years *Ai Joong Wah* was opened 6 days a week with Wednesdays as our day off. We served breakfast at 6:00 am, sometimes to waiting crowds who wanted to eat my mother's fluffy pancakes drenched in sweet syrup and melting butter (15 cents an order) or the toasty golden brown waffles, scrambled eggs, bacon, ham, and toast. We stayed open to 11 pm and then later when business was not so good we closed at 9:00 pm. Quite often, I worked the late shift. There was usually a young man who nursed a cup of coffee to keep me company until the closing.

Location of *Ai Joong Wah*

My father opened *Ai Joong Wah* only a half block away from 8th and Webster, the center of Oakland's Chinese community. On both sides of Webster Street, the main thoroughfare, between 7th and 8th Streets there were a total of 5 restaurants — *Lock Gone*, *Far East* (*Yuon Oong*), *New Home* (*Hin Slin Guey*), *Harry's Café*, and *Ai Joong Wah*. *Wing Mow*, the store that sold our Chinese school supplies was located across the street at the corner of 8th and Webster. Next door was *Leong Yiu*, a barber shop, one of several in Chinatown. Then there was *Lock Gone*, a restaurant that sold *faw op* (roast duck), and *leong foon* (Chinese black jello). Next to *Lock Gone* was the pool hall, which later became a Chinese grocery store. Next to the pool hall was the *Far East Café* run by the Fong Torres family. There was another storefront and then *Hin Slin Guey*, New Home, home of mouthwatering custard pies.

On our side of Webster Street starting at 8th was *Man Sang Wo*, a store run by Gee Guey who was thought to be the unofficial mayor of Chinatown. Next to *Man Sang Wo* was the herb store where jars of dried sea horses and other medicines were displayed in the storefront window. I use to sit in the herb store to watch the worker weigh the selected medicine on shiny scales balanced by strings. I was captivated by the floor to ceiling boxes with the names of the herbs.

Next to the herb store were other storefronts and then *Harry's Café* and *Ai Joong Wah*. Our restaurant was located next to other stores that were fronts for gambling houses. Upstairs, immigrant families had lived there when they first arrived from China. At the corner of 7th and Webster was the comic bookstand where Mr. Jin, the owner let me read comic books for free. It was there that I was introduced to the magical world of Wonder Woman, Batman, and Superman. During World War II I recall saluting a sailor in his uniform when he walked by the comic book stand. He returned my salute.

Inside *Ai Joong Wah*

The doors of *Ai Joong Wah* were flanked by windows and walls. The walls were adorned with ornate and colorful Chinese bowls. Inside, the restaurant was appointed with dark wood booths on the left side and a long Formica counter with seats diner style on the right side. Each booth had a round mirror with an ornate frame. At one time my father installed a pin ball machine to the left of his office window where players clanged and spun the pinball for hours.

My father's miniscule office, a multi-use space, was on the left side of the restaurant near the staircase and the one oval table to serve larger groups of customers. There was a second story, which housed more tables for diners, a hallway that stored food and led to the women's bathroom. We had a former banquet space that was closed off to store items we didn't use constantly.

Much activity took place in my father's office. We typed and printed our menus there. My father did his accounting on the wooden abacus there. The office was where my father introduced my brother, Bill, to the teachings of Confucius.

Neither my older sisters nor I were invited to learn. I hid under the open window of the office and recited *Kung Foo Ji, Slin Boon Slin*, a phrase about Confucius that I did not understand at all.

At the back of the dining area was the kitchen. There was an opening to the left of the steam table, which allowed male customers to go to the men's bathroom. The kitchen was divided in two. On the right side there was a large stove top, a grill, and a giant wok where the cooks, including my mother, stir-fried *chow mein, chop suey*, and other dishes. On the left side was the kitchen sink where *Lo Wong Bok* washed dishes. Next to the sink sat the large walk-in floor to ceiling refrigerator. In between the sink and the stove area was a work station where the cooks prepped.

The back of the kitchen led to a small room with a butcher block. Knives and cleavers hung above the butcher block. A scale to weigh meat was suspended from the ceiling. The men's bathroom was located to the left of the butcher block. For special occasions like Chinese New Year or someone's birthday my father worked his culinary magic there. He made his *choon goon*, eggs rolls, from the pinkish membrane of the pig's stomach and dipped whole cooked chickens to make his succulent *see you guy*, soy sauce chicken. The smell of the soy sauce floated through the air in this space. When he made his delicious stuffed fish, layered with a sweet tomato sauce, he chopped the fillings in this space.

Behind this area to the left was the pastry room, my favorite place. I spent hours there with the cooks who made strawberry shortcakes, chocolate rolls, cream puffs, Parker House rolls, baking soda biscuits, apple pies, custard pies, and cupcakes. When the cooks made cream puffs I made sure I was there. After the cream was whipped in an industrial size beater I covered my finger with the oozing whipped cream and slowly licked the sweetness into my body.

In the backyard *Cheong Sook*, one of our cooks, planted a small vegetable garden. He grew *gow ghee toy*, a stringy delicious vegetable for soup. I loved watching it grow and could hardly wait to shred the leaves while leaving the stem in the ground. *Cheong Sook* was pleased that I liked the plant. He knew that I had itchy fingers. Worried that I might tear off the leaves before they were mature he made a sign for me, which said *ngon hon sow but doong*, eyes see but hands can't touch. I obeyed the sign and I didn't shred the leaves until *Cheong Sook* or my mother said that it was okay.

The workers – cooks, waiters, and dishwasher – became members of our extended family. One of my early responsibilities was to check on the cooks, one of them, in particular, *Cheong Sook*, when he didn't come to work. When *Chell Goong*, another cook, was late I fetched him. I didn't like climbing the dusty stairs of the *slon doy*, bachelor apartment house on Eighth Street. The hallway was dimly lit and the thinnest sliver of light squeezed through a tiny window. The darkness wrapped around me. Facing my fears I knocked on Chell Goong's door. He opened it a crack and I could see his bloodshot eye peer through the opening.

 "*Hoy goong lah*, start work," I admonished him. The door shut and I scampered down the stairs to daylight.

Another cook, my favorite, *Yu Yoong Goong*, spent Wednesdays, our day off, with our family. Dressed in his white shirt and suit he accompanied us to San Francisco Chinatown to see our uncle and to eat dim sum (*chaung ngow* in the Toisan dialect). *Goong* went to see American movies with my parents. They were quite a threesome. When his grandson married, my daughter, Felicia, served as the flower girl at the wedding. After my father died in 1961, *Goong* became my mother's companion until she died of cancer. A short time later he passed as well.

Everything – weddings, holidays, and birthdays – swirled around the restaurant's schedule.. When two of my sisters, Li Hong, and Lai Wah, were married *Ai Joong Wah* stayed open. We went to their events - Li Hong's reception and Lai's wedding - in shifts. If a holiday did not fall on a Wednesday, our day off, we stayed open. One Halloween my father gave out packages of Wrigley gum to trick-or-treaters. On Thanksgiving we served roast turkey. Our cooks roasted the turkeys to a bronze sheen and sliced platters of juicy meat for entrées consisting of soup, salad, turkey, gravy, cranberry sauce, mashed potatoes or rice, vegetables, Parker House rolls, apple pie or ice cream for dessert for the grand total of $1.00. On a sheet of paper posted in the kitchen we kept track of how many turkey dinners we sold. I loved marking a line when someone shouted in a roast turkey order. On one particular Thanksgiving, we sold over a hundred turkey dinners.

My favorite time was the day after Thanksgiving. My mother or the cooks would make turkey *jook*, rice gruel, and have it ready by eleven in the morning when we came to work the next day. I ate 4 bowls at a time, sometimes dipping the *yu jow gui*, the fried donuts that we purchased from *Lock Gone* across the street. I spooned the delicious gruel topped with tiny dices of green onions into my waiting mouth. I crunched the softened *yu jow gui* as if the entire combination was nectar from the gods. I ate copious amounts. It was hard to get to work. If Christmas fell on any day except for Wednesday we kept the restaurant open. When we still lived on Harrison Street, a block away from *Ai Joong Wah*, we put up a stately Douglas fir Christmas tree in front of the window facing the street in hopes that people passing by could see it. It was a quiet and lonely Christmas at home one year because my parents weren't home to open presents with us. On the second floor of our rented Victorian home a young girl, an immigrant from China, lived there with her father or her uncle. I wondered if she celebrated Christmas. I wanted to share our tree with her but I didn't invite her to see it.

We celebrated Chinese New Year in the early days of the restaurant. I can't remember if we worked one Chinese New Year but I recall the special dishes – the *bock jom guy*, the white poached chicken, Chinese mushrooms, the greens, and the steamed whole fish - that my mother and the cooks turned out. The gingery aromas were so different from the smells of our usual restaurant fare – the soups, the brown gravy, the boiled vegetables. My father drank *ng- ka-py*, a potent wine during these celebrations. One time, he poured a shot and left it on the table. When I saw it I thought that it was tea and took a sip. The liquor burned in my mouth. I choked and spit it out. BIT . . . TER!!!!

Birthdays! What better place to have a birthday party than your own family restaurant? When I turned 14 my parents invited the entire family, married sisters, sons-in-law, and grandchildren in all to come to my party on a Wednesday when we had the restaurant to ourselves. After eating a delicious birthday meal I anxiously waited for my birthday cake to be delivered by the bakery. I had insisted on ordering the cake myself, thinking that it would be delivered. It never came. Disappointed, everyone went home and I felt terrible for years.

All this time I nurtured a fantasy that my parents would take some time off from work for a vacation. I thought that they should take trips to Reno where they could gamble. So at Lincoln Elementary School whenever I did an exercise on the back of the *Weekly Reader* I wrote of my dream. I wanted my parents to take time off for trips and to take me with them. We never did so the short trips to Lake Merritt to feed the ducks with my father and my brother sufficed. One time my father allowed me to invite some friends to come along with us. That was heaven!

I started helping at *Ai Joong Wah* around the age of 5. In addition to wiping silverware I filled sugar jars and napkin holders. On cold rainy days, I unscrewed the metal lids of glass containers and dropped saltine crackers into the sugar granules. The crackers prevented the granules from clumping together. I stuffed the white rectangle-shaped napkins with a bumpy surface into silver-colored holders. I liked pushing the springy metal piece that held the napkins in place. It was a challenge to pull a napkin out after I finished. I washed glasses at the front end of the restaurant where we had a non-functional soda fountain. Other times I squeezed glasses of fresh orange juice for customers. I sliced the oranges in half and put them on the cone of the juicer and lowered the handle to smash the fruit. The juice dripped slowly into the glass with a layer of foam at the top. I watched in surprise as customers shook salt into their freshly-made juice.

Who ate at *Ai Joong Wah*? We served Chinatown residents and other customers who came from throughout Oakland. Quite often single males (there were six sisters waiting on tables at different times) came to eat so they could chat with us. Oakland police officers came. They sat at the counter in uniform with their guns at the side. Their dark blue uniforms were a colorful contrast to the salmon-colored Formica of the counter. Henry J. Kaiser, the American industrialist, whose corporate office was located in Oakland was a regular customer. After his first wife died he continued to eat at our restaurant with his second wife, who was his first wife's nurse. A warlord from China came with his entourage. He was a Muslim who didn't eat meat. So when I spotted his rotund body ambling down the street I ran to alert the cooks. We customized his won tons, preparing them with shrimp because as a Muslim he didn't eat pork. This was a big deal for our family to have a customer with such notoriety. Lonely men, their faces etched with silence, from the Salvation Army a block away on Webster Street, stayed all day. They had nowhere to go and my parents did not make them leave. Once, one of them brought me a used crib and a doll, the only doll of my entire childhood. A Bank of America banker whose name I don't remember, Mr. Carlson, our baking goods vendor, and Mr. Stagnaro, a glass merchant on 9th Street, were regulars.

When the Korean War erupted in 1950, young Chinatown men, including many of our friends, enlisted. On the night before being shipped out they all came to our restaurant for a brief time of camaraderie. There was a feeling of heavy somberness that permeated *Ai Joong Wah* that night. I felt the heaviness of their fear as they sat before going into harm's way.

When I was old enough I graduated to the wait staff that consisted of my mother, older sisters (my brother also took his turn when he was older), and a hired waiter named Johnny Louie, a pink-faced ruddy complexioned man who wore socks that had holes in the back of his heels. During my lunch hours at nearby Lincoln Elementary School I returned to *Ai Joong Wah*. I waited on tables, scooping soup, serving entrees of fried halibut, veal cutlets, plates of beef over rice, won ton soup for 45 minutes before I gulped a quick lunch, and ran back to school before the one o'clock bell rang.

Both my father and my mother purchased groceries for *Ai Joong Wah*. My father was responsible for buying the big ticket items such as meat and baking goods – apples, flour, and sugar. My mother's job was to go to Swan's Market in West Oakland to purchase smaller items. I was her helper. We would leave *Ai Joong Wah*, walk down Webster Street and turn right at Seventh to head towards Franklin. At Seventh and Franklin I came to a dead halt, refusing to cross. At Lincoln School I heard rumors that the blacks and Latinos in West Oakland were waiting to beat me up. No matter how much my mother cajoled I wouldn't budge. She eventually went on alone. I waited at the corner. Sometime later, I'd see her carrying bags of groceries coming towards me. When she crossed the street I took the bags. I don't know if she ever told my father that I wouldn't go to Swan's Market with her.

I loved going into the kitchen when I wasn't waiting on tables, wrapping won ton or shredding fresh pods of peas in the back booth. The cacophony of pots and pans clanging, the sizzling of steaks on the grill, the banging of the *wok chon* provided familiar background sound to the rhythm of turning out meals to feed our customers – Oakland police officers, Salvation Army tenants, and workers from nearby office buildings. *Yu Yoong Goong,* my favorite cook, and I made fresh potato chips. I'd drop the freshly sliced potatoes into the bubbling oil. When the chips curled into golden brown treats, *Goong* would tell me to scoop them out. I'd scoop the chips and toss them onto a paper towel while my mouth watered.

I pretended to stir-fry in the giant wok at one end of the kitchen. I held the *wok chon* and scraped the sides of the wok, dreaming that I was a cook. Later that translated into reality when my mother taught me to cook beef so that it turned brown with a bit of juicy red showing. She and the other cooks made the most delicious *ngow nguke fon*, beef over rice. For non-Chinese customers we charged them eighty cents a plate for this dish. For Chinese customers who could read the specials written on colored sheets of rectangle paper glued to the wall or mirrors we charged them sixty-five cents.

As a teenager my job was to collect cash from the cash register. I rolled coins into paper holders and carried them along with dollar bills in a cloth bag to the Bank of America located on Broadway, two blocks away. Clutching the cloth bag as if it were a second stomach on my body I made my way to the bank, fearful to walk past the African American housing project where a childhood friend, May Kay Smith, lived. I scrunched my body and walked closely next to the building as if that stance could protect me. I was always relieved that I made it to the bank and back without an incident. I wasn't always happy working at *Ai Joong Wah*. Whenever I could, I would leave, running off when my parents weren't looking. I'd either go to *Man Loong*, the grocery store on Eighth Street that belonged to friends or to Janet Lee's house. I loved Janet's enormous second story living quarters. It was so different from the Victorian that we rented. At Janet's house I learned to play piano. We'd play restaurant, gathering up flakes of cigarette ashes and pouring them into salt and pepper shakers, pretending that we were flavoring our food. Her mother and older sisters taught me to play Poker and mah jong. While playing I would hear their doorbell ring. It was one of my sisters fetching to me to return to *Ai Joong Wah* — my idyllic escape interrupted.

My happiest time came during Chinese New Year. Chinatown had a festive air and flower vendors set up their stands to sell Chinese New Year flora and fauna. Once a year the San Francisco Chinatown lion's dance troupe came to fundraise. I made sure I got out of Lincoln School to follow the lion dancers from store to store and home to home. I forged a note from my mother, saying that I needed to be home. Once out of school I trailed the lion dancers and relished the noisy firecracker popping time in front of our restaurant. My father always hung an iceberg lettuce package filled with money for the dancers to jump up and snatch in the din of the smoky exploding firecrackers and pounding drums. It was so loud but I didn't care. All my worries were carried away by the lion dancers that came to bless Chinatown.

When I was a student at Oakland High School I worked after school and on weekends. I read when the restaurant wasn't busy. I became acquainted with the writings of Theodore Dreiser, Edna Ferber, and other authors. I read Dreiser's *American Tragedy,* Ferber's *Giant, Pride and Prejudice,* and other books. They extended my world beyond the dark brown booths, the steam table, and the concrete floor. I fell in love with the English moors, the gothic castles, and the mysterious and handsome Heathcliff. After taking a typing class at

Oakland High I joined my sisters in typing and printing the daily menus. My mother and the cooks would name the specials offered for the next day's menu. Clack, clack, clack! In my father's office I'd hit the keys of the old Underwood typewriter, typing up the specials for the day. When I finished I took out the yellowish green gelatin pad and one-by-one I printed out menus in purple ink for the next day.

As an English major at the University of California, Berkeley from 1956 to 1960 I fit my college life into my restaurant work schedule. I would go to classes and return to *Ai Joong Wah* during the day to put in my work time. In the evenings, I would drive back to Berkeley to put in hours of study at the library. Very seldom did I stay on campus long after my classes. Once in a while I could have time off to go to a football game. Mostly, I glued my ears to the radio on Friday or Saturday nights to listen to the Cal basketball games. The Erickson twins were my favorite players. Following my graduation from UC Berkeley and my graduate work at California State University East Bay I still worked at the restaurant even when I was a student teacher. Whether I wanted to or not I was always there in between school, seeing friends, going to church, and dating. I didn't have a choice. My parents needed my help.

In 1961 a few months before my July wedding we closed *Ai Joong Wah*. I was getting married and going onto an elementary school teaching career. I was moving from Oakland to Palo Alto where my future husband, Ed, was completing his doctoral studies at Stanford University. My father was dying and no one in the family wanted to help my mother run the restaurant. She was tired and ready to go on to another phase in her life. I helped close the restaurant. I found mementos - some pots, a soup ladle, two cookie sheets, and the prime rib knife to take with me. I still have most of them.

Ai Joong Wah, was an establishment that forged my identity and roots to my family and culture. It was a place where my parents, Gee Seow Hong and Gee Suey Ting, labored long hours to provide a life for my siblings and me in the United States. To this day I am fond of mama papa restaurants in various Chinatowns. When I see young children helping their parents I am carried back to the days of *Ai Joong Wah*.

I can still hear *Long Wong Bok*, calling me.

> "*Oy, mought cha!*"
> "*Oy,* wipe forks!"

Will my children and grandchildren understand that call?

On August 16, 2009 my husband, Ed, and I took our grandchildren, Ben and Sasha Wong Halperin, to Oakland Chinatown. I wanted Ben and Sasha to see where I grew up. We took them to the site of our house at 725 Harrison Street and also showed them my Chinese schools. When we arrived at 723 Webster, the location of 'Ai Joong Wah' we peeked in. Sasha wanted to go in so we did. I asked if we could take her upstairs to use the toilet. Just as we climbed the stairs I turned around to point out the office to Ben. He wanted to know where my siblings and I typed our daily menu. The four of us reached the second floor and I explained to Ben and Sasha that we had many family parties in the now-closed dining area there. It was in this space that I had drunk my father's ng ka py whiskey. It all came back to me. Downstairs, in the busy restaurant, I told Ben and Sasha to thank the woman for allowing us to go upstairs. In my rusty Cantonese I told her that my family owned the restaurant from 1943 to 1961. She wanted to know the name and I said 'Dae Joong Wah (because we spoke in sam yup, the third dialect, and not Toisanese). She asked if we sold cha siu bows. 'Not at all,' I replied.

New Shanghai Café, Lodi, California

Figure 42 Sisters Nancy, and Mary, Quong Wong, Violet & Whitlow (grandchildren), brother Jack, and sister Betty stand in front of the New Shanghai in Lodi, CA about 1946. Courtesy, Lorraine Lee Brown.

Several family members share some memories of the *New Shanghai.*[3] Betty, the second oldest daughter often helped in the café after school as did oldest son Jack.

Violet Chan, a granddaughter, also helped out in the family work and later youngest son Don took over operation of the business following his father's demise. Don operated the family business for nearly forty years including a second and more modern *New Shanghai* across the street from the original restaurant.

The *New Shanghai* opened in 1926 and was operated for nearly seventy years by four generations of the Quong Wong family in Lodi, California, a small city in the upper region of California's Central Valley just east of the large Sacramento-

---

[3] Much of the information is from interviews of several family members by Mel Brown on Aug. 3, 2009 and a letter from Violet Chan, July 20, 2009 to the author.

San Joaquin River Delta to the south of Sacramento, the state
capital. Since the earliest days of the 1848 Gold Rush hundreds of men from the Toishan region of Guangdong
Province, China, immigrated to this area. Some of them later
settled in Lodi after its founding in 1869 with the opening of
a depot for the Central Pacific Railroad. As the town grew so
did the Chinese community with its laundries, stores, cafes,
and families.

His children knew little about the earliest years of Quong
Wong's life other than that he was born in Toishan in 1894.
He first immigrated to America in 1908 and family accounts
say he initially settled in San Francisco where he worked in
his father's shoe store. Quong went back to China about
1914 to get married, returning to San Francisco a year later.
He eventually moved to Lodi where he was hired to cook for
the family of Ross Sargent, a California state senator with a
large and prosperous cattle ranching business that was one of
the area's most influential dynasties.

Chinese farm and ranch cooks usually prepared large simple
meals for the many workers on the ranch while others like
Quong Wong cooked in the family home itself. Those years
provided him with cooking skills that prepared him for later
entering the restaurant business in 1926 with two partners,
one that was a cousin named Kim Wong.

The *New Shanghai* was located in the heart of Lodi's historic
Japanese American community that started around the 1880s,
and which by 1902 had over 50 residents.

> By 1910, Lodi's Japan town was thriving next to
> the Union Pacific railroad tracks, icehouses and
> packing sheds that shipped the area's fruits and
> vegetables across the United States. On Main
> Street, Nikkei hotels, stores, restaurants, pool
> halls and bathhouses were intermingled with es-
> tablishments run by Chinese immigrants. Japan

town businesses offered an economic base for the town's Nikkei (Japanese immigrants and their descendants) and familiar goods and services to the thousands of seasonal grape pickers who worked in regional vineyards. By 1940, the area's approximately 800 Japanese residents had created a Nihonmachi that included a Buddhist Church and many social organizations, four general stores and a fish market, a drug store, six restaurants, a pool hall, a tofu maker, a laundry, and five hotels.[4]

That busy sector along Main Street across the Union Pacific tracks from the old railroad depot played a significant role in the history of the *New Shanghai Restaurant*. For many years Quong Wong's landlord was the Frank Matsumoto family, which owned the two-story building that was home to the New Shanghai for just over forty years. He converted the front part of the ground level section into a restaurant and used the back section as well as the second floor for living quarters for his family.

In this central location, the popular eatery became the place of choice for many parties and banquets held by area Nikkei. Several fruit packinghouses situated in the area employed hundreds of local unskilled workers, mostly women. Many of them frequented the New Shanghai regularly at lunchtime but income for the café was still limited especially during the economic downturn of the Great Depression. There were always enough regular customers plus travelers from the nearby railroad depot to keep business steady so that the *New Shanghai* managed to remain open while other area eateries closed. This allowed Quong Wong to support a wife in China and growing family during a stagnant national economy. This

---

[4] California Japantowns: Lodi.
<http://www.californiajapantowns.org/lodi.html> (accessed Aug. 16, 2009).

all changed with Japan's attack on Pearl Harbor on December 7, 1941. People of Japanese descent were relocated to internment camps for the war's duration but despite their absence the *New Shanghai* managed to stay in business.

Figure 43 Kim Wong (cousin), and Sing Chow (cook). Courtesy, Don & Jannie Wong.

Four of Quong Wong's five children, Betty, Florence, Mary and brother Jack were born in Lodi while Quong cooked for the Sargent family. In 1929 the Wong children were sent to China to live with their mother and to be schooled by classic Chinese education. Their mother was pregnant when she left the States so the youngest son, Don, was born in China in 1930 a few months after their arrival there. The four older kids returned to Lodi in 1939 and lived with their father in the apartments on the second floor above the restaurant.

The restaurant was pretty much a family-run business. Quong had his children, and a grandchild, Violet, work for him with as many as 7 or 8 people working at one time at the restaurant. The children usually did all the assorted menial jobs required in a family restaurant like preparing vegetables, filling small soy sauce bottles, salt and pepper shakers, sorting silverware, making pots of tea, bussing tables, washing dishes, etc. Depending on their age, the children helped in various ways in the kitchen. All kinds of meat and vegetable had to be chopped, cut, diced or sliced for different dishes. Shrimps have to be shelled. Water urns have to be filled for tea. Other chores included sweeping the dining room floor and keeping a supply of change in the cash register.

Betty, the second oldest daughter, began working in the restaurant at age sixteen and continued there until she married in 1941. She remembered that her regular after school job at the popular cafe kept her very busy each afternoon and evening through her late teenage years. She walked several blocks from school each day straight to the café for chores. Before World War II, Betty, still in her teens, was the short order cook at night because the cook was busy playing mahjong with her father. Whenever a late night customer arrived wanting a meal, Betty stopped whatever chore she was doing, took the order, and prepared it. She then packaged the order for carryout or served the dishes and cleaned up afterwards.

Extra helpers were hired in later years when business began to thrive. In one period when there were only six family members available, two hired hands were needed to help get the work done. One employee, a Caucasian, came looking for work and he became the dishwasher. These hired employees were pleasant and Betty had fond memories of them. They'd joke around and seemed to enjoy what they did while most of the family members took their work and life much too seriously.

Betty noted that the most popular dish was chow mein. The dinner combinations with a variety of dishes also were very popular. Fried prawns were another. And so was the barbecue pork. The variety of noodle soups was popular.

We had a room for making fresh noodles. The process of hand-making the dough and then running it through machines is a tedious job. The dough has to be run through the machine many times before it becomes a long, thin sheet. Another gadget has to be used to make and cut the long thin noodles. The next step is to fold them into neat balls and placed on racks and into the refrigerator so the cook can access it quickly and neatly.

The *New Shanghai* had a set printed menu, but if someone wanted some special dishes we usually accommodated them. If someone wanted authentic Chinese dishes, such as minced pork steamed with salted fish, we tried to provide them. Some of our Asian customers would order dishes such as Black Bean Spareribs, Bitter Melon, Sweet and Sour spare ribs, etc. There were no American dishes such steaks, pork chops served.

After closing, many tasks remained such as cleaning up, the dining room, putting things away in an orderly fashion, counting the money from the cash register, and recording the proceeds for the day. The cook in charge of the char siu (barbecue pork) cut pork legs into strips and marinated them overnight to barbecue the next day.

Betty recalled that the family members were all so busy with their duties that there was not much interaction on a personal level. However, we ate our two meals together, lunch at 3:30 (before we opened) and dinner (after we closed). An already long day was prolonged by the family having dinner together after closing up because there would be more dishes to wash and put away before leaving the kitchen or dining room. The business hours were from 11 a.m. to 2 p.m. for lunch and from 4:00 to 11 p.m. on weekdays and we stayed open later on weekends but we closed on Wednesdays. Night customers were usually expected since New Shanghai was known for its late hours of food service. Ordering supplies and food were pretty much routine procedures with fresh meats and vegetable being purchased locally while rice and other commodities came from Sacramento or Stockton vendors. We placed new orders ahead so that we'd not run out before the next delivery. Fortunately we had a pretty large room for storing supplies and the refrigerator we had was pretty large.

On almost any weeknight during the late 1930s and early 1940s, the unmistakable clattering sound of shuffled mahjong tiles filled the café about 8 p. m. Each evening as business slowed following the dinner rush, Quong Wong and his two partners, one of them the eatery's cook, would move into one of the café's partitioned booths to play, smoke, and discuss business matters. Friends or other Toishan cooks from local restaurants always joined to provide the needed fourth player in the curtained booth for the evening's gambling and bull session.

The year 1941 brought significant change to the *New Shanghai*. That summer daughter Betty married and left for her new husband's home in San Francisco's Chinatown. Later that year Quong Wong suffered a debilitating stroke that left him paralyzed on the left side and somewhat diminished in mental capacity. Younger daughter Mary and her brother Jack became caregivers for their father as well as responsible for the restaurant's daily routine. It was also then that oldest son Jack truly learned to shoulder the demands of managing the cafe as Quong Wong slowly recovered his health. The elder man continued to stay as busy in the restaurant as his condition allowed by becoming the chief cashier. That job kept him seated on a stool at the front counter daily throughout the lunch and dinner hours where he managed the cash register solely with his right arm and hand. Mr. Wong's presence at the register became a familiar sight to all of the regular customers.

When America entered WW II following the Japanese attack on Pearl Harbor, Hawaii, wartime conditions brought much change to the lives of all Americans but especially to the families operating small businesses such as restaurants. The most significant changes for the *New Shanghai,* according to oldest son Jack Wong, were due to rationing.

> Items like sugar, cooking oil, butter, eggs, and coffee, were rationed by the government and could only be purchased in restricted amounts set by law using special coupons and ration stamps. Chinese cooks have always known how to stretch recipes in clever ways to keep costs down so we met the challenge with only a few complaints from the regular customers.

As the war went on, Jack faced the likelihood of being drafted into the military. As the only resident male member of the family at that point in time, Jack was given a deferment based on his status as primary caregiver and economic provider for his father, sister Mary, their mother, and younger brother Donald then living in Hong Kong. After his father's death a decade later, Jack served in the military.

Following the end of the war in 1945, life slowly returned to normal for most Americans and business at *New Shanghai* continued to keep the Wong family busy. Youngest daughter Mary grew up in the firmly established café and worked there daily, as had her older siblings. Like her brother Jack, she worked after school hours at the family café. Her young niece Violet began working in the family business in the late 1940s during her adolescence. She too learned at an early age the restrictive lifestyle dictated by a family operated business.

> I think I missed out on being a typical teenager and having fun. I never had time to join in after-school activities or had the leisure of having or interacting with friends of my age because immediately after school, I'd walk back to the restaurant, change my clothes, eat, and start working

right away until 10 or 11 p. m. Then I go upstairs
to my room to study for the next school day before going to bed.

Encounters between the children and customers could have
lasting effects. Violet recalls several customers that had a
memorable impact on her.

One regular customer was an elderly Japanese
single man. I don't ever remember him coming in
sober. But he somehow managed to find a small
booth and sit down without falling. He'd be a bit
loud but never did any harm to anybody. Mr. and
Mrs. Randolph came in throughout all the years
that I worked on a regular basis. They took me
under their wings and treated me like they did
their own two daughters. I shall never forget how
loved they made me feel.

In August 1949, Mary left the nest when she and her new
husband Jimmy Lee moved to Chinatown to operate their
own noodle factory, leaving Jack completely responsible for
the family's ailing patriarch and the restaurant. Both partners
remained but Jack managed the operation and helped with
the cooking when necessary. In summer 1952, Quong Wong
passed away followed in death a few months later by partner
Sing Chow. Younger brother Don, an American citizen by
birthright, finally managed to come from China but just in
time for his father's funeral, the two never having met in person.

Following the death of his father, Jack's draft exemption expired and he joined the U. S. Air Force. His oldest sister
Nancy and her husband Phillip Wong then took over operation of *New Shanghai* in mid 1952. Since he too was eligible
for the draft, Don joined the U. S. Army and was sent to Korea in early 1953. He returned to Lodi in late 1954 and began
his restaurant business career at the *New Shanghai*. Don be-

came sole owner not long afterward as the Wong family bought out the remaining partner Kim Wong who returned to China. In 1957 Don's new wife Jannie joined him in managing the old restaurant and a few years later they began their family.

Operating a Chinese restaurant presented many challenges. Jannie noted that cooks often created major problems. Some would quit to work for other restaurants or would have arguments or conflicts with each other over the workload. A different challenge was how to get non-Chinese customers to try Chinese foods other than chop suey. Don recalled the reluctance of one customer to order fried wontons. Finally, Don offered a free sample, which the customer liked so much he insisted on paying for it!

Figure 44 Grand Opening, New Shanghai, 1966.

By 1966 the building that the *New Shanghai* occupied since 1926 needed major repairs, which its owners were not willing to make. Don and Jannie decided to move, buying a lot on the opposite corner where they built a larger modern *New Shanghai* that boasted seven woks, a staff of 10, and traditional dining booths of the original cafe. Don and Jannie Wong and their children, with able assistance from brother Jack cooking on weekends, operated that popular eatery for another twenty-five years.

Figure 45 New Shanghai Restaurant, 1990. Courtesy, Julie Wong Hornsby.

John L's Restaurant, San Antonio, Tx.

Figure 46 John L's, San Antonio, Tx. Courtesy, Dora Leung.

John L, as his customers called John Leung, and I, his wife Dora, owned and operated a popular Chinese take out business for many years. He was a second generation Chinese born in San Antonio, Texas in 1921, and I am a third generation Chinese-American, born in Duluth, Minnesota. We grew up in San Antonio, graduated from high school together, and married soon after and raised four children, three daughters and a son.

"John L" is a rather unusual name for a café that served Chinese food, but that is perhaps in keeping with the fact that our restaurant was not your typical Chinese chop suey joint. In fact, originally a retail grocery business, it received a makeover into a restaurant that not only offer Chinese dishes, but also had dishes from other ethnic backgrounds.

The story of how our grocery store was transformed into a café was not one involving a planned change but one that happened almost by surprise. When we built our grocery store, my father- in-law made it an ice station so that we could open and sell beer from the facilities on Sundays. We sold everything a small grocery store would sell, from canned goods to fresh meat and vegetables. The store was located on a large busy street in a predominantly Hispanic neighborhood. Our customers were mainly people from the neighborhood. We did all of the work ourselves. My husband did the butchering for the meat market and took care of all of the heavy work while I manned the cash register and cared for the vegetables and fruit area. We raised our children at the store, especially when they were young, but lived in a house on the other side of town.

Over the years, many large businesses and warehouses that grew up around us. Soon many of the workers and office people began to come into the store for luncheon supplies, such as lunchmeat, loaves of bread, fruit, chips and drinks. This became a good part of our business. One of the regular customers who came into the store for lunch supplies one day said, jokingly, "Why don't you just make the sandwiches for us? Then we don't have to do this everyday, John L." He began to ponder the idea and liked the suggestion, so the next day, he made some pressed ham and cheese sandwiches to see how it would sell that day. He discovered that one loaf of sandwich bread made thirteen sandwiches, which he sold for twenty-five cents a sandwich. That day, the sandwiches sold so well that we were launched into a new business.

Our time, the menu expanded to offer many different sandwiches, ham and cheese, salami or bologna with cheese, and Mexican French Roll Poor-Boys. I began to make things that went along with these sandwiches. I prepared homemade potato salad, macaroni salad, chicken salad and tuna salad. Then as the business grew, I began to make homemade chili, which became very famous, and homemade beef vegetable soup. We kept it hot in an electric soup pot in the meat market. I had always enjoyed cooking for family and friends, so my creative juices kicked into gear. John L sold all of these luncheon items out of the meat market, putting all of the varieties of sandwiches on top of the meat case where customers could help themselves and all of my salads in large white butcher pans inside of the meat case. The salads were sold by weight, at 35 cents a pound. People loved our food so much that lines began to form outside of the store from 1 1 a.m. to 1:30 p.m. John L sold over 100 sandwiches along with my salads and soup items everyday.

When business grew, I began to sell homemade fried chicken and fried fish on Fridays. We found that our customers really liked the hot lunches and that we profited from this new venture. This idea later grew into a different "Hot Plate Lunch" every day. I cooked the lunches in a small kitchen located in the storage room at the back of the store. The hot lunches were different each day, from different Chinese stir-fried dishes with white rice, spaghetti with meat sauce, beef stew over white rice, and Hungarian Goulash with macaroni.

As the number of lunch customers expanded and the grocery store business lessened, John L asked me if we should just close the grocery store and turn the business into a restaurant. We began to think of how we could do this without hiring too much help. John L and I had always worked so well with each other, that we wanted to be able to continue our success "Our Way." So after much thought, we decided to put in a cafeteria steam table line for our business. We could use the hot line for the lunches, and then provide table service at night. Using the hot line idea, I could do all of the cooking in the morning with just a few ladies to help me prepare things, and John L could serve the customers during lunch. Thus in only a month's time, we converted the grocery store into our restaurant. The cafeteria steam table was placed at the front of the restaurant. To the left was a dining room with enough tables and chairs to seat about 50 customers. To the right of the steam table was a small bar lounge for our old grocery store customers. These customers were accustomed to coming into the grocery store each evening after work for a cold beer and friendly conversation. Everyone who came to our store was more than customers; they were friends. They had been friends for many years and John L didn't want to leave them out of our new venture.

The Grand Opening was so exciting. The night before our first day, neither one of us could sleep. It was a new adventure and we were hopeful that it would be successful. We still had two children to put through college and we were concerned about making the "right choice." That morning, I cooked many of our customers' favorite items such as beef stew, fried chicken, a Chinese stir-fry, chicken fried steak, fresh mashed potatoes, and fresh cooked vegetables. I also made homemade apple and lemon pies. Included with the plate lunch special would be a lettuce and tomato salad and a beverage.

John L also made his usual 100 sandwiches, which he put on the shelf above the steam table. That day we were very busy, selling our lunches. John L worked the cafeteria line, serving the hot plate lunches. A helper dished out the salad and served the drinks. I became the cashier at the end of the line. We were very busy and felt that the restaurant was off to a very good start. There was only one problem. John did not sell one sandwich. No one wanted sandwiches when we had all that delicious hot food instead. Now... what were we going to do with 100 sandwiches. John put the sandwiches in the cooler, and that night when the old grocery store friends came for their cold beer and conversation, he passed them out as a "Grand Opening Surprise". Everyone had a great time.

Figure 47 Dora and John Leung ready to serve customers in their popular San Antonio eatery. Courtesy, Dora Leung.

The restaurant served lunch every weekday from 11 a.m. to 2 p.m. During that time, we always had fried chicken and chicken fried steak on the steam table. John L and I wanted our customers to have choices from a variety of foods. Each day I cooked different items for lunch. Some of the American dishes were chicken cooked with beer, baked chicken with dressing and gravy, spaghetti with meatballs, or meatloaf with a tomato sauce. There were also different Chinese dishes each day such as fried rice, beef with broccoli, lemon chicken, chicken chow mein, peking fish, sweet and sour pork, and homemade egg rolls. Mexican dishes changed daily also, with enchiladas, crispy tacos, soft tacos, empanadas, and homemade flour tortillas. Mexican rice and beans were a part of the fresh vegetables made each day. We also continued to serve my homemade chili. I am proud to say that many customers came from near and far for my chili. Each day, I made homemade pies. I gave my customers a selection of apple, lemon meringue, pecan, banana cream, Japanese fruit, peach and cherry pies. Each one was baked fresh everyday. I also baked homemade corn bread to serve on the lunch line.

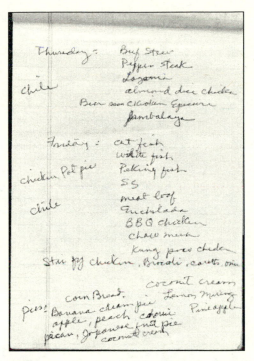

Figure 48 A Menu Plan at John L's. Courtesy, Dora Leung.

The business grew well from 1973 to 1993. During this time, he became a wonderful chef and helped with the cooking each day. He devised "Banquet Dinners" that were pre-ordered for tables of 10. Night Service only occurred on Fridays and Saturdays. Sadly John L died of heart failure in 1993. His death was such a loss to me and to the restaurant. He was always so friendly and knew all of our many customers by name. Our son, John Jr., continued working with me in the restaurant until 2001 when I retired from the business.

Looking back, it was indeed a stroke of either luck or genius that we converted our grocery business into a restaurant because it was much more fulfilling to John L and I to satisfy our customers' stomachs than to just sell groceries to them.

Midwest

Oriental Garden, Ft. Wayne, Indiana

Figure 49 Lem Chan, Fong Chen & Gong Chin. Courtesy, Joe Chan.

Joe Chan is a corn-bred Hoosier who earned a Bachelor's degree in social work from Indiana University and a Master's degree in management from Webster College. He served thirty years in the U.S. Air Force as a pilot, staff officer, commander, and air attaché. Married to the former Eliz Wong who grew up in a Chinese laundry family in Louisville, Ky. They have two children,

one a patent attorney in Atlanta, Ga. and the other a jour-
neywoman sheet metal worker in Portland, Or.

My dad, Lem Chan, immigrated to the U. S. in 1926 from Sui
Nam Village, Toishan County, Canton Province, China at the
age of 15. Detained at the U.S. Immigration Station, Angel
Island, in San Francisco Bay because of the Chinese Exclusion laws, he convinced the authorities that his claim of being
the son of a U.S. citizen was valid and was admitted into this
country. He worked briefly in a grocery store in Oakland,
California, Chinatown before moving to Chicago, Illinois to
learn the restaurant trade from other Chan "cousins."

My mom, Lucille Darling (Poy) Chan, was born in Detroit,
Michigan in 1920, and went to China with her family in 1931
when her father's business failed in the midst of the Great
Depression. Her father had owned a Chinese restaurant in
Detroit, across the street from the Sheraton Cadillac Hotel.
I've heard that his restaurant was quite popular, with a band
and dance floor, and they served liquor during Prohibition.
Henry Ford was one of his customers (but no connection between Mr. Ford and illegal liquor is intended or implied).
Grandfather Poy was an early supporter of Dr. Sun Yet-san,
the founder of the Chinese Republic in 1911, and was photo-
graphed with Dr. Sun during one of his trips to the U.S. My
mom returned to the U.S. in 1940 as a "picture bride" in an
arranged marriage (by both families) to meet my dad for the
first time. But even as a returning U.S. citizen, she was detained on Angel Island by immigration authorities for a
weekend until they could confirm her status.

By 1942, when I was born, my dad owned the *Oriental Garden
Chinese-American Restaurant* at 120 East Washington, Fort
Wayne, Indiana, in partnership with two of his contemporar-
ies, Fong Chen and Gong Chin.[5] They weren't actually

---

[5] Chan, Chen and Chin are the same surname in Chinese, but the
American English pronunciation and transliteration resulted in
different spellings.

related, as far as I know. An "uncle" in Chicago originally financed the partnership. I think that's who gave my dad his recipes, which he used throughout his 50-year restaurateur career. The restaurant was in the heart of downtown Fort Wayne, one block from the largest department store in town, Wolf & Dessauer's. Fong was in charge of the dining room, Gong was the American food chef, and my dad was the Chinese food chef, although he knew how to cook American food as well. The restaurant was quite fancy for its day with a red and white glass front exterior, leather booths on both sides of the front half of the dining room, small "rooms" each containing a table and four chairs on both sides of the rear half of the dining room, and tables and chairs running the length down the middle of both halves. The dining room decoration included a pair of art deco planters shaped like modern pagodas.

When I was six years old, after my first year of elementary school, my dad sent mom and me to Hong Kong in 1948 so I could meet both of my grandmothers. As I was an only child, I guess he thought it important to meet my surviving grandparents since it was not certain that they could ever immigrate to the U.S. My dad had not visited China since he left. We stayed in Hong Kong for a year and what limited Cantonese I can still speak today stems from that period, plus the fact that dad and I used to converse almost exclusively in Chinese. When we returned to Fort Wayne, I attended summer school and skipped the second grade; unfortunately, I then entered the third grade as a confirmed printer not having learned how to write in cursive during a "normal" second grade (I'm still a better printer than I am a writer).

I don't remember a lot about the operation of the *Oriental Garden*, as my dad and his partners tried to keep their spouses from working in the restaurant once kids were born. My mom was a stay-at-home housewife for most of my childhood in Ft Wayne. We lived in a single-family house miles from downtown on the south side; the partners worked hard to allow their children to grow up as typical American kids in a suburban atmosphere. As the only Asian in the all-white Harrison Hill Elementary School, I rarely recognized that I was "different" until a schoolmate called me a "Chinese communist" (or perhaps worse...I don't remember) during the Korean War, at which time some other schoolmates came to my defense and beat the tar out of him. I played basketball and softball, (in spite of being the last one chosen for any team because I was skinny, small and a klutz,) and won a gold and two silver medals playing clarinet in the grade school band. But my parents always stressed the importance of doing well academically in school; in fact, my dad told me that the only way I could be the equal of others in America was to be better than them.

What I do remember about the *Oriental Garden* was probably typical of other Chinese restaurants in the Midwest. One did not open a Chinese restaurant too close to another Chinese restaurant...it wasn't considered good manners to compete too vigorously with a fellow Chinese; there was enough business to go around. (The only other Chinese restaurant in Fort Wayne was four blocks away and there were also three Chinese laundries in town.) The menu was half American food and half Chinese food, and prime rib seemed to be a favorite of the customers. I remember policemen and firemen used to walk into the kitchen through the back door, spend a few minutes chatting with my dad and his partners over coffee, and then walk out munching on prime rib sandwiches. I suspect police and fire department ethics were different in those days compared with today.

In American-Chinese restaurants at that time, room and board were provided and all federal, state, and social security taxes were paid along with a monthly salary to the Chinese employees. Perhaps it was different in larger cities like Chicago or Detroit where there was a larger pool of Chinese employees to choose from, but in smaller cities like Ft Wayne, these additional benefits were needed to lure Chinese into the hinterland. My dad and his partners only hired a few Chinese to cook in the kitchen because of the additional costs. These employees slept in a room behind the kitchen. The other employees, waitresses and dishwashers, were Caucasian, although an occasional Afro-American was hired as a dishwasher. My mom and the other partners' wives also worked as waitresses sometimes, particularly after the children were old enough to take care of themselves. I remember my mom telling of how she learned to be a waitress before I was born: she walked around the dining room with a large tray on her shoulder while the three partners threw potatoes on the tray to develop and test her sense of balance … she eventually learned how to carry a full load of dishes and glasses on her tray without spilling a drop.

In the early 1950s, Fort Wayne had an NBA professional basketball team – the Pistons. Whenever the NBA Rochester (NY) Royals came to town to play the Pistons, the entire Royals team __ players, coaches, trainers, etc., __would come to the Oriental Garden after the game to eat. And eat they did…huge T-bone steaks with all the trimmings, and drinking quarts of milk and orange juice by the bottle. I remember that even while seated at the tables gorging themselves, the players were much taller than my dad and his partners who were walking around serving them. The kids of the restaurant occasionally got to sit on the Royals' bench at the Allen County War Memorial Coliseum during their games with the Pistons, and one Christmas, the Royals team gave each of us kids an Emerson clock radio…this was as desirable then as an "I Pod" is today.

In 1955, my dad left the *Oriental Garden* partnership and bought the *Mandarin Inn Restaurant* in Muncie, Indiana, from another Chinese family for $10,000. This price included all the equipment, furnishings, stock, existing lease on the storefront and upstairs apartment ($300 per month rent), and most importantly, the name. The informal Chinese restaurant code then stated that one could not open another Chinese restaurant with the same name in the same city. There was another Chinese restaurant in Muncie, the *China Inn*, only one block away, seemingly in violation of the "too close" clause of the code. The *Mandarin Inn* was in town first by several decades, and the owner protested when the *China Inn* opened, but to no avail. The cool relations between the two restaurants continued even after my father bought the *Mandarin*. During the five years I lived in Muncie before going away to college, I don't remember ever meeting the two Chinese men who owned and operated the other restaurant, even though we were the only Chinese residents in Muncie. Eventually, my dad's better food and lower prices forced them out of business.

While the name *"Mandarin Inn"* might imply cuisine from northern China in today's gastronomic world, back in those days perhaps 99% of all Chinese restaurants in the U.S. served Cantonese food because that's practically where all the Chinese in the U.S originally came from – Canton (now Guangdong) Province. Iconic dishes like Peking duck, hot and sour soup, and salt and pepper squid were unheard of back then; to most Americans, Chinese food meant chop suey, egg foo young, and sweet and sour pork. And how many of those "Cantonese" dishes were original to China is debatable.

The *Mandarin Inn*, with seating for 65 people, was probably half the size of the Oriental Garden. My dad worked in the kitchen cooking primarily American food while he hired another Chinese cook for the Chinese food. My mom ran the dining room acting as cashier, hostess and waitress, along with two or three other waitresses. The menu was split pretty evenly between Chinese and American food, and many customers claimed that Lem made the best Italian spaghetti sauce in town. The lunch menu started at 65 cents, and that would buy you a hamburger steak with mushroom gravy or grilled onions, complete with mashed potatoes or French fries, vegetable of the day, two rolls with butter, and coffee or tea. Or that same 65 cents could get you Chinese chop suey or chow mein, one egg foo young patty or two rolls with butter, and coffee or tea. The dinner menu was virtually the same as the lunch menu, but portions were larger. For $1.05, you could order the hamburger steak or Chinese chop suey, but the dinner menu included an appetizer, soup or tomato juice; relish dish with celery hearts, pickles and olives; dessert -- pie, ice cream, or almond cookies; and choice of coffee or tea.

The menu also included sandwiches and side orders, along with the complete lunches and dinners, but dad tried to discourage the "hamburger trade", because of the lower profit margins that sandwich-eaters might bring. His hamburgers were made with the same sized ground beef patty that was on the lunch menu, but he always served it on white loaf bread instead of proper hamburger buns. And his French fries were thick cut, rather than the thin cut popular at drive inns like the *new* McDonald's in town. Even though our restaurant was only two blocks from my high school, very few of my schoolmates and friends would eat lunch at the restaurant with me because our food wasn't "cool," even though our prices were lower than what they paid at other lunch counters and drive-inns.

In Chinese restaurants before 1970 in this country, chop suey was basically a stir-fry of meat and vegetables served with white rice; chow mein was the same stir-fry mixture served with crispy fried noodles, usually from the Hong Kong Noodle Factory in Chicago. The vegetables were usually bean sprouts, celery, Chinese cabbage, and a few sliced water chestnuts; "chicken chop suey" was made with chicken, "beef chow mein" was made with beef, but pork was the most prominent and popular meat in Chinese food. Egg foo young was a fried egg patty filled with pork, bean sprouts and green onions, covered with brown gravy. The same brown gravy was served on hamburger steaks, breaded pork cutlets, and mashed potatoes on the American side of the menu.

Chinese restaurants of that era were very labor intensive. Dad bought beef by the quarter, pork by the half, whole chickens by the crate, and did all of his own butchering. If customers ordered a T-bone steaks or pork chops, they were cut fresh off the loin. Nothing was wasted; the tiniest scrap of meat ended up in one dish or another, all bones went into the soup pot, and the meat fat was rendered in a large wok and the grease used for cooking. Old grease was sold to a soap company. He skinned his own almonds and roasted them in a wok full of salt; the almonds were used on almond cookies and sprinkled on Chinese dishes as a garnish. The almond-flavored salt added a nice touch to many recipes. Peanut butter was the secret ingredient in his egg rolls – it held the chopped meat and vegetables together and en-hanced the taste. He baked his own pies (apple, cherry and custard), almond cookies, and dinner rolls, mixing the dough before going to bed, letting it rise over night, and shaping and baking the rolls first thing in the morning.

Bean sprouts were the primary ingredient of chop suey and chow mein, and dad grew his own bean sprouts from mung beans, which were about the size of BBs. The growing cycle took about four days, and required soaking the beans and rinsing the growing sprouts in fresh, cold water every eight hours. Occasionally, a batch of bean sprouts would go bad, so we'd have to jump in the car after the restaurant closed and drive 70 miles to Fort Wayne to get a couple bushel bas-kets of fresh bean sprouts for the next business day. I learned years later that the mung beans were grown in north Texas, along the Oklahoma border. An enterprising Chinese farmer realized the nationwide market for the beans and found that he could grow two crops per year between the winter wheat and the summer cotton crops. He became a millionaire with a virtual monopoly on the lowly mung bean, which my dad and Chinese restaurants across the country bought by the 50-pound bag.

Food tastes change over the years, particularly in Chinese food. Today, Beijing, Shanghai, and Szechuan cuisine have joined Cantonese in most Chinese restaurants. Broccoli and carrots have replaced bean sprouts and celery as the vegetables of choice, and staples like almond duck, sub gum chop suey/chow mein, and shrimp with lobster sauce have all but disappeared from the menu. In fact, egg foo young can only be found today in restaurants that cater to the older American customers who remember the "authentic" Chinese food of their youth.

The *Mandarin Inn* opened 364 days a year from 11 a.m. to 8:30 p.m. Thanksgiving Day was the worst day of the year for restaurants in those days because everyone went to grandma's house for dinner; that was the only day of the year dad had off. Mother's Day was the busiest day of the year, with customers waiting at the door from opening until closing. Christmas, Easter, and Father's Day were also very busy. On a typical weekday, the lunch trade was busier than the dinner hours. Because of our downtown location, many local merchants, bankers, lawyers and other professionals ate at the Mandarin five days a week and often sat at the "family table;" as one person finished his lunch, another waiting customer would slip into the still-warm, empty seat at this popular, constantly-filled table for six. Our menu had a different daily special Monday through Friday – Yankee pot roast, glazed ham, Swiss steak, roast leg of lamb, and prime rib; and on Sundays, roast turkey with stuffing. We had a moderate carryout business in the evening, with the Chinese food served in the ubiquitous paper chop suey pails with wire handles.

My dad spoke enough English to manage the restaurant, which he eventually renamed *"Lem's Mandarin Inn."* I remember asking him once why he ordered food and supplies from so many different distributors. He replied that he got better prices by "shopping around", and that we got more gifts at Christmas from distributors. And every year, we'd get pen and pencil sets, boxes of candy, fruitcakes, and calendars. He truly enjoyed the workings of the restaurant trade.

In moving from a partnership to owning his own restaurant, dad took on total responsibility for the success or failure of the business. In Ft. Wayne, he got half a day off every Tuesday afternoon. In Muncie, he worked every day from 7:00 A.M. until 11 p.m., unless an emergency like a bad batch of bean sprouts or an employee suddenly quitting added to the day's toil.

Although my mom worked occasionally at the *Oriental Garden* in Ft Wayne, she worked daily along with dad at the *Mandarin Inn* after we moved to Muncie. She went from being a typical American housewife to running the front end of the restaurant. She learned to manage other employees, do basic bookkeeping and payroll, print menus, and help in the kitchen when necessary. On the busiest days of the year, like Mother's Day, we always seemed to run out of something in the dining room – steak knives or juice glasses or teapots – and whoever was least busy would to pitch in and help the dishwasher.

My life changed drastically in the move to Muncie. My home changed from a modest but comfortable two-bedroom house in a nice suburban neighborhood to a crowded two-room apartment above our downtown restaurant. No more riding my bike, playing sports with the kids in the block, bringing friends home for dinner or just to "hang out." No one else seemed to live downtown in Muncie except transients at the Hotel Delaware across the street.

After my thirteenth birthday, I spent most of my non-school waking hours in the dining room of the restaurant. That's where I did my homework, ate all my meals, and occasionally helped greet customers, wait on tables, and help with the cash register if mom was busy. Making new friends was a slow process initially, as the only people I'd see daily were either at school or in the restaurant. Eventually, I attended the nearby High Street Methodist Church and joined the Methodist Youth Fellowship (MYF), which provided a social outlet outside of school.

I was the only Chinese kid in town, and encountered Afro-American classmates for the first time in junior high and high school. Dad had always encouraged me to associate exclusively with Caucasians...I guess he was prejudiced by today's standards. As I progressed academically in this new environment and became more of a "known quantity", I found my niche in the teen-age social milieu. By the time I graduated from high school, I served as president of the Methodist Youth Fellowship and the National Honor Society, and joined in the clubs and social activities of the day. My parents constantly encouraged me to work hard in school, and being with them daily in the restaurant made it easy to keep their eye on me. I guess it paid off for them, because I was selected as a National Merit Scholar and earned a four-year scholarship to Indiana University in Bloomington

Mom voted a straight Republican ballot in every election, and dad voted Democratic. It was good business to have customers of all political stripes, but looking back at my parents' accomplishments, there was another factor at work. My parents sponsored perhaps a dozen or more relatives and friends into the U.S. from China. Due to the Chinese Exclusion Acts and the subsequent quota laws restricting Chinese immigration to this country, one way around this was to have Congress pass a special bill allowing an exception to the existing laws. A U.S. senator or congressman could introduce a bill "For the Relief of Chan Wei Hung", for example, which would allow that person to immigrate to this country in spite of the existing laws, which might delay his immigration for years because of the long quota lists. This bill would actually be a "rider" to another piece of more important legislation, and probably very few people in Congress even knew the details of the rider. That's why it was important to personally know one's U.S. senator or congressman if one was interested in getting a special bill introduced and passed, and that's why my mom and dad always split their votes so they could always be in touch with someone in power.

Even though I learned a bit about the restaurant business "by osmosis" over the years, my parents always pushed me towards the more honorable professions as a career, particularly medicine. They discouraged any thought of my becoming a restaurateur, and always belittled my attempts to learn how to cook. But dad advised whatever the future might bring, that if I was hungry and didn't have much money, I should always seek out a Chinese restaurant for a good, cheap meal.

My dad was a great chef, probably learning a lot of recipes as a young man in Chicago before going into the partnership and finally his own business. Thanks to growing up in his restaurant I think I've developed a proper sense of what's good or bad when it comes to food and service. Despite being fortunate enough to travel the world and to dine in some fine places, the flavors and aromas that originated in the kitchens of the *Oriental Garden* and *Lem's Mandarin Inn* still remain gold standards for me.

Tong's Tea Garden, Chicago, Il.

Figure 50 Tong's Tea Garden, Chicago, Il., Courtesy, Bill Tong.

B *ill Tong earned his Master's degree in Earth Science from Northeastern Illinois University. Since 1991 he has worked as a geologist at the U. S. Environmental Protection Agency (Region 5 office in Chicago). He has also been an earth science adjunct faculty at Oakton Community College in Des Plaines, Il, since 1994.*

Just as thousands of other Chinese men before and after him, my great grandfather, Yi Yuan Tong emigrated from Taishan County to America in 1906 in search of work. Foreign colonialism, civil war, and the general weakness of the Ch'ing (Manchu) national government had drained China's economic and natural resources during the late 19th century in China. After a short time working in San Francisco, he tried agricultural work in the California Central Valley, but found the work very difficult. He decided to relocate to Chicago, where there was less severe and overt anti-Chinese discrimination than on the west coast.

In 1924, after about 18 years of working as a cook at various Chinese restaurants in the heart of Chicago's original China-town, Great-Grandfather decided to retire before his 50th birthday. His son (my grandfather, Tan Sum Tong) immi-grated to Chicago just before Great Grandfather returned to China._Grandpa worked mostly as a waiter and sometimes as a cook for various Chinese restaurants in the downtown area during the mid-1920's. Grandpa later found work at several restaurants in the new Chinatown around Wentworth Avenue during the 1930's. Even during the depth of the Great Depression, he was able to find regular work. In 1930, Grandpa took a weekend job at a Chinese restaurant located in Milwaukee, Wisconsin, commuting on the Chi-cago, North Shore & Milwaukee Railroad.

World War II was the pivotal event that changed my family's history. Grandpa was drafted in 1941, and as a GI, he be-came a U.S. citizen, which gave him the right to have his family in China immigrate to America. Dad was scheduled to board a ship to America to join his father, but when he ar-rived by train from Canton to Shanghai, he found a ticket scalper had sold his reservation on the ship, and the war with Japan soon closed the port of Shanghai. Six years later, in 1947, Grandma (nee Hing Fong Lee), Dad, and Aunt Yolanda sailed for America to reunite with Grandpa in Chicago, after a 14-year separation.

Grandpa was discharged from the U.S. Army in 1945 and went back to work as a hired hand in the restaurant business, but in 1947, he decided to buy his own Chinese take-out res-taurant, known as *The Lee*, in the Hollywood Park neighborhood on Chicago's north side. Grandpa and his family lived temporarily in a GI trailer located a few blocks away. The steel trailer only had enough room to house 3 people, so Dad slept in the restaurant kitchen. During summers, when the heat was too unbearable in the kitchen, Dad slept outside on the merry-go-round in the schoolyard of Peterson Elementary School across the street. The GI trailer camp closed down in 1948 so my grandparents, father, and aunt moved about 20 miles to an apartment in Chinatown.

Grandma, Dad, and Aunt Yolanda all had to learn English from scratch by attending evening classes sponsored by a church after work. Dad told me that compared to being a farm boy in China, life and work in America was very difficult; it was like being blind (unable to read English signs) and deaf (not be able to understand English speech) at the same time. By 1950, they had saved up enough money to buy their first car, a Buick Special two-door coupe. After seven long hard years of operating *The Lee*, which was open 363 days per year and closed only for Thanksgiving and Christmas Day, Grandpa amassed enough money to build his own larger restaurant a block away at 3411 Bryn Mawr Avenue on an empty commercial lot that he purchased. To eliminate the long commute from Chinatown, he built a second floor apartment above the restaurant.

Tong's Tea Garden opened as a Chinese take-out restaurant in December of 1954. During that time, the Hollywood Park neighborhood was situated at the outskirts of Chicago. Many vacant, undeveloped lots and even a few farms were still found in the neighborhood. At that time, only one building, a corner snack shop (CV's) stood on the block of mostly vacant lots, at the southwest corner of Kimball and Bryn Mawr Avenues.

The customer waiting area was quite large, with chairs lining both walls. The order counter was located beyond the front door. Between the kitchen and the waiting area were green fiberglass panels, which hid the antique all-metal candy store register, which only went up to $3.99. Transactions over $3.99 had to be entered by ringing the $3 key multiple times. There was only one telephone in the entire restaurant, and a single extension phone located in the upstairs apartment, which my family used as living quarters. The original two phones from 1954, rented from the Illinois Bell Telephone Company, had steel rotary dials, hard rubber hand pieces, and a straight, uncoiled telephone cord.

During the early years of *Tong's Tea Garden*, the menu was limited to mostly Americanized Chinese dishes including chop suey, chow mein, egg foo young, egg rolls, fried rice, with a few staple Cantonese dishes such as shrimp with garlic sauce, shrimp with lobster sauce, green pepper-tomato-beef, pineapple chicken, almond chicken, sweet-and-sour pork (chicken, beef, and shrimp), etc. We also made a few American items such as fried chicken, French fried (breaded) shrimp, and home-made French fries. The French fries, packed into square paper chop suey cartons, were a big seller for neighborhood kids who loved them.

From the 1940's until the early 1970's, Grandpa made large batches of home-made sweet-and-sour sauce from scratch using his own recipe. I recall some of the ingredients that he used included Karo corn syrup, sugar, apricot concentrate, vinegar, and canned pimentos. Grandpa also made his own Chinese hot mustard sauce, which was simply pure mustard powder mixed with water, without the vinegar used in typical store-bought American mustard. When this later proved to be too much work, we switched to commercially made packets of sweet and sour sauce and hot mustard.

Grandpa told me the story of a competing Chinese restaurant named *Ing's*, whose owner told Grandpa sometime in the mid-1950's of his intention to drive Tong's out of business by offering delivery. Grandpa had the last laugh, however. He hired delivery staff, and within a year, it was the competitor who closed down.

Dad was drafted into the Army in 1952, where he finished his G.E.D., and was sent to Korea, where he learned to speak

Mandarin in order to assist in interrogation of Chinese pris-
oners of war from the mainland. By the time he was
discharged from the Army, Dad went to Hong Kong and
married Mom (nee Linda Chan) in 1956 in Hong Kong. Due
to bureaucratic difficulties with the U.S. consulate office in
Hong Kong, Mom was not able to join Dad in Chicago until
January of 1958, with the assistance of powerful Senator
Everett Dirksen.

When Aunt Yolanda, the first member of the Tong family to
earn a college degree (Master of Science in Mathematics,
from the University of Illinois) married David Lee, an electrical engineer and my future uncle, she left the restaurant to
start a career as a high school math teacher in the Chicago
Public School system.[6] Neighborhood high school boys were
hired to help out as order clerks at Tong's Tea Garden. One
of the neighborhood boys during the early 1960's, Ira Sutow,
later became an executive at CBS News.

After nearly 16 years as a take-out operation, *Tong's Tea Garden* added a dining room and upgraded the kitchen in a major
$30,000 remodeling project in 1970. We hired 3 professional
Chinese waiters and 2 professional Chinese chefs. Over time,
as the waiters eventually moved on to other jobs, we relied
less on hired hands and filled the gaps with family members.
For example, Mom helped in the dining room and Grandma
did a lot of the kitchen preparation work.

The official Grand Opening of *Tong's Tea Garden's* dining
room was held on May 18, 1970. Some of the major changes
to the restaurant included moving the cashier table and order
counter to the corner of the dining room near the front window. A new telephone extension was added, with a flashing

---

[6] They were pioneers as just a few years earlier prejudice prevented many older Chinese cousins and friends with college
degrees from entering professions, and they had to work in
Chinese restaurants, groceries, and laundries.

light attached to the phone. A new glass and metal display counter with sliding doors served as the new order desk. The display case housed almond cookies, fortune cookies, boxed loose tea, boxed tea bags, and for a few short years, cigars. The commercial-grade dishwasher in the kitchen could wash an entire rack of dishes in about 1 minute. To this day, I remember that I washed more dishes in a single day at the restaurant than I would wash in a month at home. New refrigerators were added in the kitchen, including an ice cream storage unit rented/loaned from the vendor. A drinking water station was installed in the dining room, including a water tap, ice cube bin, and a rack for holding drinking glasses, napkins, and silverware.

By 1971, at age 12, I was working in the restaurant regularly after school, as a cashier, take-out order clerk, and part-time dishwasher. We hired 2 neighborhood high school-aged boys to work after school as dishwashers on alternate schedules. About this time, Tong's Tea Garden switched its off-day from Monday to Saturday, so that I, and my sisters, Betty and Dolly could enjoy a day off during the weekend. In 1973, we began to hire local college and high school-aged waitresses who learned on the job. Dozens of waitresses worked between 1973 and 1980, including several of my high school classmates. During this time period, I worked regularly at the restaurant after high school, and usually worked most of the day on Sunday. I began to wait on tables during my high school years, and I served as trainer for many of the high school girls hired as waitresses. When my two younger sisters, Betty and Dolly, got older, they followed the same work pattern. After high school graduation in 1977, I attended the University of Illinois at Chicago, and continued to work at the restaurant after school and on Sundays, sometimes as much as 30 hours per week.

Work in a restaurant never ends. There was always preparation work going on. In the kitchen, there was meat and vegetables to be prepared, sliced, and stored. Inventory of supplies and food items had to be maintained; orders from commercial restaurant suppliers were typically made over the telephone and delivered through the back door of the kitchen. Used dishes were stacked on the stainless steel table connected to the commercial dishwasher; a spray nozzle was used to rinse off loose food prior to loading the dishes onto the square dish rack. In the dining room, washcloths were continually rinsed and cleaned to wipe off the dining room tables and the condiment bottles. Clean silverware, drinking water glasses, napkins, and ice were continually replenished in the dining room from the kitchen. The display counter glass and windows needed periodic cleaning, and the floors were swept every night.

When the restaurant was busy, we often had to scramble and perform several tasks for hours at a time. In a dining room full of customers, I often had to eat my meals in small bits, with a lot of interruptions. I usually covered my plate of food with a metal cover to try to keep it hot. I became used to eating food literally piping hot off the wok, which was equipped with about 3 or 4 times the number of natural gas burners found in a home cooking range. During slow times, we used the lull to complete school homework assignments, listen to the radio, or watch television on a black and white set in the dining room, a smaller black and white set in the restaurant kitchen, or a color set in our living room upstairs. Dad often played Cantonese operas on an open reel tape recorder.

During our high school years, we worked in the restaurant from after school until peak dinnertime was over (about 7:00 p.m.), or earlier, if we had to study for exams. We typically didn't eat dinner until the restaurant closed at 9:00 p.m. Unlike a typical family dinner at home, we almost never ate dinner at one common table. There was only one large round table in the dining room, while the rest were smaller square and rectangular tables designed to seat 4 people. My sisters and I were not used to the usual formal dinner table etiquette of passing a dish to other diners, or placing certain silverware on either side of a serving plate; we typically served ourselves individually from the kitchen, and sat down at whatever table was convenient in the dining room.

I eventually became responsible for handling small electric work and repairs, such as replacing worn-out wall switches, changing light bulbs, and wiring the stereo system in the dining room. I even wired a door signal system from the dining room entrance door to the kitchen, and a wired intercom from the restaurant kitchen to the upstairs apartment and the store basement. But it wasn't all work and no play for me while working in the restaurant. I still found time for hobbies. I learned from Dad how to raise tropical fish, and in 1973, we set up 4 aquariums in the dining room. Many of the customers remarked to me how soothing it was to watch the fish in the aquariums while waiting for their food to be served.

When I was in 7th grade, I also developed an elaborate model railroad in the restaurant basement, built on top of a 15' x 8' table assembled from scrap lumber by my father. Dad bought me a top of the line Lionel train set as my 8th grade graduation present. Working on the model railroad helped me to develop valuable skills, such as designing electrical circuits, solving electrical wiring problems, repairing motors, and fixing gadgets.

Growing up in an extended family household, I was especially close to my Grandfather, and I often accompanied him on his off day, when he would typically do some business at the bank (depositing the week's earnings), drop off clothes at the Chinese hand laundry, do some shopping at Sears or other stores, usually ending with a visit to his distant cousin, Hong Leong, who operated *Shanghai Inn*, a Chinese restaurant with a dining room, located at 1920 W. Lawrence Avenue. Grandpa and his cousin occasionally played mah jong. When I was in 7th grade, Grandpa won the mah jong tournament and he used part of his earnings to buy me an electric typewriter at Sears.

Largely through self-study, Grandpa was fluent in both verbal and written English to a degree that exceeded most of his peers who worked and lived in Chinatown. He loved to read, and he always had handy newspapers and magazines in both English and Chinese. I loved to listen to stories he told of his childhood in the home village in China, his early days as a waiter in Chicago, humorous incidents during his years in the U.S. Army, and stories of certain customers. I was devastated when Grandpa passed away on Christmas Day in 1979, because I had grown up with him and had accompanied him for years on his errands and shopping trips on his off days.

Dad told me similar stories, because like his father, he also was very fluent in verbal and written English, and loved to read. Dad encouraged me to learn about Chinese history and culture by taking me to the local public library when I was in fourth grade and checking out books about China. I was encouraged to speak our local Taishan dialect of Chinese, which I practiced by calling out customer orders at the restaurant in Chinese. Dad also encouraged my sisters and me to earn college degrees so we could make a better living away from the restaurant business.

By 1981, our local neighborhood had changed drastically; Chinese food had competition from hamburger, fried chicken, and pizza restaurants, and due to our reduced business volume, we staffed the restaurant with just family members. Dad cooked, while Mom, my sisters and I waited on tables during school lunch breaks and after school. Grandma helped with the food preparation work in the kitchen. By then, I was in graduate school studying geology at Northeastern Illinois University, which was within walking distance of home, so I still helped cover the dining room during the day. I took my classes at night when my sisters came home from school to help in the restaurant.

On April 15, 1984, Dad decided to retire at age 57, and he made plans to lease the restaurant to other Chinese. The new tenants, the Ng family, changed the name of the restaurant to *Hong Won*. In 1996, he leased the restaurant to Chinese from Fujian (Fukien) Province, who changed the restaurant name to *Hunan Wok*, which still operates today, but by a different family. My parents still live upstairs above the restaurant, and Dad is still the landlord.

Largely due to our upbringing, my sisters and I took pride in our family history and Chinese roots. While growing up working in the family restaurant business, Grandpa and Dad told us many stories of their endeavors, hardships, and racial discrimination that occurred during the pre-Civil Rights era. We learned, through personal experience, the Chinese immigrant work ethic, the importance of good behavior, and the importance of education as my sisters and I all eventually earned college degrees.

Guey Lon Restaurant, Chicago, Il.

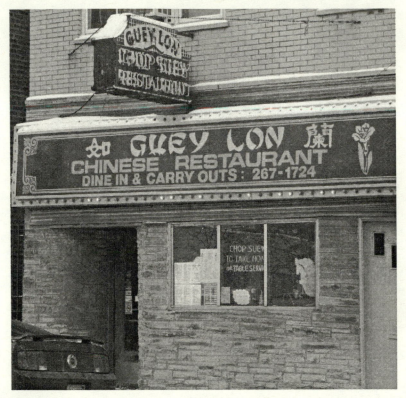

Figure 51 Guey Lon Restaurant, Chicago. Courtesy, Jessie Pena.

Darren Lee worked as an ad agency copywriter in Seattle for four years, and then left the Pacific Northwest in support of his partner, Jasmine, whose dream of attending grad school, strangely brought him back to the Midwest in 2005. A mere 400 miles up I-94 from his hometown of Chicago, Darren now lives with Jasmine and their dog, Zoe, in Minneapolis where he works as a freelance copywriter, and he can now cook almost as well as he eats.

My earliest memories are saturated with the smells and noises of my family's restaurant. Some of my most crystallized recollections are housed in the senses as much as events: the clang of metal utensils working the surface of huge two-handled woks, cleavers chopping their purposeful rhythm, the haze of cooking oil hanging in the kitchen air, the smell of garlic, ginger, pork fried rice.

"We live across the street from McDonald's!"

This was the first positive development of a moving day in 1977 that had uprooted my family from California and rudely repotted it in Chicago. Peering out the front window of my family's restaurant, I could see, almost within touching distance, the golden arches of the Irving Park Mc Donald's. In the entire four years of life that had preceded this moment, McDonald's was by far my favorite restaurant. Basking in its branded red and yellow glow, I had yet to realize was it would no longer be the restaurant at the center of my universe.

To me, and my younger brother Devin, the restaurant of my "other" grandparents was a place brand new. For my dad, our arrival in Chicago was a homecoming. He and his two brothers had grown up in the midst of the very same kitchen, dining room and upstairs apartments. Touring the restaurant, already closed for the night, before seeing our living quarters upstairs we got our introduction to our new life.

With six booths on one side, four booths on the opposite wall, and three large tables down the middle leading to the kitchen, the empty, half-lit dining room felt cavernous. Mc Donald's gleamed in the distance through the large front window by the entrance where a small stone statue of a woman encircled by landscaping rocks stood watch. The kitchen, oddly bisected by a wall with a doorway at each end, divided the side used for storage and food prep from the "cooking" side. While the walk-in refrigerator and numerous stocks of bottled soda did catch my attention on the prep side, the three giant woks and massive steam table on the cooking side were clearly the engine of whatever went on here. The sheer scale of this strange new place shocked me. Moreover, I was not aware of the lesson in my ancestry that the building and its contents had to tell.

Four Generations in Chicago

Moving to Chicago transformed Devin and I into "restaurant kids." From the perspective of the family, my brother and I, along with our cousins (daughters of our dad's older brother, David) represented a possible fourth generation of restaurateurs. Not only was our father's father, "John" Tse Kin Lee a restaurant man, but his father Tse May Kun[7] was as well.

Sometime around 1920, Tse May Kun had arrangements for work as a servant in America, but thinking he might do better for himself and his family still in China, he jumped ship in the port of New York. Settling eventually in Chicago, May Kun ran many restaurant and food-related enterprises, including the Chinese & American restaurant, the *Mayflower Inn* on Irving Park Road and the lunch counter at the original Goldblatt's department store on Ashland Avenue. It was at Goldblatt's that our great grandfather, Tse May Kun wrestled with one of the Goldblatt brothers over an electric fan on the final day of his tenancy. The fan, an expensive piece of equipment by 1920's standards, was to be taken in lieu of unpaid rent. As family legend has it, great grandfather would not surrender the fan and a struggle ensued in the store. In his "retirement," he would live and work alongside his son in his restaurant.

My paternal grandfather, "John" Tse Kin Lee was second born of four, but the oldest of three surviving siblings when he arrived in America during the Great Depression. Having immigrated to help with his father's business efforts, father and son originally, had plans to return to China after amassing sufficient wealth in America.

---

[7] *May Kun* is an approximate spelling.

The Origin of the "Lee" Family

"John" Tse Kin Lee, and my grandmother, Sue Toy Lee, established Guey Lon Restaurant in 1947. "Guey Lon" was named in tribute to my grandfather's late mother and was their second restaurant. Their first venture on Lincoln Ave was dubbed with my grandfather's American name, "*John Lee Chop Suey.*"

When asked about her late husband's background in the restaurant business my grandmother Sue Toy (now 96 years old) asserted that "Your grandfather had no business experience." To clarify, Sue Toy did indeed have more business experience than her husband when they married and went into business together. The first of eleven children, she had worked in her father's restaurant, "the Shangri-La" in Phoenix, Arizona, which Guey Lon was largely modeled after in menu and décor. Her prevailing attitude in life is that she is in charge.

A good example of this view is that she changed her husband's surname when they married. Sue Toy had no interest in becoming "Mrs. Tse" which was oddly spelled making it difficult for many English speakers to pronounce. Instead, she decided "Lee," the last part of my grandfather's given name, should be the family's legal surname. Hence, she became "Sue Toy Lee" and her husband "'John' Tse Kin Lee"

The Lee Boys

My brother, Devin and I were the second generation of Lee children raised at Guey Lon. Our dad, Daniel, the middle child of three boys, was 8 when Guey Lon opened in 1947.
Knowing the hardship of restaurant life I believe our dad spared Devin and I some of the labor obligations and swift justice he and his brothers endured as kids.

One family tradition Devin and I were happy to carry on was the consumption of hearty, meaty foods at any hour of the day. As my dad recalls, "When we were kids, whenever we had meat, we always had two steaks or two chops on each of our plates." When deciding what business path to pursue years earlier, my grandfather, who had already lived through lean times in China and America, decided that at the very least he and his future family would never go hungry in the restaurant business.

Indeed, the kids in the Lee family ate well and ate often. After school snacks for Devin and I consisted of various comfort foods, Chinese and American. Pork fried rice, roast pork and mashed potatoes, beef and gravy over rice, oyster sauce beef, fried chicken, egg rolls, and won ton were among the house favorites. If our young palettes were unrefined, it was not for a lack of trying.

We did of course make it across the street to McDonald's on a weekly basis for Happy Meals and the like. Nonetheless, the eating habit most puzzling to our parents was our appetite for TV dinners. In their compartmentalized aluminum trays, TV dinners were an incongruity in a Chinese restaurant that our parents would just as soon not have customers see. Thus, they suggested we eat them in the kitchen. But being highly portable, the TV dinners sometimes still found their way into the dining room.

A Typical Day

"Everybody did everything," my father recalls, describing the family division of labor. Both grandparents, uncle David, father, and in later years my mother were the core group. Non-family workers included additional wait staff and kitchen prep/cleanup help. Once open from 11 a.m. to 11 p.m., seven days a week, the hours of operation over the years at Guey Lon became shorter, closing at 9 p. m. instead of 11 p. m. and closing on Mondays, when I was a kid. My parents regarded the shift as "the progression from a "Chinese work ethic" to a "Chinese American work ethic." The ebb and flow of a business day still remained much the same, except for the disappointment of a few diners expecting service after 9 p.m.

Preparation starts roughly an hour before opening. Busy, but relatively empty, the restaurant shakes its sleep off. Produce is washed. Meat is cut. Rice steamed. Soup stock is put on using a pot so big I could fit inside. At 11 a.m., as it's always been, opening involves an inspection of the dining room, turning on the lights and neon sign, and unlocking the door. It's show time.

With the kitchen and dining room in full gear, primed by diners taking an early lunch and mounting take-out orders, the lunch rush begins in earnest around noon. Though high in number, the Lees are not always the most coordinated group. Fortunately in the restaurant universe, sheer force of will and hustle are enough to clear the board of order tickets.

The afternoon lull following the lunch rush includes a quick yet often, incomplete lunch break, small talk, and the completion of busy work like drying silverware or (my all-time least favorite) de-stringing pea pods. Coinciding roughly with the end of the 9 to 5 workday, the dinner rush embodies the same mayhem as the lunch rush but the portions and orders are a bit larger.. The rest of the day, closing, and clean up, are all downhill. Nonetheless, the aftermath of dinner and the fatigue of the day drain the last drops of energy from staff and the owner/operators.

By 9 p.m. the neon signs and lobby lights are turned down and straggling dine-in customers are "locked in." While non-family help finishes and departs, family members continue indefinitely until clean up is completed. A 10 p. m. dinner and midnight bedtime being a bit late for a kindergartener, the afterhours family meal was abbreviated a year after my arrival when I started school.

A Child's View of Restaurant Work
Living above the restaurant, I initially had no concept of what a workplace was. To other kids, seeing a parent "at work" might have been a factory tour or a visit to an office. For

me, seeing my dad at work simply meant finding my way downstairs. After school and during summer vacation especially, Devin and I would spend long stretches of time hanging out and observing. If there was an order, the adults sprang into action, cooking and serving the food. Then things would revert back to the "less busy" state.

During these lulls at work, we could visit and play with our dad and other adults. Interested in participating and emulating our dad, Devin and I would volunteer to work. Miniature work stations were set up for us (usually with a booster seat or crate) to appease our wishes to "help" but our earliest real "jobs" included putting fortune cookies and almond cookies into wax coated bags and folding the bags shut. Washing pots and pans in a separate sink was another low risk duty we assumed. By the time I was seven I had graduated to cutting and pitting green peppers with a steak knife.

"The Outside" or Dining Space

Over the years the fear of looking unprofessional to American customers caused our grandfather much needless anxiety. Having started his business in an era when the perception of cleanliness and order was critical to survival for any Chinese restaurant, "Grampa," believed in keeping the children out of sight. "The outside" as he called it, was public space during business hours. At least by Grampa's rules we were not to be seen, and if we had to be seen, we shouldn't be heard. The exclamation "Customer!" and the lobby door chime were our cue to vanish.

Thankfully, our grandmother and parents were as unconcerned with Grampa's rules as Devin and I were. Hence, they only worked to the extent that Grampa (still nimble in his sixties) could personally enforce them, chasing Devin and me around the dining room and back into the kitchen. While running from our angry grandfather was exciting, it was through guile that my brother and I were able to circumvent the rules whenever our cousins visited.

"The girls" were Uncle David's kids, and the four of them (later five) could do little wrong in our grandfather's eyes. Knowing this, whenever our blameless cousins visited, my brother and I tailored our indoor play to whatever they were doing. Strict but no hypocrite, our grandfather could hardly punish the boys for anything he would let the girls do openly. Under this loophole, our most outlandish dining room sport was roller skating - the ample space and long aisles becoming the family roller rink.

Generally well-behaved, relatively unsupervised

With food and people often moving in every direction, it's easy to see how even four or five adults might all be busy at the same time. As Devin and I got older (around 6 and 8 years, respectively) and more comfortable with our surroundings, our abilities to entertain ourselves using ordinary restaurant items began to show promise.

Of course, this wasn't always looked upon kindly by the elders, grandfather in particular. Actually, Devin and I were far tamer in our schemes than our dad and his younger brother, Ron, had been. When he was fourteen, our dad got busted, not for taking the family car out, but for letting his ten-year-old brother take a turn behind the wheel!

With ample storage space for hiding, dangerous equipment, and unlimited stocks of soda, the kitchen in particular inspired some truly unique mischief. Among my favorite capers was the novelty "bug ice" that we decided we would make do-it-yourself style. The store-bought version of this prank used a plastic bug encased in clear plastic "ice." Knowing how hilarious it would be to slip one of these into someone's drink, Devin and I attempted to make an even funnier "improved" version, using real bugs and real ice. Successful in swatting enough flies in the alley to fill our borrowed ice tray, we were surprisingly unsuccessful in disguising our operation. Our flies and water barely had a chance to cool off before they were spotted on the lower shelf of the freezer, and we were spanked and lectured by our mother.

"The people that we meet each day"
A favorite TV program of mine, "Mr. Rogers' Neighborhood" was populated by people like the mailman, the policeman, and an assortment of other archetypical figures. Growing up in the restaurant, not only did the neighborhood come to us, it included a slew of colorful and previously unheard of characters. Bob, the gregarious owner of nearby Casa Luna Pizza was a customer of ours. His restaurant had a player piano and pinball machine. Tony, our elementary school janitor, could make the "hula girl" tattoo on his arm dance by flexing his bicep. Perhaps most remarkable, Frank the meat deliveryman, was a cousin of Eric Estrada from "Chips," one of my other favorite shows.

The cast of players that flowed in with deliveries and out with food orders ranged from wholesome to questionable, working class to middle class, some families, and many bachelors. Most of them were white, but almost all ethnicities were represented. In this endless parade of customers and vendors the one constant was storytelling. Being kids, the old timers of the neighborhood always wanted to tell us how things were when they were growing up. These stories usually included scary or self-aggrandizing embellishments. Possibly exploiting what he saw as Chinese superstition, one old man swore that our restaurant had formerly been a funeral home decades earlier. Though I could never tell if it was for effect or senility that the man insisted it was true, images of dead bodies and ghosts raced through my agitated mind until my dad confirmed the claim to be untrue.

"What's Behind the Kitchen Door?"
To outsiders, the kitchen, behind its port-holed swinging door, is a tantalizing, unseen sight. My brother and I realized that a tour of the kitchen held curious value for our non-Chinese friends. While I can't say what they expected to see,

judging from how TV and the movies portrayed Chinese, we knew that reality was bound to disappoint the average 8 or 9 year-old non-Chinese boy. As expected, the woks, stove, and steam table fell short of our friends' expectations that they might gaze upon gambling and cat harvesting. To blunt their disappointment, free egg rolls and pop were served.

One boy, Mark, the son of our church pastor reciprocated by letting me see the "secret tunnel" connecting the parsonage to the church.

Serving Chinese & American Cuisine

"Hey kid, this restaurant's your bread and butter," my grandmother would shoot back, whenever a complaint about the restaurant passed my lips. "Bread and butter" not "gold" or "rice," is how my grandmother described our livelihood. A truly Chinese American stew, my family's English slang and Toisan Cantonese were trapped in the 1940's. According to my dad, this didn't matter much on the Toisan side, because a lot of the old village expressions were too vulgar to pass down or translate for the kids anyway.

Like our manner of speech, the Guey Lon aesthetic was also "dated," Chinese and American. Perhaps born out of the lunch counter/diner aesthetic, it was strictly utilitarian with its white tiled floor and speckled tabletops. Still, however, Guey Lon had evidence of Chinese decoration, calendars, zodiac, figurines and vases. The menu, evenly split between Chinese and American for many years, by the 1980's was 90 percent Chinese food. This evolution was the result of additional competition from American restaurants, as much as the rise in popularity of Chinese food.

While the majority of Guey Lon's patrons have been white over the years and its Chinese menu has increased, the Chinese customers, about 10 percent when the restaurant opened, have dwindled. This was one thing I picked up on as a kid, seeing so few customers that looked like us. Did these Chinese move away to other neighborhoods, or had they switched from chop suey to seek restaurants with more "authentic" Chinese food? The Chinese side of the Guey Lon menu wasn't about to change. If there was one thing the Lees do with determination it's *not changing*. Having stayed the same since the 1940's, the headline items, chop suey, egg foo young, fried rice, and egg rolls maintained their popularity through my childhood years.

"Chinese don't change the menu," my dad declared. "Even if you bought [the restaurant] from another guy you'd be afraid of losing business if you changed the menu." While *never* changing might be an overstatement, his theory for spotting other Toisan restaurants of our family's era was highly reliable. "Anyone with fine-cut chop suey on the menu is from the older generation."

Except for the style of sweet & sour sauce that our grandfather invented, our menu and family recipes held few true secrets. However, like the gong fu masters of old, the practitioners of the Lee family craft passed down their knowledge from teacher to student. Our exceedingly vague recipes (though not by design) were useless if the initiate was not present to see and taste the correct result. "This much salt, this much ginger" was hardly a formula any spy or competitor could steal by eavesdropping.

Consistent with this method, my mother's "Toisan spreadsheet" was used for years to discourage salesmen bent on selling us inventory software or terminal systems. As she put it, "If I want to know my inventory, I just go to the shelf and count...one, two, three...three cans."

A Switch in Menu Offerings
Although the Chinese side of Guey Lon's menu was etched in stone, by the early 80's, the American menu had slimmed down to only a handful of items: steak, fried chicken, fried pork tenderloin, fried shrimp, hamburger, and few more. The critical mass needed to keep some American menu items on

was disappearing; and when a customer ordered something that was listed but seldom made, it disrupted the rhythm of other orders.

All of this came to a head one early afternoon when I was about ten or eleven years old. From the other side of the kitchen my dad signaled me over to where he was cutting meat. His voice lowered, he handed me some money and said, "go out the back door to McDonald's and get me a Quarter Pounder." He emphasized, "Don't come back through the dining room. Sensing a peculiar urgency I didn't ask questions. Discretely leaving and returning with the Quarter Pounder, I was floored to see my dad unpack the McDonald's burger, switch the bun, and send it out to the dining room to be served! Peeking into the dining room I could see it was for another kid, a boy a little younger than me, eating with his mother.

The switch undetected, I felt both appalled and invigorated that we had pulled it off. Far below any standard of professionalism, this was something that could never happen again - and it didn't. The hamburger was removed from the menu soon after. "I wasn't going to chop a steak in to a hamburger and we were too busy at the time for me to do it," my dad later said in his defense.

Chinatown

Far removed from the conventions of our family's restaurant, Chicago's Chinatown at Cermack and Wentworth represented a world strangely different from our own. To my brother and me, the restaurant and surrounding neighborhood was a universe where *we* were all things Chinese to everyone, at least, everyone our age. Never mind that we couldn't speak any Chinese and had parents that had never even been to China. From our last name (which hinted at a possible family relation to Bruce Lee), to the fortune cookies we brought to school for parties instead of candy, we *were* the Chinese.

In Chinatown, however, we were anything *but* universally Chinese. In fact, unable to understand what anyone was saying to us, we were reminded at every turn that we were "jook sing" or "hollow bamboo," Chinese who had no Chineseness on the inside.

Not only were we no longer Chinese, our restaurant food was no longer Chinese either. We quickly learned "real" Chinese food, was served with the head still accompanying the animal's body. This point we actually appreciated, as my brother and I never missed an opportunity to perform some sort of puppetry with the unclaimed duck or chicken head during the meal. With "chow fun, sui mai," and the like added to our Chinese vocabularies a dish at a time, my "food-speaking" brother and I were still always happy to return to "our" restaurant.

"I'm going upstairs."
Since our first days in the restaurant, falling asleep laying in a booth or across three chairs wasn't uncommon. When Devin and I were smaller, if we waited until the end of cleanup, it might be near 11 p. m. when all the work was done. As we got "older," we fortunately gained an out.

Living in the apartment above the restaurant afforded my brother and me more flexibility than restaurant kids who had to stay at work with their parents all day (or stay home as latch key kids). When we were about 9 and 7 years old respectively, we were allowed to go upstairs without adult supervision.

If we wanted to get away from the circus that was Guey Lon, if we got too tired, or wanted to watch TV in color, we now had the option to go upstairs. In all the years that followed, Devin and I exercised the option to go upstairs countless times, but never once said, "I'm going home."

East

Aux Sept Bonheurs, Montréal, Québec

Figure 52 Aux Sept Bonheurs Restaurant, Courtesy, Karen Tam.

K**aren Tam** *is a Chinese Canadian artist (MFA, 2002, The School of the Art Institute of Chicago), currently in England pursuing a Ph.D. in Cultural Studies at Gold-smith College, University of London.*

Her Gold Mountain Restaurant series of museum installations portrays the history of the North American Chinese restaurant, combining experiences of restaurant workers with commonly held misconceptions and stereotypes about the Chinese. "Gold Mountain" refers to the name given by the Chinese to North America, reflecting the dreams and hopes of immigrants engaged in gold mining, railway construction, and eventually restaurant and laundry businesses. They faced intense discrimination, exploitation, economic and social barriers, and separa-

tion from their families left behind in China. Karen's art pays homage to their blood, sweat and tears by documenting the old-style family-run restaurant, chop suey houses, which are slowly disappearing from our foodscape and cultural landscape.

Using interviews of owners and retired restaurateurs, both within and outside of Chinese communities, she compared their experiences and the décor of their restaurants. This collaboration enabled her to construct an idealized Chinese family restaurant to capture western views of China. Over the course of the project, it also became a search for family and for community as it also reflects her own experiences growing up in a restaurant environment.

My family has been in the restaurant business in Canada for just over a hundred years. My paternal great-grandfather, Hum Kim Jam, born in 1888, was the first in the family to immigrate from Toishan to Canada in 1908. Similar to other Chinese immigrants at the time, he operated and worked at various laundry businesses and restaurants from Vancouver to Charlottetown. He finally settled in Montréal where he ran a laundry business on Notre-Dame West.

I really enjoy hearing my grandfather, Tam Yui Lui, talk about our family history, both in China and Canada, as the stories sometimes changed depending on his memory. On the back of my great-grandfather's head-tax certificate, it is written that he was the owner of a Chinese restaurant in Charlottetown, Prince Edward Island. My grandfather had told me several times that his father used to work in Halifax (Nova Scotia). When I was doing my first artist residency in Halifax at the Khyber Centre for the Arts in 2003, I had met Greg Fong, owner of the oldest operating Chinese restaurant there, *The Garden View*. We discussed family origins and the fact that my great-grandfather had run a restaurant in the city in the 1940s. Greg later excitedly informed me that my great-grandfather was possibly the mystery partner of another Halifax restaurant. Mystery solved? When I returned to Montreal and started chatting on the phone with my grandfather, I discovered that he had misremembered a fact: his father never worked in Halifax!

Born Tam See Ak (Shu Duk in Cantonese) in 1923 (Luen Hen Li Village, Toishan), my paternal grandfather acquired his generational poem name[8], Tam Yui Lui, when he married and "became a man" in 1940. In 1964 when my oldest aunt, Tam Mui Chee, was 19, she married and settled in Montréal. She sponsored her parents and siblings who were living in Hong Kong to immigrate to Canada during Expo '67. It must have been a bittersweet reunion for my great-grandfather as his wife had passed away years ago in 1954, the Chinese Exclusion Act[9] having prohibited her coming to Canada, and then later due to Mao's Communist Party's grip on China.

Man and His World
My grandparents started working right away, at the legendary Jewish-owned Chinese restaurant, *Ruby Foo's* on Décarie Boulevard, as dishwashers. My grandfather later advanced up to the position of cook and was an employee there until its

---

[8] Each character of a generation poem is assigned to the name of a generation. Each succeeding generation would take the next character. Once the last character of the poem had been reached, the cycle would begin again with the next generation named after the first character of the poem. Whenever people from the same lineage meet, they would be able to tell a person's rank or generation In my family as in others, it had been a tradition for males to have two names— one being the birth name, and the second a new name adopted from the generation poem when he got married. Women were not assigned names from the poems and were left out of traditional genealogies since they would marry out and be considered part of her husband's family.

[9] The Parliament of Canada passed the Chinese Exclusion Act on Dominion Day, July 1, 1923 to ban most Chinese immigration until its repeal in 1947. Chinese Canadians referred to the anniversary of Confederation, or Canada Day as "Humiliation Day." Families were separated during the Exclusion era making the Chinese Canadian community a largely "bachelor society."

closure in 1984. He worked at other restaurants (owned by relatives) such as *Montréal Chop Suey Café* (three generations of my family worked for "Han-sook" who owned the place- my great-grandfather, my grandfather, as well as my father), Sun Ling in Laval and Sun Wah in St. Bruno, until his retirement in 1990 at either the age of 66 or 67. My grandmother, Wong Shuet Fong, was able to help me out for this text but like many other "old-timers" I had interviewed for my previous restaurant projects, did not see the reasons for my questions. They believed that their experiences were of no consequence and because they did not see their restaurant as more than just a workplace, do not have photographs nor kept any memorabilia.

Figure 53 Gordon Tam in Aux Sept Bonheurs kitchen with Norman Lum, friend and former boss at Yangtze Restaurant, ca. 2004. Courtesy, Karen Tam.

My uncle Kwanchee was born in about 1947. Two days after the family immigrated to Canada from Hong Kong in 1967, he got a job as a waiter at an uncle's restaurant, Lee's Café in Ville St. Laurent for eight months. During high school and

CEGEP,[10] he also worked part-time as a waiter in China-town's *Nanking Café* on the weekends, and in the kitchen at Norman Lum's *Yangtze Restaurant* during the summer. Following college, Uncle Kwanchee went down to Boston and got a job as a waiter for Richard Yee's *China Blossom Restaurant* in North Andover. As it was good money, he decided to keep working instead of returning to Montréal. He ended up staying at *China Blossom* for three years and only returned to Montréal to get married. At the same time, he introduced my father to take over his position at *China Blossom*. My father worked there until Kwanchee opened *Restaurant Kim Moon* on Papineau Street in Montréal's east end in 1975. My uncle recalls that the following year (actually, 1978), my father acquired *Restaurant Aux Sept Bonheurs*. In 1988, Uncle Kwanchee and his family moved to Toronto and invested in a Chinese restaurant on Dundas Street as well as worked in a *Mandarin Restaurant* for a few years before becoming a partner in one of the franchises. With the Mandarin buffet experience under his belt, Uncle Kwanchee went back down to Boston to open his own buffet restaurants (*Mandarin Super Buffet* and *Jade Palace Super Buffet*) with local American partners in 1995. In 2003, he sold the restaurants and moved back to Toronto. My father, Tam Kim Soon (*aka* Gordon Tam), was a teenager when the family moved to Montréal. He was born in Hau Nam Chuen Village (Toishan) around the year 1949. The family fled to Hong Kong in 1951 but returned to China one year later because he was homesick. The next few years were spent shuttling back and forth between Hong Kong and Toishan. Finally in 1959, they returned to Hong Kong with his brother. Unlike my uncle, when the family immigrated to Canada, my father went to school first, finishing secondary education at Rosemont High. He spent his summer holidays working for the Lums' at the Yangtze where he began as a general kitchen worker and it was here that he learnt to cook

---

[10] CEGEP (Collège d'enseignement general et professionel), the Québec post-secondary education system founded in 1967 is required for entry at the university level.

chop suey cuisine. I believe that if it were not for family obligations, my father would have gone on to study photography
at Dawson College.

I was ten-months old when my parents bought *Restaurant
Aux Sept Bonheurs* with my aunt (Mui Chee) and her husband
in 1978. Situated in east-end Montréal in a working-class
neighbourhood on the corner of 23rd Avenue and Rosemont
Boulevard, we were across from the Botanical Gardens and
walking distance from Hôpital Maisonneuve. The location
was good as it was on two bus routes. There were two apartments above the restaurant, and we lived in the smaller one
until my aunt, uncle, and cousins moved out of the larger
one, to Scarborough in Ontario. We lived in the apartments
above the restaurant, which was very convenient. I grew up
spending a lot of time in the restaurant, and as a child would
like to pretend that I was cooking food in the giant woks in
the kitchen. After I started school, I would have my snacks
and do my homework in the back dining room. In 1987,
when I was ten years old, we moved to a house about 10
minutes away.

*Figure 54 At a young age, I enjoyed pretending to stir fry in the wok.
Courtesy, Karen Tam.*

My uncle sold his share of the restaurant to my father and my parents ran the business themselves for the next 26 years. My father did everything from waiting tables to taking phone orders and cooking the food, to delivering, while my mother was in charge of the dining room. Sometimes she would have to cook whenever they were short of staff during the lunch or dinner rush. There used to be a midnight rush as well, but with customers becoming more health conscious and changing their lifestyles, business became quiet after 10 p.m. in the last few years. The hours of operation were from 10:30 a.m. to 2 a.m. (and closing at midnight on Sundays). Looking back, my parents were incredible to be able to run the business themselves, sacrifice a social life, their health, and to endure the long hours and discriminatory behavior from patrons and employees, and give up close to half of their lives to the business.

There were a few other chop suey restaurants in our area, *Miss Hong Kong* (owned by distant relatives), and *Restaurant Wah Do*, which was owned by Mr. Hoi Jun Yee who had also worked for Norman Lum at *Yangtze Restaurant* and learnt to cook there. Whenever any of the kitchens ran out of an ingredient during the lunch or dinner rushes, they would borrow supplies from one another. They also sold their restaurants around the same time as my parents in the early 2000s, with the intention of retiring.

Mets Chinois & Canadiens / Air climatisé!

Aux Sept Bonheurs' brown-orange-red-yellow bricked building at the corner of 23rd Avenue has a large red sign with *"Restaurant"* and *"Bonheurs"* in black, *"Sept"* in pink lettering, and the Chinese name in white. At night it would be lit and the encircling bulbs would flash to attract customers. There were two Bell telephone booths on the south side, which users would come into the restaurant to get change. I think my parents got some kind of commission from the phone company for the number of calls made at the booths. The three large windows (one on the south side, and two on the west side) had pink and blue neon signs, *"Mets Chinois & Canadiens" "Chinese and Canadian Food,"* and was hand-painted at the top to look like icicles with a polar bear saying, *"Air climatisé."*

The interior of our restaurant was not overly ornate nor was it bland. When you walked in past the front door, the interior door (which prevented the wintery air blasting in and the heat escaping) and the interior glass partitions were hand-painted in red, black, gold with designs of bamboo leaves, thunder-scroll border patterns, and the characters for "harmonious," "spirit," "Spring," and "wind." The windows were fitted with orange lace curtains, which I used to believe had "happiness" as its repeating motif. The front half of the dining room had eight sets of booths with red vinyl seats and brown-yellow speckled tables, and fake brickwork. The rest of the area held black-metal framed red vinyl chairs and more speckled tables. The pink textured wall used to hurt me with its volcanic points when I leaned on it too much. The black and orange counter at the front was where people ordered take-out, where we answered phone orders, and where customers paid their bills. Following a do-it-yourself aesthetic and approach, as well as practicing some sensible Chinese thriftiness and common sense, my father would build shelves and other ap-paratuses to suit his and the restaurant needs. After we stopped having a cigarette machine, my dad built a cigarette shelf behind the counter. Next to the counter was where our weekend waitress, Jeannot Michaud, used to sit on the week-ends, underneath the large "double happiness" character made from bricks. My parents' table was the one next to the swinging doors leading to the kitchen. We did not have much artwork hanging, only two large shell pictures of birds. We also had wall and hanging lanterns with intricate and detailed paintings of Chinese ladies and landscapes, complete with tassels. My favourite feature of the restaurant was the floral wallpaper in the back dining room, a place where I would have my snacks and do my homework after-school. Another was the quiet quality of the light that filtered through the or-ange curtains, especially in the early afternoon after the lunch crowd had gone, which was even better during the winter. The overall décor of *Aux Sept Bonheurs* had a good blend of Chinese and tavern-esque elements.

Too Darn Hot! (Prep Work)

Prep work in the mornings in the dining area included vacuuming the wall-to-wall carpet, setting the tables, putting money in the cash register ($100), and brewing coffee. In the winter, it also meant shoveling the snow out in the front and the roof/balcony as occasionally if it was too packed with snow and ice and temperatures rose, the melted snow would leak into the smaller dining room ceiling.

Although the restaurant opened at eleven, my parents would always arrive at 10:30 a.m. to do prep work. For my father, morning preparations in the kitchen meant switching on all the lights and equipment, making stock for the won ton soup, boiling rice and once dry, frying it in one of the large woks, bringing stuff out of the fridges, preparing food for the lunch crowd, reheating the "sauce rouge" (aka "red sauce," also known on the menu as cherry sauce) as well as the dried garlic spareribs, and taking the egg rolls out of cold storage, before enjoying a cup of coffee. The weekly schedule of orders and deliveries of food supplies involved:

- Mondays: Order vegetables from Garlick, chicken from Lay Fung, meat and spareribs from Canada Packers. Delivery of egg roll skins, rice, flour, MSG, and sugar from Wing Fung
- Tuesdays: Delivery of vegetables from Garlick
- Wednesdays: Order egg roll skins, flour, won ton skins, chop suey (bean sprouts), take-out containers[40] and paper bags from Foo Lay. Delivery of chicken from Lay Fung. Prep the chicken.
- Thursdays: Delivery of meat supply and spareribs from Canada Packers. Prep the meat.
- Saturdays: Order egg roll and won ton skins, Cantonese mein (noodles), bean sprouts from Wing Fung.

My dad would also make the plum sauce on Mondays and "sauce rouge" on Wednesdays. He and the other cook would wrap wontons from Mondays to Thursdays whenever there was nothing else to do. He made egg rolls on weekdays, and almond cookies every second Saturday. My father would take a few hours off Sunday afternoons to go to Chinatown, pay his membership dues at the clan associations, do some groceries, and pick up BBQ pork and roast duck for our dinner as the busy Sunday dinner rush did not give him enough time to cook our own meal.

Closing tasks in the kitchen included moving everything back to the fridges, washing floors, woks, sinks, and equipment. If I was still awake and at the restaurant during closing time, I would usually keep my dad company while he cleaned up. Sometimes I would be asleep in the back dining room on three of the vinyl chairs parked together. In the dining area, my mother would make sure all the tables were clean and set, the coffee pots were washed (crockery and cutlery would have been done after the dinner rush by Jeannot). Once he was done in the kitchen, my father would tally up all the bills, dividing them up into take-out orders, dining room orders, and deliveries. He would then add or subtract gas costs and pay the delivery guys, or as we referred to them "ngoy mai jai." If it were the weekend, one of them would give Jeannot a lift home. My dad would then empty the cash register, leaving only the pennies. When we got home, whether it was the upstairs apartment or our new house, I would fall fast asleep to the soft rhythmic shuffle of money as my dad counted how much the business made that night. On average, it would be $7,000 a week, and up to $12,000 after the distribution of flyers (twice a year, 100,000 each time). When they first opened the restaurant, a flyer distribution company did not exist so my mother and cousin, Hartwell, would pound pavement and put flyers in all the neighbourhood mailboxes.

My father and uncle were the sole cooks at *Aux Sept Bonheurs* in the beginning. During the busiest years though in the '80s,

before the recession, my father hired three cooks. The recruitment method back then was to post up an ad on the wall
or windows of grocery stores in Chinatown The last few
years, it was just himself and one other chef, and recruitment
was usually through word of mouth plus ads in the local Chinese papers. The kitchen would be extremely hot in the
summertime since there was no air-conditioning. It got more
oppressive while cooking, so the cooks would open up the
back door for fresh air and in hopes of a breeze. While the
kitchen was sweltering in the summer, the opposite was true
in the wintertime. It would generate its own heat when meals
and dishes were being cooked, but otherwise it was quite
cold. My father would have to wear two heavy sweaters,
sometimes donning a down vest as well. I remember that he
would escape out to the dining room (heat) whenever he finished cooking and my father's hands would be extremely red,
dry, and chapped.

The kitchen was long and narrow, divided into 4 main areas:
1) the front where dishes and food would be put out for the
servers and delivery guys to pack- this area contained a
wooden table to make sandwiches and toast, a yellow fridge,
an orange Arborite counter where packed orders for delivery
were placed, shelves full of bowls, plates, cardboard, paper
bags, round aluminum containers, plastic yellow containers
for soups, pu pu platters and related items, paperwork, bills,
staplers, other miscellaneous things, fried noodles in a red
plastic bin, boxes of almond cookies, pre-packed Styrofoam
cups of plum sauce, packets of soya sauce, a bain marie for
the wonton soup and red sauce, a bowl of fresh chopped
green onions for the won ton, large stainless steel sinks; 2)
the main cooking area with a wok range for 3 chambers,
stove, deep-fryers, sink, shelving with plates and bowls; 3)
just beyond this was the prep work area (chopping block table, stainless steel industrial fridges, chest freezers, more
Arborite counters, a radio tuned to CBC Radio Two) where
the cooks would wrap won tons, chop vegetables and meat,
where my father would make the egg roll fillings, and wrap

egg rolls; 4) just before this area were a few stairs leading up to more storage. There were three doorways, one door leading to the small dining area, the second to a closet, and a third to several smaller rooms and a toilet with stained glass windows. The first had large wooden shelving units built by my father and held bins and bags of rice, flour, sugar, MSG, tins of pumpkin sauce and tomato sauce, the Kitchen Aid meat grinder, and a sink. There were two smaller rooms, one with long a Coca-Cola fridge, also filled with food supplies and which used to serve as sleeping quarters for employees.

Health and Safety

A few years ago, after my dad finished making a huge vat of "sauce rouge," he was moving it over to where he usually installs it. Unfortunately, the new cook had spilled some water on the floor so my father slipped and got degree burns on his arms from the still bubbling sauce. Even after applying balm it took months for the huge blisters to heal. Every time my father got a cut, burn, blister, or bruise, my heart would jump a little and I would catch my breath. I would feel the pain for him, even though he was used to it. He would even point out how it didn't hurt by putting pressure on or slapping his wounds, "See!" In the mid-90s, my mother slipped on the wet floor and injured her back. She was in constant pain and had to wear a back brace for a number of years. Every night and occasionally in the morning at home, I would give her a back massage in hopes of alleviating the pain somewhat. Prior to the tobacco law banning smoking in restaurants (the first and second times), all workers at the restaurant, except my parents, as well as the customers were heavy smokers. My mother would experience coughing spells from years of inhaling the smoke from cigarettes and would encourage them to not to light up.

My mother was the sole waitress during the week and on the weekends we would have another server, Jeannot Michaud, who was like a grandmother to me. She worked for us since the restaurant's opening up until her seventies. I remember she used to spread plum sauce on her toast in the mornings because it reminded of her childhood growing up on a farm in 1930s Québec, and having pumpkin jam on toast. She also told me that as a teenager and young adult, the Chinese restaurant was considered the sexy place to take a date. Jeannot's children and grandchildren used to visit and eat at Aux Sept Bonheurs quite frequently and were recruited to help out during the busiest day of the year (Mother's Day). She passed away at age 75 in 2003. We did have other waitresses over the years that had been regular customers but they never seemed as dependable as Jeannot. We tended to have one delivery guy during the week with two more during the dinner rushes and on the weekends. The ones I remember the most were: the young Chinese "older brother" who later worked for and delivered supplies from Wing Fung, "Crazy" Luc who was a full-time employee for CN Rails, "Big Jack" and "Little Jack" who worked for the post office, "Ti-Guy" who constantly aggravated my parents (my dad would say, "There's no cure for stupidity.") but was quite reliable, André whose love affairs and family drama we would all know and sympathize with, Italian-Canadian "Danny-boy" who had ties to the Rock Machines biker gang, William who used to eat at *Aux Sept Bonheurs* when he was a boy, and Michel "Garbage Man" who pretended to do weight-lifting with the garbage cans.

Because it was mostly my parents who worked the restaurant and they felt they could not rely on anyone else to look after it if they were away, they never took vacations or holidays. The only times I remember them stepping out of the restaurant for trips was for my uncle's funeral in Toronto in 1987 and my grandfather's funeral in Hong Kong (only my mother and I went) in 1986. Since it devoured most of their waking hours and lives, it also meant that they were unable to take me to Chinese school in Chinatown, or to participate in other activities, except for swimming at the local YMCA and piano lessons where my music teacher came to our house. Later when I was in high school, my parents would take turns in having half days (nights) off. My mother had Monday and

Wednesday nights, and my dad had Tuesday and Thursday nights (but he would always return to the restaurant to close up). A few years afterwards, they would also take Saturday mornings and afternoons off, as well as Sundays during the day. It was great to spend time with them individually, although my father tended to sleep his evenings off, as he was always tired and exhausted. No matter who came home or if I was home alone, my father would always 'deliver' dinner since our house was on his delivery route. Saturdays would be spent together, maybe going for dim sum in Chinatown, shopping, and running errands. When I was in CEGEP, I would go to the Chinese school in St. Henri for a double-header of learning to speak Mandarin and reading/writing Chinese at the same time. My mother would attend the tai-chi classes there as well. During my art school years, I would frequently recruit my parents on their days off to be my models and to provide sweatshop labour for my art projects.

August would be the slowest time for business as it was "Construction Holiday" and many of our customers were out of town on vacation. Another slow period during the year would be in January- people did not have as much money to spend after Christmas and the New Year. The busiest days of the year were (in order): Mother's Day, Christmas, New Year's Eve, New Year Day (because all other non-Chinese restaurants were closed), and Valentine's Day. Only once a few years ago, in 1998, the restaurant was closed down due to the Ice Storm. During the best years, we would have to recruit family members like my grandfather and uncles, and even Jeannot's daughters, Lynne and Monique, to help out for Mother's Day. The dining room would be packed for hours with diners and a long queue that went out on the sidewalk for take out orders.

Un numero 4 pis un Pu Pu platter (Menu)
The menu changed over the years to reflect demand or lack of demand. The most popular order, whether it was take-out, delivery, or eating in, was the "numero 4" meal (6 egg rolls,

dried garlic spareribs, pineapple chicken, chicken chow mein, chicken fried rice, almond cookies at $14.25 + tax for two), followed by the No. 2 meal (6 egg rolls, dried garlic sparerib, chicken chow mein, chicken fried rice, almond cookies at $12.00 + tax for two) which my dad can still reel it off with a French accent. À la carte, customers tended to order chicken fried rice, then pineapple chicken, won ton soup, egg rolls, dried spareribs, and beef macaroni. A few years ago, my father and I thought I would be funny to include poutine on the menu, but Chinese-style. Instead of the traditional cheese curds, French fries and gravy, it would be fried taro root with fermented tofu and black bean sauce!

We used to serve fish & chips, BBQ chicken, pu pu platter, doré fish, hamburger steak, and hot chicken sandwich. Fish and chips was the first item to go, followed by the hamburger steak. This was hamburger beef shaped by hand in the form of a piece of steak with a toasted bun, fries, gravy, and coleslaw on the side. The reasons for taking it and the BBQ chicken off the menu was that there was not enough demand and that it took too long to make. Doré fish (known in Toronto as pickerel fish) became too expensive. Hot chicken sandwich, consisted of two pieces of white bread, crusts removed, with gravy and slices of cold white chicken meat in between. Gravy would be poured over the whole sandwich, topped with green peas, French fries and coleslaw on the side. We also stopped serving pu pu platter (a Tiki house staple) which had a selection of fried chicken wings, fried wontons, bacon-covered chicken liver, breaded shrimp, and garlic sparerib.

Other western fare that one could have at *Aux Sept Bonheurs* included French fries, club sandwich, Chef's salad, grilled cheese sandwich, chicken sandwich, bacon and tomato sandwich, and French fries with gravy. The most popular Chinese dishes were Cantonese chow mein and shrimp with lobster sauce. *Aux Sept Bonheurs* house specials included seafood *wor bar* (hot sizzling crispy rice with seafood and vegetables), *moo goo har kew* (breaded shrimp balls with mushrooms), *moo goo guy kew* (breaded chicken balls with mushroom), and *moo goo har peng* (shrimp with mushrooms and Chinese greens).

Of course my parents and I would eat food that was not on the menu- more home-cooked style meals with the requisite Chinese soup. My favourite dish was the Chinese-style long garlic-honey BBQ spareribs my dad would make on a monthly, sometimes bi-monthly basis. Another was what we would term "village food," a Toishanese meal of stir-fried Chinese fungi *"won yee"* and vegetables like celery heart and *"si gwa,"* with shrimp. I also loved to eat stuff off the menu like my dad's egg rolls, beef macaroni, Cantonese chow mein, won ton soup (especially the crunchy fried noodles that came with it), and seafood fried rice. Our delivery guys wolfed down plates of brown gravy spareribs, and without fail, every single one of them would eventually sport a "sparerib belly."

Until the third year of high school, I would go to the restaurant after school to have a snack, do my homework, and have dinner before going upstairs when we lived in the apartment above the business or wait for my parents until closing time to go home together after we moved to a house. Saturday nights were spent packing the almond cookies, which I enjoyed very much doing with our waitress, Jeannot. First, we did packs of ones, using the same packaging as for egg rolls. Once they came out of the oven and were placed in Sunkist Orange cardboard boxes, we proceeded by opening one of the wax sacs and placing the hot cookie within, folding the top corners in to meet up at the centre, folding the flap down, stapling, and tossing it into a light blue plastic container. Afterwards we would make packets of two and place those into another blue container. Almond cookies came free with the phone and take out orders. They were also given to diners who ordered numbered meals and to small children. While we were packing cookies, the delivery guys would pour fresh hot plum sauce into Styrofoam cups for take out and phone orders.

Another chore I enjoyed helping with was drying the cutlery and setting the tables (unlike some restaurant children, I did not work at the business from a young age). I also liked to go exploring in the back. There were smaller rooms that were used for storage, and doors that led back to the small dining room, and had a door leading outside, but which was bolted at all times (prior experience with thieves, and maybe dine & dash?). When we still lived above the restaurant, I liked to play occasionally in the back alley, listening to my Walkman, playing badminton with my mom, biking through the connecting alleys or in the parking lot across the street, pretending I could do kung-fu on the patio, and mixing my own concoctions of water, soya sauce, and cream to make 'coffee.'

Jeannot and I used to play 'Bank' when she taught me about money and how to count. I had a red plastic and vinyl box with a see-through lid, decorated with pictures of Miffy, in which I kept all the money and coins I had. I also liked to sit behind the counter, at the cash register, and pretend that I could take orders and handle money. Mostly, I pretended to tidy the bills, the books on the shelves, and went through the radio dial (from Q92 to Cité Rock Détente) while discovering new objects behind the sliding doors. That's where we kept cassette tapes, a couple of coconut jars, bundles of bills, a small cash box, and who knows what else!

Nearby was a police station and frequently, police officers would come to have take-out, and whenever they did, we would put their order on a separate bill and not charge them tax. One regular face from the law enforcement world was a detective who was convinced that we had Triad contacts and could help him bust some Chinese gangs.

Crime and Racism Threats
Besides cars being stolen (including two of my father's, leading to speculations that it was a Russian mob job) over the years, our corner used to witness occasional car and truck

collisions. We were only burgled twice. The first time occurred (when I was still in kindergarten) after closing when
we were asleep upstairs. I remember waking up, becoming
conscious of my parents whispering frantically. My mother
had heard glass being broken, and so my father got dressed
and went down to the restaurant to investigate before calling
the police. The restaurant's side glass door had been smashed
in and the burglars had left with less than $100 from the till. I
don't remember the second burglary, but my father tells me
that the thieves had come through the small window of the
kitchen bathroom and only took the small cash box. I had
never been told that we had been held up before, the robber
wielding a knife to my mother's neck sometime in the 1980s
(again because we never kept more than $100 in the till, we
did not lose much).

As most of our customers were "pure laine" (French Québe-
cois) and pro-sovereignty,[11] there were tense occasions,
especially around St. Jean Baptiste Day (Québec's national
holiday) when many people flocked to the nearby Parc Maisonneuve for the annual celebrations. The police would close
off most of Rosemont Boulevard for the revelers, and we
would have to lock the front door, with the delivery boys using the back door to go in and out. We would only let
customers and the police cadets come through to eat and use
the bathroom. My parents had learnt from previous incidents
that revelers would do drugs in our toilets, or be extremely
rude and confrontational, asking why my parents did not
speak French well, or telling us to go back to China. We were
also targeted by graffiti during the passage of Bill 101 because
we had neon signs in two of our windows: *"Mets Chinois et
Canadiens / Chinese and Canadian Food."* Some fervent support-
ers of the language law deemed our signs illegal and ordered

---

[11] The pro-sovereignty movement advocates an independent Québec, to be a separate country from Canada due to its unique
history, culture, and French-speaking majority.

my father to take the English sign down. My father removed both the French and English neon signs.

One summer I was hanging out at the restaurant when a few of the delivery guys started talking smack about "les Chinois" (my parents) behind their backs. I was shocked at their language, the racist things they said, not to mention that they seemed to have forgotten I was in the room and could understand French. I regret now that I did not have the courage to speak up, to defend my parents, or even to tell the employees off. The creepiest experience I had with one of the deliverymen, a middle-aged Polish immigrant, was when I was still a teenager. He kept asking me to take walks in the park with him. He even had the temerity to ask my father if he could take me out to the cinema! Needless to say, he did not work for us very long. One thing I hated the most, a sentiment shared with my mom, was when certain delivery guys would just sit facing us at the furthest booth from our table, and just stare and watch us as if we were their entertainment. It was extremely disconcerting, and even if you glared at them, they would still be transfixed.

Days of Our Lives (Entertainment)
We had a television that picked up more channels than anticipated since the apartment building nearby (owned by cable-company Vidéotron) had huge satellite dishes. Sometimes we could get PBS and if my dad was lucky, the rabbit ears picked up ABC and he would be able to watch the NFL Super Bowl. My parents were not soap opera fans, but since there was nothing else on in the afternoons, they were pretty well up on what was happening on "General Hospital", "Days of Our Lives", and "The Bold and the Beautiful". Of course during hockey season, everyone was glued to the TV set (Go Habs Go!). My dad finally hooked up a VCR to the television when I was in high school, which meant that my mom and I could watch voraciously tapes and tapes of extremely cheesy yet addictive Chinese soaps.

"Monkey" and the Rock Machines

Of all the customers who passed through our restaurant, quite a few have eaten with (and even antagonized) us for close to 20 years. Many of our regular lunch crowd worked at the Botanical Gardens and the nearby hospital. For years, even after Hôpital Maisonneuve was transformed to a long-term care facility, the 'Hospital Director" would come in for lunch and dinner. He was a great contact as we would never have to make an appointment if one of us was sick or had medical questions. His youngest children went to Sécondaire Jean Eudes (a nearby private school) and would have tutorial sessions in our back dining room.

Robert was a friend of a few local police officers who did house renovations on the side and they frequently lunched together at our place. Once my parents were frantic due to an emergency with the pipes in the kitchen. They asked if Robert could fix them, which he did for a mere $10. After that, he was our regular plumber, at home and at the restaurant, and we would repay him in meals and eggrolls. "Monkey" was an old fellow who lived in the apartment complex across the street ("4050"). He would always order won ton soup, 3 egg rolls, 7-up, and when he had the money a half order of chicken fried rice. He was quite grouchy, blunt, and outspoken and could rub people the wrong way. He called my dad "Monkey," and in return, we would refer to him as the original "Monkey." One of his favourite pastimes was going to the Expos baseball games at the "Big O" (Olympic Stadium). "Big" Lynne and "Small Lynne (whose nickname was "Chicken") both started out as customers and later worked for us. "Big" Lynne was a gorgeous statuesque Italian-Canadian and had a daughter, Nadia, who would play with me whenever they came to eat. "Chicken" also had a daughter, Sylvie ("Chick-chick"), with whom I had gone to preschool. Both Nadia and Sylvie kept dining at our restaurant when they were working professionals. Couples would come for a date at *Aux Sept Bonheurs*, choosing to sit in the darkened corner booth. There was one businessman who brought both his wife and mistress (of course, on separate occasions)!

We would occasionally get orders from Cirque du Soleil's headquarters in St. Michel, as well as the Rock Machines (one of Hell's Angel's rival gangs in the east end). My father told me that once he delivered to the Rock Machine bunkhouse, which had security cameras everywhere. He had to walk past growling guard dogs and to a bald burly man waiting at a pool table with a scantily dressed lady on his lap.

Gold Mountain Restaurant
Only after they sold *Aux Sept Bonheurs* in 2004 did my parents take their first proper holiday, touring China up and down the coast (fulfilling one of my father's life-long dreams). I tagged along on this trip organized by the Chinese Restaurant Association of Québec, and the other tour members were retired Chinese restaurateur couples. Since then, they have gone on a few more trips to China together. After selling the business, we experienced quite a few firsts. I have a vivid memory of the first time we had dinner at home together as a family, and the walk afterwards (a first), our first family road trip (although just to Toronto) without stress or worry about the restaurant, my father's first day of sitting at home and the joy of doing absolutely nothing, our first Christmas with the extended family, and of course our first holiday to China.

My family experience in our Chinese Canadian restaurant was, and continues to be, the basis of much of my art. My parents occasionally work on my projects with me and I have spent the past few years traveling across Canada with my chain of "Gold Mountain Restaurant" installations. I have participated in several artist residencies where I have had opportunities to meet many Chinese restaurateurs (both working and retired), to record their stories, and to collaborate with them. Since their "retirement," my parents have still worked in other restaurants owned by relatives, but are now pursuing other activities. One summer, my father worked as a gallery attendant at the Montréal Biennale. My mother, pursuing her own art interests in Chinese painting and calligraphy, has taught a few drawing and painting classes to children.

積善家國重學業廣成芳
宗傳世澤遠晉本立道隆
爾昌友延嗣捷開文裔光

"If your life is prosperous and flourishing, even your friends will continue refurnishing or establishing temples in remembrance of you and your family. This helps to establish a cultured and civilized society.

If your family continues to be successful generation by generation, it continually benefits the world and makes it more beautiful. Its success is secured only while you are an honest, truthful, and virtuous person with a moral life.

Doing kindly deeds is very helpful for your family and country. If you are successful at this and study well, it may help you to be remembered for generations."

(Translation of the Tam generation name poem)[12]

---

[12] Tam generational poem and its translation from: http://mysite.verizon.net/vzepzaui/genealogy01.html (accessed October 8, 2009).

Mandarin Restaurant, New York

Figure 55 Mandarin Restaurant Plates, Teapot, and Box of Jasmine Tea on Chinese Emperor's Chair, Courtesy, Gilroy Chow.

Gilroy Chow, *born in Cleveland, MS, grew up in Queens, New York. He earned a B. S. from Mississippi State University and an MBA from Florida State University and is an engineering manager making steel conveyor components in Clarksdale, Ms. Married to Sally Chow, a high school teacher, renowned cake decorator, and church organist, their daughter is a CPA/Controller in Oxford, Ms. and their son is Director of Operations for a large medical practice in Norfolk, Va.*

I've often wondered how my father, Joe Tong Im came to the restaurant business. His formal schooling only ran to the 3rd grade before he came to the U. S. as a lad (Joe Tong Im) of 12 in 1912. Story has it the immigration officer asked him his name: he recited "Joe Tong Im," with his family name first (the surnames "Joe and "Chow are two different angli-

cized spellings of the same Chinese name) followed by his
given name. That what the Officer wrote and that's what it's
always been. Later, when he married, he gave his family the
appropriate last name. Coming to America alone from
Guongdong province, Hoy Ping county, Hen Gong village,
he initially settled in Greenville, MS. working and living in his
"uncle's" store. We're not quite sure who "uncle" was, but
most likely a paper relative from our native village.

He worked until he saved enough to start into partnerships
with some "cousins" to form the Joe Brothers Store and
Modern Store (grocery stores). He worked diligently in the
grocery business, even selling meats wholesale for the Black-
hawk Amour Company, travelling all of North Mississippi
and then finally managing his own businesses in the Mississippi Delta area. It was in Cleveland and Memphis, TN where
he made many contacts with wholesale cotton brokers looking for markets for the cotton produced in the region.

In 1945 a delegation of Chinese Government officials visited
Louisiana State University to learn about American agricul-
ture. There they met a Chinese student, our cousin Jack
Chow. He was a student at Louisiana State University on the
GI bill after having served in the OSS in WWII. In conversa-
tion, one thing led to another and eventually to Dad's
beginnings as an entrepreneur. These contacts connected him
with some financial backers so he could start the Ho Chong
Company, an export-import business. After a very successful
start in 1946, Dad moved the family from Mississippi to New
York. He became the Executive Vice president and General
Manager of the Ho Chong Company. Initially we lived on
Riverside Drive overlooking the Hudson River in Manhattan,
until Dad purchased a modest house in the Kew Garden
Hills district of Queens. He commuted daily by bus and train
to his office in the Empire State Building. He always told his
clients "I'm easy to find on the directory by the elevators. It's
the shortest name, "Im" in the tallest building in the world."
The Ho Chong Company exported cotton and was the exclu-

sive agent in the Far East for the Phillips 66 Chemical and Petroleum Company of Bartlesville, Ok. He engaged the American Victory Lines (steamships) to transport bales of cotton, oil, and chemicals to the Far East and then return with teas (oolong, jasmine, black, and others) silks, fine porcelain figurines, and other Chinese goods. Business was quite rosy for several years as trade expanded.

However, with the rise to power of the Communists in China in 1949, a "Bamboo Curtain" imposed a national embargo on trade with Red China ending all trade with the U. S. I know now it was probably the greatest disappointment of Dad's life to see that the thriving business that he had built came to a halt through no fault of his own. Not to be discouraged he was resolved to start again. Dad had to find a way to provide for the family until trade could be resumed. A family friend recommended a place called the *Mandarin Restaurant* that was available and a deal was brokered for Dad to purchase the business and lease from Dr. Deutz, the dentist on the first floor that owned the building. Those are the events that got Dad into the restaurant business. He had done many things, but cooking was not one of his areas of experience or expertise, nor was food service. What enabled him to eventually become so successful in the restaurant business?

Nowhere in his background was there anything about prepared food, but he took to it quite readily. His command of the language was commendable. He was a voracious reader of the New York Times each day and Time magazine each week. He could get along well with people. You might call him a penultimate "smoozer," a charmer. We realized what a special aura he had when he was invited to pose for commercials (Hathaway shirts, subway billboards) and model for illustrations and pictures on a number of occasions. Perhaps it was the sparkle in his eyes or the quick, sly grin he gave when he connected with a person. He had a way of making each customer feel special and that the food was selected and prepared especially for them and their families. Often people would ask for him to make their order, "something not from the menu," but even if he recommended pedestrian menu items, they would comment "How wonderful." His recommendations for "exotic or specialty" dishes might include subgum wonton (mixed Chinese vegetables surrounded by fried wontons), Moo Goo Gai Pan, Shrimp Cantonese, or Pepper Steak, but never, never truly authentic cooking because American taste buds were probably not attuned to the really exotic seasoning and condiments of the old country. Most might find the taste of *hom yee* (salted fish), *foo gouy* (fermented bean cake), or *nam yee* (fermented red bean cakes) too strange. Only the occasional Filipino doctors from the hospitals would order something with black beans.

"The restaurant," as my siblings (Happy, Pearl, Lilly, Lucy, and James) called it was located on 305 First Avenue, between 17th and 18th Street, nestled among Beth Isreal Hospital, New York Infirmary, NYU Hospital and the massive Bellevue Hospital complex in the Lower East Side of Manhattan, several miles from Chinatown. It was strictly a neighborhood restaurant with typical "Chinese American" fare served to the many native New Yorkers who would come in for a quick lunch or a family dinner for as many as eight people. Yes, it was the day of one from Column A, one from Column B, choice of soup, one egg roll per person, tea and dessert (choice of candied kumquats, pineapple, fortune cookies, almond cookies, jello, or ice cream in any of four flavors) for a fixed price. If you were a regular, you might get away with a substitution for a modest price.

Across First Avenue were the enormous apartment complexes of Stuyvesant Town and Peter Cooper Village covering 80 acres. They included over 11,000 high-rise apartment units varying in size from studio to 4 bedrooms. They mostly housed professional and white collar or upper middle class working families. Behind the restaurant were some 6-story walk-up tenements, some brownstone homes and many hospitals. So the clientele on any given day would include many doctors, nurses, interns and hospital workers for quick lunches and later in the evening families, large and small. Union Square, famous as a place for public soap box oratory, was just 5 blocks away. The toney Gramercy Park area, with its buildings attended by doormen, was just to the North.

Other neighborhood Chinese restaurants included *Look's*, primarily a smaller take-out and delivery style restaurants on First Avenue and another one on Avenue C and 14th Street. All served similar Cantonese cuisine suited to New Yorkers' Chinese American taste of the time. Thinking back, most customers ordered the same items week in and week out. It was before the days of many TV advertising, much less the Food Network, dedicated food magazines and extensive world travel that have introduced people to the different tastes and styles we know today.

Not far away was Greenwich Village, with many artsy types, writers, actors, hippies, and students from NYU. I remember Cliff Robertson double parking in front in a big Buick, ordering take out, with Dina Merrill waiting out in the car. Another memory was waiting on Carl Sandburg with his wife Lilian. He had ordered a simple meal, but was careful to call me back to the table after I had given him the check. He pulled out a small black coin purse, opened it, took a dime and placed it in my hand, "That's for you, young man." I should have kept that dime and framed it. He came several more times from his home in North Carolina, even to the point that my niece Susie was used to model for illustrations for one of his books of poetry.

The customer base for this neighborhood restaurant was quite diverse with many Jewish people, but also Italians, Irish, other Europeans being "regulars". There were bank and corporate executives, and office workers, but also stevedores, dock laborers and truck drivers in the mix. Quite a remarkable cross-section of the city would gather for lunch or dinner. Fridays' menu special always included non-meat (shrimp or vegetable) items for the practicing Catholics. There were very few Chinese customers at the Mandarin. Thinking back, most Chinese didn't even think about eating out, except for the laundry families that went to Chinatown on Sundays. All those in the restaurants business were working 7 days a week and didn't go out at all.

Before the days of McDonald's, fast food consisted of pizza or deli sandwiches and then there was "Chinese food," which was quick, convenient, hot and cheap! You didn't need a knife and fork to get it to your mouth. A good bit of the Mandarin's business was take out and delivery. Whenever it rained, you knew that there was going to be a lot of takeout and delivery business and the phone lines would be ringing off the hook.(our phone number was GRamecy 3-2064,5). Food was sold in pints and quarts, although specialty dishes were served by the "order," more than a pint, less than a full quart. For the delivery boys the dreaded order included won-ton or egg drop soup going any distance. The cardboard containers used then couldn't take the shock of a bike ride on the cobblestones of First or Second Avenue. Some customers would offer the 10 cents bus fare to accommodate the extra distance. Tips were 10 to 25 cents and the eye raising big tipper would give a dollar. I recall we had to chain our bicycles with the big baskets in front of the store or at our destinations walking up to each apartment, if we wanted our bikes to still be there after making deliveries. It was still the Lower East Side of Manhattan.

Organization of the kitchen was similar in all Chinese restaurants in the New York Metropolitan area. The *"How Chuy"* or head chef was in charge of everything, and I mean everything. Often temperamental, he ruled the kitchen and determined who worked where and did what and when. No questions, no suggestions, just do it! (If you didn't know who he was you could tell by the fact he the one who had Monday off). He had the responsibility of phoning in the meats, vegetables, and special grocery order from the Chinese purveyors each week. He had to know not just what to order, but how much. The second cook(s) (chow wok), there could be several depending on business levels or day of the week, but just a single third cook. He always manned the steam table, fried egg rolls and broiled the barbecue spare ribs and roast pork. The dishwasher didn't just wash dishes, but also had the responsibility of peeling onions, cleaning celery, and washing and cooking the huge tubs of white steamed rice. Everyone seemed to be very skilled in the cutting, slicing, dicing and chopping the meats and vegetables during the ingredient preparation times prior to each rush hour.

The daily preparation schedule included: bringing up enough refrigerated foods from the walk-in cooler in the basement up to the kitchen for preparation before the rush hours of 11 a.m. and 5 p.m. Cook the complete "steam table fare" of egg drop soup, broth, steamed rice, roast pork fried rice, chicken chow mein, egg foo yung, and wontons. Preheat the serving dishes and change the prep area for actual cooking of specific orders. Put out and fill all the seasoning bowls, including a pot of prepared cornstarch to thicken the sauces.

There was also a weekly schedule: Tuesday a.m., make the Chinese Barbecue spare ribs and roast pork in "closet size oven." It involved trimming the meat, marinating the meat in home made sauce and roasting in a slow oven for several hours. Saturday a. m., egg rolls to be made and "pre-fried." First the egg roll stuffing including celery chopped, boiled, and pressed to remove water, and meat which was the crackling made from the rendered fat (trimmed from whole hams, the primary component of *char sui*). I think the oddest ingredient in the egg rolls was a generous portion of peanut butter. The old Chinese did not waste any part of the meat. The bone was put in the giant stockpot that was constantly heating through out the day. Neck bones, chicken bones were added as they became available through out the week. Always simmering, never boiling.

Communication in the kitchen was quite verbal, with food orders being called out for food by the waiters and waitresses, as well as the take out person. I marvel that there were not many mis-orders or duplications of dishes with the heavy traffic during the busy periods, lunch and dinner. They had to be called loud and clear in Chinese only. The chef(s) took delight in telling us that Chinese that couldn't speak Chinese were "mo yung" (useless). To this day, I blame the chefs that we encountered over the years that impaired my Chinese language skills development. They came from many different villages in Canton, China, and each used their native dialects, hence my own broken Chinese. Again, responsibilities were clearly delineated, as to who did what and what sequence things were called, garnishes added, serving dish selected, appropriate lids and covers were precise. Nothing was random about the many actions taking place in the kitchen. You were quickly corrected if anything wasn't to protocol. No one wanted to have the reputation for producing bad or poor food. The chef wanted every dish to be pleasing to the palate, the eye, the nose and the pocketbook.

Sometimes there was good-natured repartee between the ABC's or <u>A</u>merican <u>B</u>orn <u>C</u>hinese or those that were FOB or "<u>F</u>resh <u>O</u>ff the <u>B</u>oat" immigrant Chinese workers. Another derisive term was to be called a "jook sing" or literally 'hollow bamboo' meaning 'no brains'. The opposite would be a "jook kok" or the hard joint of the bamboo or 'smarter' native-born Chinese. Like any social interaction, it was more difficult for some than others. As the saying goes, "You just had to be there."

The *How Chuy*, or head chef, would put all the ingredients for each called order in a small pan and pass it along to a second chef, who would actually fire up his wok, combine the ingredients, in careful sequence and time, seasoned and sauce up and placed over the steam table for quick pick-up. Woe be to the waiters or waitresses that didn't pick-up their orders in a timely fashion. The cooks did NOT want their food to get cold or the crispy food to get soggy waiting to be sent to the patrons in the dining room. Back then, there were no microwaves to reheat the dishes.

Help for the kitchen was not hard to find by just calling the "Chinese employment agency.' You just gave the position you needed filled and the next day a man would show up with a piece of paper, showing the job he was filling and the rate of pay he was to receive. Now finding good help was another matter. Could he understand the dialect of others on the kitchen staff? Did he chop, slice and season to the liking of the "*how chuy*"? Was his wok heated to the right level each time and was his timing appropriate as each ingredient was added to the dish? Was his gravy and sauce the right consistency? I don't know how many times Dad had to send someone back after just one day, or even how many times the *How Chuy* gave notice that he wasn't coming back after the weekend. Another problem with help was the immigration issue. I vividly remember staff taking off out the back, over the fence, and down the alley with their white aprons being tossed as they ran at the dreaded word "Immigration." Again, in my naïveté as a young man, I didn't know about those cooks that had "jumped ship" to have an opportunity to work in "Gum Saan," the Gold Mountain.

Our family part took place in the "front" of the store, where we functioned as waiters, waitresses, cashier, maitre'd (host and hostess), as well as the aforementioned take-out and delivery. The *Mandarin* could seat 115 people at one time according to the sign posted by the NYC Fire Marshal. Like the kitchen there was a fine tuned schedule of responsibilities, never written, but well understood by all. Depending on the expected business (weekends were always busier) the table assignments could be split 1, 2, 3, or even 4 ways. Due to the shape of the floor, there were tables for 2, 4, or 8.

Happy (Joe T. Imm, Jr.) was the oldest child. After returning from Japan, he served in the U. S. Army after finishing his

Business degree at Mississippi College. He was newly married to Joyce and worked initially at Luria Brothers in the scrap metal business during the day. In the evening he would handle the takeouts while Joyce waited tables. Their two girls were the first grandchildren in the family. Happy's work later took him to the offices of TWA (Trans World Airlines), where he worked until his retirement after 30 plus years of service.

Pearl would also wait tables, but was the primary bookkeeper making daily entries in the books, doing weekly payrolls, and sales tax reports and monthly closeouts. She worked during the day in the home offices of the Celanese Corporation on Park Avenue. While she couldn't officially hold another job while employed there, she could attend evening classes at Queens College to earn her business degree. Lilly and Lucy's early tasks were to answer the phone, cashier, or act as hostesses. Gilroy and James took care of deliveries while in junior high and high school days. Mom and Dad did a little of everything in a training or troubleshooting mode to keep everything and everyone caught up. One rule comes to mind "Do not go to the kitchen or return to the front empty handed." I still marvel at the way that huge trays of steaming hot food were carried and balanced, one-handed, out of the kitchen. I can still carry multiple dishes, nestled in one hand from learning the "tricks of the trade." Surprisingly, broken dishes or glasses were a rarity. Over the years roles and responsibilities shifted to fill every task to accommodate our daily schedules.

Mom and Dad made a early morning twice weekly trip to the farmers' market on the West Side near the Hudson River to purchase vegetables wholesale. The back of the Cadillac got loaded down with cases of celery, yellow onions and cabbage. What a sight that was to see that big, shiny car loaded like a delivery van. Everyone had two scheduled days off a week except our parents. They worked every day, every week with the exception of one day a year when they went to Radio City

Music Hall to see the Christmas Extravaganza. Dad said it was the biggest bargain in town, with a first run movie, as well as a live stage show.

I think it a wonder that we didn't have any more arguments over who would do what when. James and I had Boy Scout activities that would include camping at Alpine, NJ Scout Camp or Ten Mile River upstate, and track, fencing or cross country at Parsons Junior High School and Forest Hills High School. Lilly and Lucy had Arista, piano lessons or Girl Scouts while going to school, besides church activities at the Lutheran Church of the Ascension. There was also time for dating and participating in activities and functions that the various Chinese organizations around the city held regularly. Mom and Dad encouraged these activities, but we were reminded that we were to be at work on schedule and on time. Pearl recounted that to this day a recurring nightmare of being at the Mandarin at rush hour having a full house with no other help in front. I told her that I think it had happened to all of us at one time or another but incredibly everyone got waited on and served. No unions, no computers, no help, no excuses, just get it done! I think we all felt a familial duty to do our part for everyone else in the family and nothing was begrudged then or even now.

Over the years our perspectives of that 'restaurant' period have changed a lot mostly for the better. I can distinctly remember 38 years ago my mother-in-law asking me after Sally and I had moved to Clarksdale, Mississippi whether I would be interested in opening a restaurant there, with my background at the Mandarin. After having worked as an engineer at the Kennedy Space Center during the Apollo years, there was absolutely no appeal for me to return to serving and feeding the general public in a restaurant anywhere. Little did I know that in 1995 Sally and I would be doing Southern Chinese cooking demonstrations at the Smithsonian on the National Mall in Washington, D. C. and again in 2005 for the Festival of American Folk Life.

Waiters and waitresses had the responsibility of folding wontons twice a week. The opening wait staff prepared the tank
of black tea each day (20 gallons). The mustard (dry English
mustard to me mixed and stirred), duck sauce (home made
sweet and sour sauce), had to be brought out for quick service to put on each table, depending on what was ordered
from the menu. There was salt, pepper, and of course a bottle
of soy sauce on each table that had to be filled and cleaned
each night. Napkins to be folded just right, silverware to be
dried, polished, and put out to server stations.

In my early years, a favorite part of the night was to count the
tips that had been pooled in a pint take-out soup container
just inside the kitchen from all the waiters and waitresses. At
settling up time, the container was passed around for all to
"weigh" by hand that container and guess how much was the
night's take. Over the years, it was amazing how close we
could get considering the variety of coins inside. As a family
business, we were not paid a salary, but we did get to keep
the tips. It made the 33 minute "E" subway train ride from
Forest Hills to Manhattan each day after school seem more
worthwhile.

Another aspect of the business was the occasional catered
affair. We did not offer full service catering, but would prepare the food, delivered in 5-gallon oil cans. The Society of
Illustrators was one such customer and another was the
Knickerbocker Beer Company. The station wagon would pull
into the brewery, and we would be directed to a large meeting
hall. In the brewery, everything was spotless, but there was
beer dripping from the spouts that loaded the tanker trucks.
When you went to the break or rest room, there were taps
dispensing draft beer seemingly everywhere. I don't know
how the help stayed sober.

Dad enjoyed entertaining large groups. He had a knack for
being able to invite a cross section of people of various backgrounds for an evening of dining and visiting. I can recall one

such evening where there were many prominent cartoonists along with some customers from the community. I remember meeting the cartoonists John Prentice who drew "Rip Kirby" and also Leonard Starr who drew "On-stage." I found out they shared a studio and Leonard Starr actually looked like the character "Rip Kirby," but more remarkably that his wife was actually the main character "Mary Perkins," a stunningly beautiful woman. Amazing, to see and meet these people, as I was a comic and cartoon aficionado.

After the initial success in the restaurant business, Dad looked at expanding from the city out into the suburbs using the successful model of the original Mandarin. By 1955 there was an upscale version of the Mandarin in Cedarhurst, Long Island and soon after, one in Long Beach, Long Island. The Long Beach restaurant was quite a change from each of the others. It was in a resort community two blocks from the beach and Atlantic Ocean. The front of the building was a classic diner, the Rio Rita. It had a long counter with stools and then a few booths in front. The chef was a big, jovial Chinese man that cooked short order breakfasts, made wonderful muffins, pies, cakes and other pastries, as well as hamburgers, pot roast and other diner menu items. Here you had to call your orders in English.

The Long Beach restaurant was much larger than the Manhattan or Cedarhurst operations. It had an extensive dining room as well as covered outdoor seating. It was complete with a full service bar. Located over two hours from NY's Chinatown, help had to be provided with housing during the week. A house was purchased just to accommodate the large number of cooks and waiters in near dormitory style sleeping arrangements. This business did not survive, not so much for the lack of business, but the extremely cyclical nature of summer resort activity. Other expansions included boardwalk concessions where egg rolls, fried rice and chow mein were served to sunbathers among the games and rides of Rockaway Beach, Brooklyn and Long Beach out on Long Island.

Life in those days wasn't all just work and school for my siblings and me. The Chinese social scene included many dances and parties at the many colleges and universities. Invariably, each school (Hunter, CCNY, NYU, Columbia, etc.) had a Chinese social club that gave big dances, some with orchestras or DJ's spinning 78, 45, and 33 rpm records. There was hardly a weekend or holiday that didn't have something going on. There were also social clubs (Jade's, Long Island Chinese Circle, etc.) that gave parties where Chinese could meet and socialize. We would go *after* our restaurant closed at 10 p.m., then party, or go bowling, and then invariably have "*sleuw yeah*" (small snack to eat) in the wee hours in Chinatown's tea and noodle shops. We had a rotating work schedule to accommodate one another's personal calendars.

After Dad succumbed to a heart attack in 1965, coinciding with the end of the lease for the Mandarin, it was decision time for the family. By then each one of the brothers and sisters had other plans for their lives. Happy, Lily, and Lucy had married and started families of their own. Pearl, James, and myself had finished our initial college degrees and were ready to pursue other interests. The "restaurant" had been good to us and for us. It allowed us to spend time as family, as co-workers, and as responsible owners of that enterprise. We grew in so many ways that have certainly influenced our lives and our very beings in an extremely positive way. It gave us a work ethic and family that has carried a long, long way. It was the springboard for our careers and families across the country in banking, finance, travel, engineering, computers, and other fields of endeavor. I know that we have great reminiscences and memories of those times, but I don't know if anyone would like to go back to the old days.

South

How Joy Restaurant, Greenville, Ms.[13]

Figure 56 How Joy Restaurant, Greenville, Ms. Courtesy, Raymond Wong

Raymond Wong *and his wife, Cathy, ran the How Joy Restaurant started in Greenville by his parents in 1968 until it finally closed in 2005. He has been actively involved in civic activities, serving as* board member and President of a local theater group, Delta Center Stage, board member of the Greenville Chamber Commerce, Rotary Club member, and host of a local morning TV show, *Good Morning Mississippi on WABG, an ABC affiliate.*

My father and mother, Suey Heong (Henry) and Pon Lum

---

[13] Thanks to Russell Wong for his able assistance in recording the history of our family restaurant.

Wong, began the *How Joy Restaurant* in the summer of 1968. They immigrated to Greenville in the heart of the Mississippi Delta in the late 1940s from Toisan, China, where my father was born in 1922 and my mother in 1930. They started a corner grocery, Wong's Food Store, in a black neighborhood that they operated until 1970.

I am the third child in the family with an older sister Betty in Jackson, Ms., an older brother Herbert, in Berkeley. Ca., and a younger brother, Russell in Houston, Tx.

Family Background
Family members of my father, Suey Heong (Henry) Wong, have been in the U.S. since the 1850s to 1860s. One of Henry's ancestors became a U. S. citizen so that Henry's father and Henry were both automatically citizens even though they were born in China.

Henry moved to the U. S. as a young boy of sixteen to live with his brother Suey Chong (Slim) Wong in Chicago. Unfortunately, Henry's father was mistaken as a gang member in Chicago and gunned down before Henry made it to Chicago. Later they moved to the Mississippi Delta where their sister, Yet Yue, lived. Her family had a grocery store in Drew, Mississippi, a small thriving town among the cotton fields of the Delta.

After serving in the Army Air Force during World War II, he went back to Toisan to be married. The family elders determined that Pon Chu Lum from a neighboring village would be a good bride for Henry. Henry agreed to this arranged marriage and they wed in the late 1940's and came to the Delta. Pon Chu and Henry moved to Greenville, a much larger town than Drew, soon after arriving in the U.S in 1948 to open a grocery store and raise a family. Like many of the Chinese in the Delta, Pon Chu and Henry opened their store in a black neighborhood.

The Impetus for Opening a Restaurant

In the 60's, the civil rights movement was in full gear and fomented unrest in the black communities. Desegregation of the school system was forced upon the Delta, as elsewhere. In light of the turbulent racial unrest at that time, my parents became concerned for our family's safety, especially since we spent most of our time in the back of the store. That was where we ate our meals, did our homework, and watched TV there. We also slept there until we built a small house behind the store.

My parents decided they either should move to a safer neighborhood or maybe relocate to another city. Although my parents had already been in the grocery business for over 20 years, they considered a different business. Henry's older brother, Slim was a great cook and suggested opening a Chinese restaurant. However, that probably meant relocating, possibly to another state, because Chinese restaurants were rare in the South and found only in major cities, such as as Memphis, Atlanta, and Birmingham. It was certainly not clear that a Chinese restaurant could be successful in the heart of the Mississippi Delta. In fact, all other attempts had failed.

My parents thought that Greenville might be a good place for a Chinese restaurant. In 1968, Greenville had a population just under 50,000. We had a thriving downtown with a population roughly, 35% White and 65% African- American but most businesses were owned by Whites. There were approximately 300 Chinese-Americans in the predominately black neighborhoods. Having lived in Greenville for almost 20 years, my parents felt pretty comfortable in dealing with all segments of the community. Of course, they were very familiar with the black community because they lived there. Their main exposure to the white community was through their grocery store and the First Baptist Church, which opened their doors to Chinese immigrants in 1934 by way of the Chinese Mission, and became a focal point of the Chinese community in Greenville.

At that time Henry had a good friend, Maan Chong Seid (Allen Lee), whose brother-in-law, Raymond Cheng, was working as a chef for the Joy Young Chinese restaurant in Memphis, TN. He had been brought from China to cook there but Henry persuaded Cheng to partner with him to open a Chinese restaurant in Greenville. At first they wanted to lessen their risks by making it a take-out only restaurant, which would not require as large a building or investment in fixtures and furnishings as a full service restaurant would. But after careful deliberation, they decided to go ahead and have some sit down service, opening with nine tables. It was the first full service Chinese restaurant in the interior of Mississippi. Since they realized "good luck" would be needed to succeed, they decided to use the Chinese words for that concept as the restaurant name. "Good luck" is pronounced "*haw choi*" in their dialect of Chinese, but that might be too difficult for the locals to pronounce so they decided to anglicize the name to *How Joy*.

Our building was originally a Burger Chef fast food restaurant. During the remodeling of that building, many people would come by out of curiosity. There was even a group that came in to make sure Chinese people would be operating the restaurant to assure its authenticity.

When we first opened the business we were still in the grocery business at Wong's Food Store. My mother and I were often left alone to run the store. My older brother and sister were already away at college. Because of concern about the family's safety at the store and the success of the restaurant after several months, we soon sold Wong's Food Store. We felt confident that the How Joy Restaurant could sustain itself.

How Joy Opening
How Joy opened in the summer of 1968. At first, we didn't know if people would like the food or would even come in.

Would they be scared to try Chinese food? After all, this was Mississippi in the 1960's.

Our very first customer was Mrs. Lourene Wells, a long-time family friend. She was very well respected in the community and very active in the Chinese Mission. During the 1960's Mrs. Wells would visit Chinese women in the back of their grocery stores to teach weekly Bible lessons. On that first day, we watched excitedly through a small square window in the door between the kitchen and the dining room as Mrs. Wells placed her order. Our new business was a reality! Our first order was coming in. Back came the waitress through the swinging doors. She yelled out the order. Mrs. Wells wanted tea. In our rush and excitement of opening, we had not made any tea. So we rushed to make hot tea. The tea brewed quickly and we poured it into a teapot. The waitress loaded it on a tray and took the tea out to deliver it to Mrs. Wells. One emergency handled. But then, seconds later, back came the waitress. Mrs. Wells wanted iced tea! Fine, let's get some ice for the tea. But we didn't have any! Luckily there was a store almost next door. Someone rushed out to get the tea. By the time we got the ice to the restaurant, Mrs. Wells had already begun eating her meal. We quickly served iced tea to Mrs. Wells. There was a conversation between Mrs. Wells and the waitress. The waitress came back into the kitchen. Mrs. Wells needed sugar and lemon for her tea. Sugar we had, but no lemons, so someone dashed back to the supermarket. By the time we got the lemon to Mrs. Wells she had completed her meal. Despite this ice tea experience, Mrs. Wells became a long and loyal customer of our restaurant.

Mrs. Wells was our first customer that day, but not our last. We had opened at 11 a.m. People continued to trickle in until approximately 5:30 p.m., and then the bottom fell out with a rush of customers. We ran out of prepared ingredients by 7 p.m. We hadn't prepared enough vegetables. We were not prepared for that first day. The first evening we ran out of sitting room and our mother showed some ingenuity and quickly converted two small plant tables to provide seating for single occupancy.

People had to wait as much as an hour and a half to be served so we were worried if these customers would ever come back. One customer, in particular, Mrs. Weathers, did come back the next evening with more friends. She was so impressed with the food and we were so impressed with her accepting us. The opening was a tremendous success, and the timing was great. We had full occupancy every night for the first week. My father was an ideal manager for the restaurant because he had the ability to make people feel welcome.

We initially started with just one waitress. When we got busy, everyone chipped in. We had cousin Mary Dong Lau come from San Francisco for a couple of days and cousin Margaret Wong came from Drew for a couple of weeks, for example. After a year or so, my father enlarged the seating capacity to almost 100 people. We ended up having 4 waitresses or wait people including myself, and a friend, Danny Wong.

Initially we had only Chinese cooks. They lived in the back of the restaurant. But they were difficult to keep in Greenville. There was not much for them to do when they were not working. Frustrated with often having to find Chinese cooks to replace the old ones, my parents decided to train locals to cook the food. My mother trained several Black women to cook our dishes. It worked out well.

After living in Mississippi for so many years, my father had formed a deep appreciation of the tastes of the local community and developed a Chinese menu accordingly, which proved to be extremely popular. The most popular items on our menu were the How Joy Steak and the Butterfly Shrimp. The How Joy Steak consisted of either rib eye or sirloin steak sliced and served on a bed of stir-fried vegetables cooked with a special sauce. The Butterfly Shrimp consisted of shrimp, split and opened, laid on bacon and fried in a wok.

The Butterfly Shrimp was served on a bed of sautéed onions covered with sweet and sour sauce, and topped with almonds and green onions. The Butterfly Shrimp was time-consuming to cook and we often fell behind. My parents eventually changed the recipe. Instead of wok-frying the shrimp, the Butterfly Shrimp was dipped in batter and deep-fried. It solved the slow cooking process of cooking in the wok. And guess what? It was just as popular. Another innovation, another hit.

We also offered such items as moo goo gai pan, green peppered steak, chicken almond ding, shrimp and lobster sauce, and Cantonese lobster, among others. The menu also included American dishes such as steaks and fried shrimp. In the early 70's, we started serving lunch plates. In the late 70's we started a lunch buffet. At home, my father loved to eat southern food like collard greens, grits and cornbread, but felt he could not serve them in a Chinese restaurant. The buffet gave him the chance to offer good southern dishes like fried chicken, catfish, and stewed cabbage.

All of the Chinese dishes were served family style. The entrée was served in a stainless steel compote dish and covered with a stainless steel top to keep the food very hot. We tried placing chopsticks on the tables at first, but they just got in the way as most customers did not have a clue how to use them.

When we opened the restaurant, and for at least the first decade, Chinese ingredients and vegetables like *bok choy* were not widely available. We had to order *bok choy* from San Francisco and have it delivered by air. Eventually we were able to order ingredients from Chicago. We also ordered bean sprouts and Chinese spices from California & Chicago. Later, Asian suppliers came from Atlanta and Houston every 2 weeks. Now you can get supplies from local vendors, but Asian vendors often have better prices.

In 1976, we moved to a larger location that served up to 250

people.   We had 6 waitresses and a kitchen staff of 5, including 2 Chinese chefs.   Chinese cooks understood very little
English and the waitresses could speak no Chinese - quite a
dilemma.   But since both groups understood numbers, we
solved the problem using a system where a number on a
chart identified each dish.

In the mid 70s business in Greenville was very good as cotton
was king and the towboat industry in the Delta was also very
prosperous. In 1978, my father decided again to increase capacity by adding a banquet room that could seat 150 and
including a theater-like stage. We opened 7 days a week from
11:30 a.m. to 10:00 p.m., except Saturday when we didn't
open till 5 p.m.

In 1991, we introduced karaoke to the Delta. Besides having
it for special parties, we offered it to guests in our bar area
every Saturday night, with amazing success. Everyone enjoyed themselves. One evening as we were about to close, a
surprise guest showed up. Dick Cavett, a late night national
TV talk show host, walked into our restaurant. He ordered
dinner and then sang karaoke. He gave a rousing rendition of
"On Top of Spaghetti," otherwise known as "On Top of Old
Smokey."

Prior to the opening of *How Joy*, when Chinese had big parties
everyone would pitch in to do all the cooking and everything
else needed for the events. Eventually *How Joy* began to serve
Asian American parties, banquets, weddings, and things like
that. One of our biggest events was a Chinese wedding held
in Arkansas where we catered for a party of 900 at the con-
vention center.

How Joy became a preferred venue for entertaining foreign
visitors, especially those from mainland China and Japan that
came to explore setting up different industries in the region.
Companies would bring their foreign visitors to eat at *How
Joy*. The visitors liked the food so much that they would come

back after work because they missed Chinese food after being fed fried catfish and fried chicken for many days. Henry Wong's special Chinese recipes appealed because the visitors were brought up on that type of cuisine. *How Joy's* acceptance was quite evident during election campaigns when local politicians would campaign there, including during several elections for governor.

Figure 57 Henry Wong chats with diners. Courtesy, Raymond Wong.

Overall, *How Joy* provided more acceptance and visibility for us and for the Chinese community. My father was a great ambassador. He got along with everyone and he was well liked. The old cliche of "he never met a stranger he didn't like, black or white, rich or poor" fit him well. He often offered "*ng ka py*" rice wine to special friends. My father made it clear that the restaurant wasn't just a place of business, but also a place for people to come together to socialize. Once after many years, we tried to close on Mondays for my father to rest, but we quickly found out that he didn't want us to close any day because " if we're closed my friends don't know where to find me. If I'm at the restaurant they always know where I am."

Canton Restaurant, Savannah, Ga.

*Figure 58 Canton Café and Canton Restaurant, Savannah, Ga.
Courtesy, P. C. Wu.*

P. C. Wu is a member of the Pensacola City Council and is active in numerous community and civic service organizations, serving once as District Governor of the Rotary Club. He earned a Ph.D. at Florida State University and is Professor Emeritus, University of West Florida.

Lancy Te Sheng, my mother, was from Shanghai, China. She completed nursing school there shortly prior to coming to the U. S. It so happened that the head of her nursing school had a friend, Yu Lung Pang, that she knew was seeking to marry. He was from Chekiang, China and as Ambassador from China to the United States he was in New York to attend the 1939 World's Fair. The couple exchanged photographs and started a correspondence across the ocean that led to a proposal, and acceptance, of marriage. However, my mother's entry into America was not an easy one. The Chinese government presented the first series of roadblocks. You would think that with my father being an Ambassador/Counselor that it would be easy, but it wasn't.

She had to return for papers over and over again. I would later remember hearing my mother say, "nothing in life ever came easy to me."

When all the papers were finally in order my mother came to the U. S. to meet my father. On the way the ship stopped in Hawaii and passengers disembarked to do some sightseeing. My mother was told you cannot get off "you are on your way to get married and there is nothing for you to see." My mother arrived in San Francisco on August 28, 1941 and made her way by train to New York. On September 5, 1941, Lancy Te Sheng and Yu Lung Pang were married at the Chinese Consulate General's Office at 30 Rockefeller Plaza, New York with a reception at the Port Arthur Restaurant at 7 Mott St. in New York.

T. S. Chu, Father's Friend

When my father Yu Lung Pang first came to America, his best friend, T. S. Chu, came over with him from the same village in Chekiang. Whereas Pang settled in New York, T. S. Chu ended in a small place called Tybee Island about 25 miles from Savannah, Ga. T. S. Chu started a business in which he would buy knick knacks from a J. C. Penny's store in Savannah and take them to Tybee Island (a resort area in the summer) to resell from his station wagon.

When I was four, my father unexpectedly died. One of my earliest memories was that of my mother crying. The sobbing seemed constant and very puzzling to a child of four. How was I to understand that my father had just passed away? How could I, only four years old, understand the loneliness and abandonment my mother must have felt after traveling to this foreign land- to marry, and suddenly find herself all alone. To make matters worse I believe she spoke very little English. So here was this woman who barely spoke any English all alone in a country very foreign to her in so many ways. The language, food, smells, and customs were so different from China. And here she was with a small child with only the little money she made from her small curio shop.

Introduction to John Wu

T. S. Chu, after an appropriate time has passed, invited my mother and I to Savannah where he introduced her to John Wu, a recently divorced Chinese who owned a restaurant there. He had come to the region from Canton, China, now renamed Guangzhou. John Wu's father and some other relatives all had a different surname, Ng. I believe there may have been some paper relatives in the mix because in those days the only way a Chinese could come to America was to claim to be related to someone already here.

John Wu left China when he was only 13 years old, having only 25 cents and a seventh grade education. John originally was in Jacksonville, Florida, where he worked for several years learning the trade of cooking. According to him, his salary was taken from him because the people there thought being taught a skill, cooking, had value in itself. Although they took advantage of him, this skill proved invaluable in two ways. First, it taught him the value of an education. He would often say, "if you get an education no one can rob you of it. It was unlike other possessions that could be taken away." Second, it enabled him to open his restaurant in Savannah in 1930, which is thought to be the first Chinese restaurant there. Soon after opening the *Canton Café,* later renamed *Canton Restaurant,* John Wu married a Caucasian woman, I believe named Helen, who worked as a waitress in the restaurant. However, as mentioned earlier, they eventually divorced.

Following this introduction, we returned to New York and my mother and John courted by correspondence. They eventually decided to marry and we returned to Savannah where they married in about 1951. She was a perfect match for him as their personalities complemented one another. He was quiet whereas she loved to talk, he was introverted while she was extroverted, etc. My parents were not social butterflies-matter of fact I only remember them attending one dance.

One obstacle they had to overcome was that he was from Canton, now Guangzhou, and spoke Cantonese while she was from Shanghai and spoke Mandarin. She, of course learned Cantonese, but continued to speak Mandarin to her best friend, Mrs. Yao. Together they ran the restaurant, he as the cook and she as the hostess. Mother also displayed and sold her curios and porcelain figurines in the restaurant as my father built a display case along one wall.

My sister Diana was born in 1952 and my brother Daniel in 1954. Both grew up to help as chefs in the restaurant and we were proud that they would both win the top ranking in newspaper restaurant polls.

Canton Tea Garden
My father's restaurant, *Canton Tea Garden,* was in a building he rented at 128 Drayton Street. My father's business was different than my other uncles in that it was in the middle of town in the Caucasian business section. As for my uncles, often it was difficult to tell if there was a blood relationship because Chinese called all older Chinese male friends, "uncle." Most of these uncles and aunts had businesses in the inner city.

The restaurant was located just across from the county courthouse. A few blocks away was the birthplace of Juliet Low, the founder of Girl Scouts, so on any given day the restaurant would be full of lawyers, judges, *and* Girl Scouts.

The food served in the restaurant was not really Chinese, but food that was cooked to appeal to the American palate and given exotic names. These dishes were found in any Chinese restaurant serving mainly Caucasians such as Chop Suey and Chow Mein, Egg Foo Yung, Sweet and Sour Pork and Chicken, Fried Rice and Mo Kwat Gai. The latter is a good example of fare that was American food that was given an exotic Chinese name. It was simply slices of fried chicken breast served on a bed of lettuce and covered with brown gravy. For appetizers we had Egg Rolls and either Won Ton Soup or Egg Drop Soup. There were also several gourmet dishes such as Sizzling Seafood Wor Ba, Gung Bo Gai Ding, Canton Sizzling Steak and Imperial Chicken.

We also offered American dishes like fried chicken, steaks, hamburgers, fried shrimp and great french fries. A constant comment was that my Father served too much food for the price! Drinks were limited to hot and cold tea, beer, and coke cola (only in the 8 oz bottle.) My father had a passion for Coke and would only serve the small bottle claiming the formula had been changed in the larger bottle. Desserts included the free fortune cookie, or ice cream, and almond cookies.

Our family ate meals that were very different from the restaurant items. My father did all of the cooking for family meals. We did give the best cuts of meat to customers, but there was always a lot to eat and very good. In the mornings my mother would get us ready for school, and breakfast would be the previous night's dinner reheated. Often I would dream of pancakes or scrambled eggs.

I did not realize till later how difficult my father's life was. He was not a warm person and he did not smile very often. On top of that he was very quiet- speaking only when necessary. Looking back I wonder whether he smiled at all. His work hours would start around 8 a.m. and continue until around 3 a.m. These hours were put in over three gas-fired woks running full blast in a kitchen that was not air-conditioned. In the summer the thermometer could easily reach 120 degrees. In the beginning the only two days the restaurant would close were Christmas and New Years. Later they would hire an additional cook but for years it was just my Father. There was no such thing as a sick day when you are the only cook.

One vivid memory I have of my father is when he showed the door to a salesman selling a new device called a pizza oven. I was dismayed at the time as I thought it was an opportunity to make a fortune. Pizza was not yet popular but then again, it may not have been well-suited for a Chinese restaurant.

My father was a very honest and generous man. Anyone who could not afford the food in the restaurant would be quietly fed at the backdoor, without any fanfare. Perhaps it was for this reason, among others, that when he died over 400 people showed up for the funeral of this quiet, soft spoken, and honest man.

Growing up in the restaurant I, like my siblings, had constant duties to perform as anyone who grew up in a Chinese restaurant can attest to. My father was never told that the child labor laws existed. Chopping, prep work, cooking, clearing tables, and the list goes on and on. Looking back I believe these experiences were the perfect motivational system to make you serious about college.

A restaurant was an interesting place to grow up in. You learned to be outgoing and to be comfortable dealing with many people. One shocking discovery was finding that some people thought nothing of eating and then leaving without paying the bill. Another appalling fact was that some people would talk with a mocking imitation Chinese accent in our presence as if we were not standing there or if we were deaf.

Living in a Caucasian community where there were few Chinese, I often felt like a duck that was raised with a herd of sheep. My upbringing included being raised Presbyterian, attending Catholic Schools, and having a Jewish best friend (in high school.) I was in Boy Scouts and I am very proud of my Eagle, God and Country award, and Demolay membership.

My elementary school years were difficult as I was in a fight,
it seems, almost every day. I can't say it was the main reason,
but being Chinese I felt I was often the target of prejudice.
Strangely, many people I later became closest to were people
I had fought. It was though mutual respect came following a
physical confrontation. I participated in both football and
basketball. I especially enjoyed football because on defense
you could vent some pent up hostility in a socially accepted
manner. This early fighting, which has not occurred since the
8th grade, taught me not to back down from any challenge.

My parents constantly emphasized the importance of education. When I entered college my father emphasized a degree
in either medicine or engineering. I know I was a disappointment for although I earned a Ph.D., but it was in
Education.

Canton Restaurant

While renting the building that housed the *Canton Gardens
Restaurant,* my parents purchased a building on the corner of
Abercorn and York St. It was zoned commercial and the bottom floor was rented to an opthalmologist. When his lease
expired my parents announced their intention to move their
restaurant to that location, 134 Abercorn. Neighbors started a
petition to block the move. Opposition included bank presi-
dents, a prominent Episcopal minister, and several
community leaders. My mother claimed it was racially motivated. My parents prevailed but before opening the
restaurant, renamed *Canton Restaurant,* they were required to
put a fake brick exterior over a real brick wall. The irony is
that when the building was later sold for condos, one of the
first things they did was to remove the fake brick exterior.

A major problem any restaurant faces is an occasional need
to hire a cook, either a replacement or an addition. We had to
go through an employment agency in New York but there
were not many cooks available although the pay was good
and included room and board. Indeed they were so rare that

when we took vacations, we took the cook, whoever it was, with us in the back seat of the car. Chinese restaurant owners lived in constant fear that their cooks would be lured away by other restaurants. Over the years (we closed in 1991), my parents treated the staff well and in return they were very devoted as many were with my parents for over 25 years.

On our vacations we usually visited our cousin Ava Eng (Chung) in Miami. Her family owned—you guessed it, a Chinese restaurant. When we returned from vacation, people would ask what we saw, and the answer would be "very little." Our vacations essentially involved leaving one restaurant, driving around 500 or so miles to sit in another Chinese restaurant, and then driving back to our restaurant. Nonetheless we enjoyed this 'change of scenery' very much.

My mother was extremely religious and a devout Christian, which may explain her passion to help other Chinese immigrate. She did her immigration work in the late evening and early morning when the restaurant was being cleaned. It was a difficult task, for her English was poor and so she would sit with a Chinese-American dictionary slowly looking up words. She would take the most difficult cases, often ones that had been denied for she loved a challenge. Never once did she charge a cent from the estimated 400 immigrants that she assisted until her passing in 2006. None of this got to her head.[14] When invited to join the Savannah Rotary Club, possibly the first woman so honored, she declined, as she did not want to leave the restaurant at the busy lunch hour.

---

[14] She received numerous awards from prestigious groups for her immigration work that enabled my parents to meet U. S. Congressmen Prince Preston, Herman Talmadge, and Sam Nunn. In 2009, the Federal Court in Savannah fittingly recognized her efforts with Chinese immigrants by mounting a plaque in her honor in the court lobby.

Conclusions

Many similarities exist in these narratives about the lives of Chinese restaurant families that date from around 1950 or earlier. After entering the United States or Canada, and working in different regions in varied employment, some immigrants found work as a waiter or cook, often in restaurants owned by a relative. Later, some formed partnerships with other relatives, friends, or co-workers to open their own restaurants. After establishing a business, many bachelors returned to China to marry and start families, which were typically left in the village while the husbands returned to North America to work and send money back to them.

Years later, if they had not already succeeded in bringing their families from China, they arranged to buy false immigration papers to enable young sons or other male relatives to come help work. When a father retired, it was common, at least until the middle of the last century, for one of his sons to take over the restaurant. Racial discrimination gave Chinese few alternatives in that era for employment outside of family-owned businesses. Starting in the 1950s, children received better work and career opportunities so they were less likely to follow in their fathers' footsteps.

Family-owned restaurants were utilitarian and practical in their furnishings and decor, not elaborate or expensive, and typically located in economically marginal neighborhoods. Families commonly lived near, if not in the back or above, their restaurants, as did laundry and grocery families during that era. The austere, and often crowded, living quarters were barely adequate to house large or growing families.

Many of these eateries were located in neighborhoods, or towns, where few Chinese lived. The owners had to be inventive and resourceful to succeed in a business that was new to many of them. Since most customers were non-Chinese, many offered few, if any, authentic Chinese dishes. Chop suey and chow mein, popular dishes with non-Chinese, defined the Chinese menu; other offerings were typical western favorites like steak, pork chops, and hamburgers, and regional items like enchiladas or fried chicken.

Work was demanding, with long hours each day. As children got older, they were assigned more responsibility with tasks like cleaning floors, bussing tables, washing dishes, doing food prep work, cashiering, and serving orders. Between these chores, school-age children commonly did their homework in a corner table or booth. These demands gave them little time for after school or extracurricular activities, which often impeded their assimilation to western ways.

The restaurants often served as neighborhood gathering places where congenial interactions with most customers fostered improved attitudes toward Chinese. Yet, the association of Chinese with restaurants also invoked stereotypes that limited their opportunities to advance in society. Furthermore, rude or condescending customers created problems and taught restaurant families valuable lessons about societal prejudices toward Chinese.

Growing up in constant proximity to their generally authoritarian parents who held Confucian values like filial piety, children and parents often had conflicting views. They were expected to be "seen but not heard," obey parents unquestioningly, and embrace Chinese customs and traditions.

Being assimilated to Western values by adulthood, many adopted individualistic goals and entered careers that were new to Chinese youth. However, the values of their parents were not entirely lost. The necessity of working together to survive taught them the value of interdependence. They also learned the value of hard work, thrift, and self-discipline. These skills, acquired daily from their restaurant experiences, proved beneficial to success in their future endeavors throughout life.

Children witnessed the resilience and persistence of their parents in dealing with their hard life, eloquently described in these narratives honoring their common roots. These narratives illustrate common as well as unique ways by which growing up as part of a family business produces significant impact on personal growth and development.

9. As One Era Ends, Others Begin

Chinese family restaurants, like Chinese laundries, provided one of the few viable means of economic independence for several generations of immigrants from Guangdong villages in North America as well as in many other parts of the world for over one hundred years starting from the middle of the 19th century. Chinese were so strongly associated with these livelihoods that they became stereotypical images of all Chinese to the general public even after many Chinese entered other occupations and professions.

During the early 1950s the popularity of Chinese family restaurants offering Americanized Cantonese dishes began to decline. While some prospered, many struggled. The earlier success of these restaurants contained the seeds of their downfall because the quality of the cooking became more variable as they increased in number. There were just not enough skilled cooks to go around, and many cafes had only inexperienced and untrained cooks.

In earlier years, and in regions where Chinese food was new, even mediocre cooking could pass muster because most diners had no standard for comparison due to their general unfamiliarity with Chinese cuisine. These family restaurants managed to survive because their prices were cheap, the food portions were large, and the service was usually prompt.

Over the years, however, increased sophistication of diners led to the recognition that what many Chinese family restaurants

served was not comparable with dishes prepared by chefs trained
in China.[1] After decades of success being viewed as exotic and
even daring fare, Cantonese cuisine was no longer interesting or
novel to adventuresome diners seeking new gustatory delights. As
one critic lamented:

> Just reading that same old roster of dishes, from or-
> ange-flavor beef to mu shu pork, is enough to give
> anyone an advanced case of ennui.[2]

One entrepreneurial San Francisco restaurant owner,
Johnny Kan, attacked the problem head on in 1953 with a style of
operation that was new for a Chinese restaurant, accompanied with
much fanfare. His innovative menu offered new "authentic" Chinese dishes. Served by trained and attentive wait staff in an elegant
setting, his restaurant prospered and attracted many celebrity diners, which further enhanced its prestige.[3]

> Our concept was to have a Ming or Tang dynasty
> theme for décor, a fine crew of master chefs, and a
> well-organized dining room crew headed by a courte-
> ous maitre d', host, hostesses, and so on. And we
> topped it off with a glass-enclosed kitchen. This would
> serve many purposes. The customers could actually see
> Chinese food being prepared, and it would encourage
> everybody to keep the kitchen clean.[4]

Other restaurant owners, responding to the need for innovation, adopted a Polynesian theme first made popular in the 1940s
by non-Chinese restaurants, notably *Don the Beachcomber* and *Trader
Vic's*. Overnight, "tiki Chinese" became the trendy fashion in

many Chinese restaurants, featuring a South Seas décor with flaming torches and tiki Gods to promote the fantasy of an escape from a stressful industrial society to dine in a carefree paradise. This style featured highly profitable tropical *mai tai* alcoholic beverages accompanied by *pu pu* platters of appetizers. Despite these cosmetic changes, the main food offerings were still familiar Cantonese standbys like egg rolls, won ton soup, almond chicken, and tomato beef.

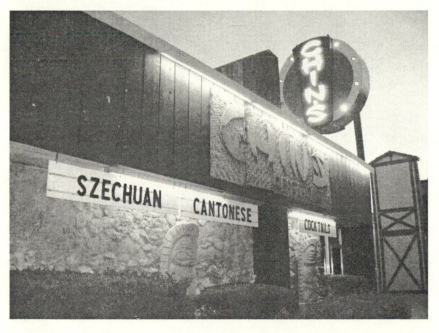

Figure 59 Chin's Restaurant, Livonia, Mi. offered both Szechuan and Cantonese food in a tiki setting. Courtesy, Chris Jackson.

But as with all fads, the Polynesian theme itself had a limited life.[5] It began to die out in the 1970s as the next new Chinese cuisine, Szechwan, took center stage. Suddenly it seemed as if almost every Chinese restaurant had revamped its Cantonese menu, and

spicy kung pao dishes had become the rage. Many Cantonese restaurants even quickly changed their names, to something that
combined northern China sites like Shanghai, Hunan or Peking
with names of settings like Palace, Garden, or Pagoda.

Hunan, Peking, Shanghai, and Szechwan cuisines that had
been long established styles in northern China did not receive wide
attention in North America until the 1960s even though they had
been offered as early as 1911 in Chicago.[6] These cuisines from
northern China, collectively referred to by restaurateur Cecilia
Chiang as "Mandarin," were featured in her upscale restaurant located outside of San Francisco's Chinatown.[7] By the 1970s, this
cuisine was promoted as more authentic than "Americanized"
Chinese food and seriously challenged restaurants that previously
served only Cantonese dishes from southern China.

Beginning of The End

The earliest Chinese emigrants that departed to many
places in the world originated from rural areas of the Cantonese-
speaking Guangdong province. However, sources of Chinese immigrants changed drastically after the 1965 U. S. Immigration Act,
which established a new quota system giving each country the
same quota of 20,000 per year, with the majority of Chinese immigrants to the U. S. coming from mainland China, Hong Kong, and
Taiwan. In 1979, Taiwan was allowed its own allotment of 20,000
slots in addition to the 20,000 for mainland China, with another
600 slots given to Hong Kong. Furthermore, many immigrants
from other Pacific Rim nations were ethnic Chinese.[8]

The post-1965 immigrants came from regions that differed in linguistic, cultural, and *socioeconomic* characteristics from the pioneering Guangdong immigrants. Moreover, many newer immigrants were educated professionals in their homeland who found that their education and skills were not readily marketable in the U. S. and Canada, especially if they did not have good English skills. Consequently, they had to work for low wages and long hours in restaurants, garment factories, and domestic jobs.

The 2000 U. S. census showed that the Chinese population approximated 2.9 million, of which a high percentage was born outside the U. S. These demographic shifts were a mixed blessing. On the positive side, it corrected gross injustices of the past exclusionary laws and allowed reunification of many families. On the culinary side, the cuisine became more varied and offered a greater variety of China's styles of cooking than had previously been available. However, on the negative side, the increased Chinese immigration after the 1965 immigration reform created more competition for work in areas with large Chinese populations. New immigrants that lacked professional skills or English proficiency could only find work under adverse conditions such as in restaurants, which involved long daily hours at below minimum wages with no fringe benefits.[9] [10] Union efforts on their behalf were limited because many immigrants, here illegally, were fearful of deportation and reluctant to join unions.[11] In addition, the increased competition for housing raised rents in the already crowded and inadequate quality housing in Chinatowns.

Owners of larger restaurants defended themselves against

charges that they exploited workers by noting that patrons would not pay the higher prices they would have to charge to pay higher wages.[12] Adding to the predicament of Chinatown restaurants, Chinese gangs extorted protection money from them, crimes that persisted as they were rarely reported for fear of reprisals.[13]

The Chinese family-operated cafes and restaurants that featured Cantonese cuisine began to decline more rapidly over the 1960s just as the Chinese laundry did a generation earlier. Whereas the Chinese laundry vanished partly due to the widespread availability of home washers and dryers, the Chinese restaurant did not so much disappear as much as it was transformed. In the wake of the new wave of immigrants from Asia following the 1965 immigration law reforms, the Cantonese style of cooking that the earliest Chinese immigrants popularized soon gave way to the Szechwan, Shanghai, Hunan, and Fukien cuisines of new Chinese immigrants from Asian areas other than Guangdong.[14] Furthermore, immigrants from other Asian countries such as Thailand, Vietnam, Cambodia, India, and Korea opened competing family restaurants. Pan Asian or fusion cuisine also emerged to attract adventurous diners seeking new culinary experiences. The rediscovery of Japanese cuisine, and the popularity of sushi, provided another rival for restaurants featuring Cantonese style cooking.[15]

The past success and popularity of Chinese food in the U. S. and Canada fueled a substantial expansion in the number of Chinese restaurants during the last third of the twentieth century.

However, by the 1980s there was a shift from small family-owned facilities of the mid-twentieth century back to larger ones with ornate décor and furnishings. Investor syndicates in Hong Kong and Taiwan financed many of these new restaurants during the 1980s, fueled by anxiety over their uncertain future in the region with the impending return of control of Hong Kong to China in 1997.[16]

The small family restaurants could not compete against these large Chinese restaurants owned by partnerships and corporate chains.[17] The luxuriously decorated larger restaurants were in better locations and hired professional managers and large service staffs trained to deal effectively with non-Chinese diners. They recruited experienced chefs with culinary training in Hong Kong and mainland China to improve the quality and increase the variety of authentic offerings to meet the tastes of the increased percentage of Chinese patrons born in China and Taiwan as well as to satisfy those non-Chinese diners seeking new gastronomic experiences. They focused on creating gourmet delicacies for sophisticated diners than on the more common fare for working class and family clientele.

Small family-run restaurants were also challenged by the expansion of restaurants at the other end of the spectrum, low cost operations such as fast food franchises and all-you-can-eat buffets.[18] Caught in a squeeze between the high-end and low cost establishments, the family-run restaurants barely survived mainly with their long-term customers whose loyalty they had cultivated over the years.

Perhaps, however, even without these threats from industry developments, the family-run Chinese restaurants featuring Cantonese cuisine would have declined naturally as their owners aged and retired. Before the end of World War II, their adult children would have likely taken over the operation of their parents' businesses because of discriminatory hiring practices against Chinese in many fields, even those with college degrees.[19] Fortunately, social attitudes toward Chinese and other minorities have greatly improved since World War II. By the 1950s, Chinese had much greater opportunities and acceptance in white-collar professions and careers. These improved prospects were ironically made possible largely through the financial support from the earnings of the very businesses that the children later declined to operate. When their aging parents retired, their educated children no longer needed to take over their family restaurants to earn a living.

Legacy of Chinese Family Restaurants

The legacy of the Chinese family restaurant has both positive and negative aspects. Clearly, this opportunity for self-employment proved to be a vital economic lifeline to Chinese immigrants in the early twentieth century when they had access to few other means of earning a living. They managed to create an ethnic "product" that was attractive to the general population, which made Chinese restaurants a profitable business. Delicious food was certainly important for their success, but their low prices also contributed to the competitive edge that Chinese restaurants achieved, an advantage achieved by the long hours and hard labor that these families endured. But, there was a negative side to this victory, as Chinese "trapped" themselves by their low prices made possible by their family efforts. Chinese restaurants gained a reputation for inexpensive meals and they were never able to charge the higher prices that some other cuisines could command.

Another price of Chinese restaurant success was that it fostered an ethnic stereotype that created barriers for their children seeking to advance beyond the restaurant. Chinese gained respect from the general public in the middle of the last century, but primarily for their culinary skills. This stereotype initially reduced access of their children to careers in other businesses and professions. However, by the 1960s, the academic achievements of Chinese who grew up in their family businesses such as restaurants finally helped them break free from these restrictions to enter many professions and occupations previously denied to them.[20]

The Future for Chinese Family Restaurants

Despite the demise of many older Cantonese family restaurants, as long as there are new immigrants with meager finances and poor English skills, new small family-run ethnic restaurants will open to take their place. Newer family-owned and operated Asian restaurants can be found in all parts of the country, mostly run by immigrant families, many of ethnic Chinese ancestry, from other Asian countries such as Korea, Thailand, and Vietnam, and other parts of Southeast Asia. Similarly, these countries are new sources of immigrant owners of other small family-run businesses like grocery stores, convenience stores, and dry cleaners.

Small business success requires hard work and cooperation of all family members in making sacrifices to work in their restaurants and other family businesses. Some will survive, but some will fail, often due to circumstances beyond their control such as competition or the overall economy. Nonetheless, like the earlier Chinese immigrants, many Asian immigrants still regard establishing one's own independent business rather than working for someone else as the best way to get ahead economically. The success of past generations of Cantonese family restaurants stands as evidence that they too may achieve their goals following this path.

Figure 60 The Cook At the End of the Day, Silver Wing Café, San Francisco. Courtesy, Leland Wong.

REMINISCING ABOUT A CHINESE RESTAURANT

NELLIE WONG

Last night I ate dinner
in a Chinese restaurant
roast pork and mashed potatoes,
rice and corn, a wedge of custard pie.

Others were eating rice
with bean cake and *cha siu*
One man ate corned beef and cabbage
and shimmering Jello cubes

Glasses clang, silverware shook,
Oil sizzled to another Chinese restaurant
to Chinatown, a girl who washed glasses, wipe forks, knives and
spoons,
who typed the next day's menu,
who squeezed oranges for juice,
large, small,
but always fresh.

In the back kitchen in the damp air
a man bakes apple pies and banana shortcakes
a cigarette dangles from his mouth,
his eyes half closed.
When the afternoon off comes,
he shuffles off to his rented room, pulls up his sleeve,
sticks a needle into his arm.

He escapes, orange, delicious,
and I run upstairs, stuffy myself
with strawberry pie.
My skin rises in hives,
my skin wants orange, wants delicious.
I awaken. More dishes, more menus.
I refill the sugar jars.
Granules sparkle, I cover them up
and salt shakers take precedence
on the Formica counter
in wooden booths.

Slide and run, run and hide,
wait on those who inhabit
this Chinese restaurant.
A man with a crutch and one leg
Limps downstairs from the Aloha Hotel,
sips his dinner of black coffee
and sugared "bombs."

A shriner and his wife, with wide smiles,
eat halibut steak, rice and gravy
and apple pie.
The shriner shakes his tassel with authority.
He splits one 60-cent dinner
for his two young daughters.

Three slices of whole-wheat bread
for a glass-eyes customer
who smears catsup on each slice,
thick, juicy, oozing over the plate.
This man paints red in my father's eyes
who shouts to me:
Give him the bottle with the quarter-inch catsup
or we will not survive, we will not survive.
A young gypsy girl and a sallow old man
sit in the back booth.
He lifts her skirt, caresses
her thigh, feeds her a spoon of rice.
She shivers. I look away.

A gas station attendant peeps
behind the American menu,
one eye on the other waitress.
His lips parted, he orders leg of lamb
with mint jelly.
his money is good, is green.
He pays to eat and look
at the other waitress.

And I eat and my skin itches,
knows nothing, not its hives,
its questions marks.
I return to the Chinese restaurant,

its blinking coffee-cup neon sign.
I read the menu, examine it
inside out. The ink spills.
The calligraphy sprawls.

This Chinese restaurant demands love,
demands attention. Its walls expand,
I slither inside.

What would the glasses, the ovens
and chopsticks tell, what grease
on uniforms, what language
beyond food?

Nellie Wong © 1986. Courtesy, Nellie Wong

Figure 61 Restaurant Illustrations, Courtesy, Flo Oy Wong

Endnotes

[1] Madeline Y. Hsu. "From Chop Suey to Mandarin Cuisine: Fine Dining and the Refashioning of Chinese Ethnicity during the Cold War Era." In *Chinese Americans and the Politics of Race and Culture,* edited by Sucheng Chan and Madeline Y. Hsu, 173-194 (Philadelphia: Temple University Press, 2008).

[2] *Washington Post,* Nov. 29, 1987, 37 Cited by Lu, "Ethnic Enterprise."

[3] Johnny Kan with Charles L. Leong, *Eight Immortal Flavors* (Berkeley, California: Howell-North Books, 1963).

[4] Victor and Brett de Bary Nee, *Longtime Californ': A Documentary Study of an American Chinatown* (New York: Pantheon, 1973): 110.

[5] Sylvia Lovegren. *Fashionable food: Seven Decades of Food Fads* (Chicago: University of Chicago Press, 2005): 276-279.

[6] Display Ad 9 –No title. *Chicago Tribune.* Aug. 16, 1911. Proquest Historical Newspapers Chicago Tribune (1849-1986), 11. See p. 44 for Mandarin Inn, Chicago, ad reference to "novelty of its Mandarin dishes."

[7] Cecilia Sun Yun Chiang with Allan Carr, *The Mandarin Way* (Boston: Little, Bown, 1974).

[8] Zhang, "Transplanting Identity," 188.

[9] Ivan Light and Charles Choy Wong, "Protest or Work: Dilemmas of the Tourist Industry in American Chinatowns," *American Journal of Sociology,* 80, no. 6 (1975): 1342-1368.

[10] Adding to their problems, the Immigration Reform and Control Act of 1986 required employers to check the immigration status of workers, with fines for failure to comply. Unannounced immigration raids during peak dining hours hurt their businesses but family-run restaurants were less affected. Karlyn Barker, "Chinese Restaurant Owners Complain to INS About Worker Restrictions." *Washington Post,* Oct. 18 1988, D3.
 Refugees received legal status if they had lived continuously in the U. S. since 1982, benefiting 13,752 previously undocumented immigrants, many of them restaurant workers. Chinese from one of the poorest provinces, Fukien, tried to enter illegally, and then apply for asylum. Among those succeeding, some used savings to open restaurants, adding to an oversupply. Such conditions ensured worker wages stayed low while diners had low prices. Zhang, "Transplanting Identity," 188-191.

[11] Lin, "Reconstructing Chinatown," 70-74. Since the 1970s, New York Chinese restaurant waiters had mixed union success to counter management taking part of their tips and not giving benefits or overtime pay. In

the 1990s, some restaurants fired, locked out, or black listed waiters, which led to pickets as well as counter-demonstrations.

[12] Florence Fabricant. "Can't Have Chic Chinese Restaurants If the Diners Won't Pay," *New York Times*, April 23 1997, B5.

[13] "A Gang Is Preying on Chinese Restaurants on L.I." *New York Times*, Jan. 5 1986, Part 1, 26. "Chinese Restaurant Owners Are Targets of Extortionists," *New York Times*, Jan. 4 1981, Part 1; 20.

[14] Wu, "Improvising Chinese Cuisine Overseas"

[15] Larger Cantonese restaurants in or near urban areas gained new life when non-Chinese "discovered" dim sum starting around the 1970s, with continuing strong interest. Dim sum, an assortment of small steamed and fried items such as dumplings and buns filled with meats or vegetables is served with tea in mid-morning; dim sum was not new but had not been previously promoted or marketed to non-Chinese.

[16] Fred Ferretti. "Chinatown at New Year's: A Hong Kong Connection," *New York Times*, 1986, Feb. 5. C23

[17] Although based on Honolulu, this analysis applies to restaurants in large mainland cities as well. David Y. H. Wu "Improvising Chinese Cuisine Overseas." In *The Globalization of Chinese Food*, edited by David Y. H. Wu and Sidney C. H. Cheung (Honolulu: University of Hawaii Press, 2002): 61-62.

[18] Jacqueline M. Newman. "Chinese Buffets: A Trend Worth Noting," *Flavor and Fortune*, 1999, 6 (4), 27-28.

[19] Haiming Lui. "The Identity Formation of American-Born Chinese in the 1930s: A Review of Lei Jieqiong's (Kit King Louis) Master's Thesis," *Journal of Chinese Overseas*, 3, 1 (2007): 97–121.

[20] Such successes ironically fostered a new stereotype of Chinese, and other Asians, as "model minorities."

Bibliography

Abraham, Terry. "Class, Gender, and Race: Chinese Servants in the North American West." Paper presented at the Joint Regional Conference Hawai'i/Pacific and Pacific Northwest Association for Asian American Studies, Honolulu, Hawaii, March 26, 1996. Anderson, E. N. *Food of China*, New Haven: Yale University Press, 1988.

Bancroft, Hubert Howe. *History of California.* Vol. 6. San Francisco: A. L. Bancroft, 1888.

Barbas, Samantha. "I'll Take Chop Suey: Restaurants as Agents of Culinary and Cultural Change." *Journal of Popular Culture*, 36, 4, (2003): 669-686.

Beck, Louis J. *New York's Chinatown: An Historical Presentation of Its Peoples and Places.* New York: Bohemia Publishing, 1898.

Boggs, Grace. *Living for Change: An Autobiography.* Minneapolis: University of Minnesota Press, 1998.

Bonner, Arthur. *Alas, What Brings Thee Hither: the Chinese in New York: 1800-1950.* Madison, N.J.: Fairleigh Dickinson University Press, 1996.

Bronson, Ben and Chuimei Ho, "1901: The Boom in Chinese Restaurants Begins." Chinese American Museum of Chicago. http://www.ccamuseum.org/Research-2.html#anchor_90 (accessed Aug. 16, 2009).

Brookhiser, Richard. "Eats from the East." *National Review.* Sept. 25, 2006.

Carter, Susan B. "Celestial Suppers: The Political Economy of America's Chop Suey Craze: 1900-1930." Cliometrics Conference, Gettysburg College, June 5, 2009.

Chan, Loren B. "The Chinese in Nevada: An Historical Survey, 1856-1970." In *Chinese on the Western Frontier*, edited by Emil Dirlik and Malcolm Yeung. Lanham, Md.: Rowman & Littlefield, 2003: 85-122.

Chao, Tonia. "Communicating Through Architecture: San Francisco Chinese Restaurants as Cultural Intersections, 1849-1984." Ph.D. diss., University of California, Berkeley, 1985.

Chen, Yong. *Chinese San Francisco: 1850-1943. A Trans-pacific Community.* Stanford, Ca.: Stanford University Press, 2000.

Cheng, David Te-Chao. *Acculturation of the Chinese in the United States: A Philadelphia Study.* Ph.D. diss., University of Pennsylvania, 1945. Foochow, China: Fukien Christian University Press, 1948.

Chiang, Cecilia Sun Yun with Allan Carr, *The Mandarin Way.* Boston: Little, Brown, 1974.

Cho, Lily. "On Eating Chinese: Diasporic Agency and the Chinese Canadian Restaurant Menu." In *Reading Chinese Transnationalisms: Society, Literature, Film, edited by* Maria Ng and Philip Holden. Hong Kong: Hong Kong University Press, 2006: 37-62.

Chong, Raymond. "Gim Suey Chong: From Hoyping to Gum Saan." *Gum Saan Journal* (2009) 31, 19-52.

Chu, Louis H. "The Chinese Restaurants in New York." M.A. Thesis. New York University, 1939.

Coe, A. *Chop Suey: A Cultural History of Chinese Food in the United States.* London: Oxford University Press, 2009.

Doherty, Sue. "Sonoma Stories And The Song Wong Bourbeau Collection: A Model For An Exhibition And A Public Outreach Program— An Innovative Approach To CRM." Master's Thesis. Sonoma State University, 2005.

Donzheng, Jin. "The Sojourners' Story: Philadelphia's Chinese Immigrants, 1900-1925. " Ph.D. diss., Temple University, 1997.

Food Bureau. Cafeteria Management. Jan. (1928): 18.

Fuller, Sherri Gebert. "Mirrored Identities: The Moys of St. Paul." *Minnesota History*, 57, 4 (2000): 162-181.

Hancock, Emory. "Making the Small Town Restaurant Pay." National Restaurant News Jan. (1925): 26.

Hsu, Madeline Y. "From Chop Suey to Mandarin Cuisine: Fine Dining and the Refashioning of Chinese Ethnicity during the Cold War Era." edited by Sucheng Chan and Madeline Y. Hsu, *173-194. Chinese Americans and the Politics of Race and Culture.* Philadelphia: Temple University Press, 2008.

Kan, Johnny with Charles L. Leong, *Eight Immortal Flavors.* Berkeley, California: Howell-North Books, 1963.

Kwan, Cheuk. *Chinese Restaurants.* 2004.
        http://www.chineserestaurants.tv (accessed June 1, 2009).

Larsen, Jane Leung. "New Source Materials on Kang Youwei and Baohaunghui." *Chinese America: History and Perspectives*, 7, (1993): 151-198.

Lawson, Robert *At That Time.* New York: Viking, 1947.

Lee, Jennifer 8. *The Fortune Cookie Chronicles: Adventures in the World of Chinese Food.* New York: Hachette Book Group, 2008.

Lee, Joanne. "What is real Chinese food. *"Flavor and Fortune,* 2, No. 3 (1995): 17 and 21.

Lee, Rose Hum. *The Chinese in the United States of America.* Hong Kong: Hong Kong University Press, 1960.

Leung, Peter C. Y., and Eileen Leung. "Mr. Frank Fat, a Legendary Restaurateur in Sacramento." In: *150 Years of the Chinese Presence in California,* Sacramento, Ca.: Sacramento Chinese Cultural Foundation and Asian American Studies, University of California, Davis, 2001. 96-119.

Li, Li. "Cultural and Intercultural Functions of Chinese Restaurants in the Mountain West: 'An Insider's Perspective.'" *Western Folklore* 61, no. 3/4, (2002): 329-346.

Libby, Gary W. "Historical Notes on Chinese Restaurants in Portland, Maine." *Chinese America: History & Perspectives* (2006): 47-56.

Light, Ivan, and Charles Choy Wong. "Protest or Work: Dilemmas of the Tourist Industry in American Chinatowns." *The American Journal of Sociology* 80, no. 6 (1975): 1342-1368.

Lim, Imogene. "Chinese Cuisine Meets the American Palate: The Chow Mein Sandwich." In *Chinese Cuisine/American Palate: An Anthology,* edited by Jacqueline M. Newman and Roberta Halporn. New York: Center for Thanatology Research and Education, 2004, 130-139.

Lim, Imogene. "Chinese Restaurants As Cultural Lessons." *Food and Flavor* (1997): 13-14.

Lin, Jan. *Reconstructing Chinatown: Ethnic Enclave, Global Change.* Minneapolis: University of Minnesota Press, 1998.

Ling, Huping. *Chinese St. Louis: From Enclave to Cultural Community.* Philadelphia: Temple University Press, 2004.

Ling, Susie. "Dreamer in the Kitchen: Richard Wing." *Gum Saan Journal,* 30, (2007): 21-32.

Lister, Florence C. and Robert H. Lister. "Chinese Sojourners in Territorial Prescott." *Journal of the Southwest,* 31, 1, (1989): 1-111.

Liu, Haiming. "Chop Suey as Imagined Authentic Chinese food: The Culinary Identity of Chinese Restaurants in the United States." *Journal of Transnational American Studies,* 1 (2009): 1-24.

Liu, Haiming. "The Identity Formation of American-Born Chinese in the 1930s: A Review of Lei Jieqiong's (Kit King Louis) Master's Thesis." *Journal of Chinese Overseas,* 3, 1 (2007): 97–121.

Liu, Haiming, and Lianlian Lin. "Food, Culinary Identity, and Transnational Culture." *Journal of Asian American Studies,* 12, 2 (2009): 135-162.

Lovegren, Sylvia. *Fashionable food: Seven Decades of Food Fads.* Chicago: University of Chicago Press, 2005.

Lu, Shun and Gary Alan Fine. "The Presentation of Ethnic Authenticity: Chinese Food as a Social Accomplishment." *Sociological Quarterly*, 36, No. 3, (1995): 535-553.

Lu, Tzu-ching. "Ethnic Enterprise in the Kansas City Metropolitan Area: The Chinese Restaurant Business. Volumes I and II." Ph.D. diss., University of Kansas, 1990.

Lui, Andy. "Small Business in the United States: A Field Study of Three Chinese Restaurants in Midland, Texas." Master's Thesis, Oklahoma State University, 2006.

Mar, M. Elaine, *Paper Daughter: A Memoir.* New York: Harper Collins, 1999.

Mariani, John. *America Eats Out: An Illustrated History of Restaurants, Taverns, Coffee Shops, Speakeasies, and Other Establishments That Have Fed Us for 350 Years.* New York: William Morrow, 1991.

Mayer, Grace M. *Once Upon a City: New York from 1890 to 1910.* New York: Macmillan, 1958, 417-418.

McKeown, Adam. *Chinese Migrant Networks and Cultural Change: Peru, Chicago, and Hawaii 1900-1936.* Chicago: University of Chicago Press, 2001.

McLeod, Alexander. *Pigtails and Gold Dust.* Caldwell, Idaho: Caxton Printers, 1948.

Mo, Timothy. *Sour Sweet.* New York: Adventura, 1985.

Nee, Victor and Brett de Bary, '*Longtime Californ': A Documentary Study of an American Chinatown.* New York: Pantheon, 1973.

Newman, Jacqueline M. "Chinese Buffets: A Trend Worth Noting." *Flavor and Fortune,* 1999, 6 (4), 27-28.

Nie, Phonsia. "Chinese in Chicago's 'Levee:' Chinatown before 1912." Master's Thesis, Northwestern University, 2009.

Pfaezer, Jean. *Driven Out: The Forgotten War against Chinese Americans.* New York: Random House, 2007.

Pillsbury, Richard. *From Boarding House to Bistro: American Restaurants Then and Now.* Cambridge, Ma: Unwin Hyman, 1990.

Pillsbury, Richard. *No Foreign Food: The American Diet in Time and Place.* Boulder, Co.: Westview Press, 1998.

Siu, Paul C. P. *The Chinese Laundryman: A Study of Social Isolation. edited by J. K. W. Tchen.* New York: New York University Press, 1987.

Smart. P. L. Josephine. "Ethnic Entrepreneurship, Transmigration, and Social Integration: An Ethnographic Study of Chinese Restaurant Owners in Rural Western Canada." *Urban Anthropology and Studies of Cultural Systems and World Economic Development*, Sept. 22 2003.

Song, Miri. *Helping Out: Children's Labor in Ethnic Businesses.* Philadelphia: Temple University Press, 1999.

Taliaferro, Patricia J. "Monosodium Glutamate and the Chinese Restaurant Syndrome: A Review of Food Additive Safety." *Journal of Environmental Health*, 57, 10 (1995): 8-13.

Eleanor Wong Telemaque, *It's Crazy to Stay Chinese in Minnesota*. Nashville, Tn: Nelson, 1978,

Tow, J. S. *The Real Chinese in New York*: The Academy Press, 1923.

Tsai, Henry Shih-Shan. "The Emergence of Early Chinese Nationalist Organizations in America." *AmerAsia Journal*, 8, 2, (1982): 121-143.

Veniard, Clara. "Immigrant rural entrepreneurs: Chinese restaurants in rural New Hampshire and Vermont." Geography Honors Thesis, Dartmouth College, 2001. Advisor: Richard Wright.

Wah, Fred. *Diamond Grill*. Edmonton, Alberta: NeWest, 1996.

Whitfield, Ruth Hall. "Public Opinion and the Chinese question in San Francisco, 1900-1947." Master's Thesis, University of California, Berkeley, 1947.

Wing, Richard C. "General George Marshall and I." *Gum Saan Journal*, 30, (2007): 33-44.

Wong, Janice. *Chow: Memories of Food and Family*. Vancouver, B. C.: Whitecap, 2005.

Wong, Marie Rose. *Sweet Cakes, Long Journey: The Chinatowns of Portland, Oregon*. Seattle: University of Washington Press, 2004.

Wong, Wayne Hung. *American Paper Son, A Chinese Immigrant in the Midwest*. Urbana, Il., University of Illinois Press, 2006.

Wu, Ching Chao. "Chinatowns: A Study of Symbiosis and Assimilation." Ph.D. diss., University of Chicago, 1928.

Wu, David Y. H. "Improvising Chinese Cuisine Overseas." In *The Globalization of Chinese Food*. edited by David Y. H. Wu and Sidney C. H. Cheung. Honululu: University of Hawaii Press (2002): 56-66.

Yu, Renqiu. "Chop Suey: From Chinese food to Chinese American food." *Chinese America: History and Perspectives* (1987): 87-99.

Zhang, Jie. "Transplanting Identity: A Study of Chinese Immigrants and the Chinese Restaurant Business." Ph.D. diss., Southern Illinois University, 1999.

Zhu, Liping. *A Chinaman's Chance: The Chinese on the Rocky Mountain Mining Frontier*. Boulder, Co.: University Press of Colorado, 1997.

Zhu, Liping. "Ethnic Oasis: Chinese Immigrants in the Frontier Black Hills, " *South Dakota History*, 33, 4 (2003): 289-329.

Index